Augustus Jessopp, Alexander Harris

The oeconomy of the Fleete

An apologeticall answeare of Alexander Harris

Augustus Jessopp, Alexander Harris

The oeconomy of the Fleete
An apologeticall answeare of Alexander Harris

ISBN/EAN: 9783337113216

Printed in Europe, USA, Canada, Australia, Japan

Cover: Foto ©Suzi / pixelio.de

More available books at **www.hansebooks.com**

THE

ŒCONOMY OF THE FLEETE:

OR

AN APOLOGETICALL ANSWEARE OF ALEXANDER HARRIS

(LATE WARDEN THERE)

UNTO XIX ARTICLES SETT FORTH AGAINST HIM
BY THE PRISONERS.

EDITED,

FROM THE ORIGINAL MS. IN THE POSSESSION OF

HIS GRACE THE DUKE OF WESTMINSTER, K.G.

BY

AUGUSTUS JESSOPP, D.D.,

HEAD MASTER OF KING EDWARD VI. SCHOOL, NORWICH.

PRINTED FOR THE CAMDEN SOCIETY.

M.DCCC.LXXIX.

COUNCIL OF THE CAMDEN SOCIETY

FOR THE YEAR 1878-79.

INTRODUCTION.

I.

In the month of January, 1876, I obtained permission from His Grace the Duke of Westminster to examine certain MSS. at Eaton, which the third Report of the Commission on Historical Manuscripts had made known to the public. The noble mansion was under the dominion of an army of builders, and some difficulty was experienced in finding the volumes I especially desired to see. While looking for them I came upon the MS. from which the following pages are printed. I was first attracted by noticing many names of the Recusant Gentry with whose misfortunes and hard treatment I had become familiar in the course of my researches into the working of the Penal Laws against Catholics during the reign of Queen Elizabeth; and it was not long before I discovered that it was a document of some interest and value furnishing us with a picture of the condition of a London prison in the seventeenth century such as can, probably, be found nowhere else.

The volume had evidently been almost exactly in its present condition when the scribe finished his copying into it; it is a folio volume which some diligent compiler of the latter half of the seventeenth century had used for transcribing into, and can hardly have been opened for two hundred years. The sand which the writer had sprinkled is still liberally distributed over the paper, and in some cases the pages had slightly stuck together from the ink being scarcely dry when the writer had turned over the leaves. The book contains 660 pages, which are numbered to the end, though several have never been used; the writing is beautifully clear and neat, and rarely presents any difficulties.

It is evident that the original from which the Eaton scribe copied was imperfect, and that one or two leaves—perhaps more—on which Harris had written his particular answer to Coppin and Kennel, had been torn off. What more Harris's " Defence" may have contained it would be idle now to guess. All that follows from p. 152 to p. 159 appears to have been of the nature of an " Exhibit," which the defendant " put in" when he presented his defence to whatever court of appeal it may have been originally intended for.

On my bringing the MS. to the notice of Mr. Gardiner, the Director of the Camden Society, he suggested that the Duke should be applied to for permission to print the volume, and he invited me to undertake the editing of it for the Society. With prompt and delicate courtesy his Grace, in reply to my application, sent the MS. by return of post: no questions were asked, no conditions imposed; and since February, 1876, the volume has remained in my custody.

I was not able to set to work at my task as early as I hoped, and when I began I was surprised to find that I had quite under-estimated the amount of trouble it would involve. I had assumed that I should find abundance of materials ready to hand if it should prove advisable to draw up a brief account of the Fleet Prison; and had a vague idea that such stray notes as I had set down from time to time, in the course of my own desultory reading, might be easily supplemented by references to the more accessible sources of historical knowledge. I soon discovered to my dismay that nobody could tell me much about the history of prisons in England, and that I should have to break ground and explore with little or no help from previous inquirers.

I fear that some members of the Camden Society will be inclined to complain that I have not done more to illustrate this MS. I cannot hope that many will give me credit for anything approaching the amount of research it has really involved. I regret I could do no more; I have done what I could.

I have to express my gratitude to many friends for many kind services. The fields of historical research are so very wide that a man cannot hope to achieve anything of permanent value in that domain except he be *en rapport* with his fellow students; and how freely they help one another they know best who work hardest.

It is enough to say that I have frequented the Record Office to make it quite certain that the officials there have been of incalculable service to me. We have heard much of late of an " English School of History," and of the good work it is doing and has done. It would be difficult to estimate the influence exercised upon Historical Literature in England by such chivalrous guides and helpers as Mr. Bond and Mr. Selby, though it seems almost invidious to mention any names.

II.

When the massive stone walls which used to abut on Farringdon Street, and the gloomy buildings which they inclosed, were pulled down thirty years ago, the last vestiges of an institution were swept away which had existed on the same spot certainly for eight hundred, and probably for more than a thousand years.

It was an institution such as could only have existed so long in this the most tenaciously conservative country in Europe, an institution which, as we look back upon it now, appears to us "picturesque" chiefly for its indefensible badness, and for that amazing vitality which even the most enormous and flagrant abuses (under the plausible name of vested interests) have always exhibited among ourselves.

The first mention that I have discovered of the Fleet is of the date A.D. 1197, when (9º Ric. I.) "Nathaniel de Leveland and his son Robert — fined in lx. marks. To have the custody of the King's Houses at Westminster and of *the Fleete Prison which had been their inheritance ever since the Conquest.*"[a] Four years after this the same Robert applied to King John for leave to hand over the wardenship of the palace at Westminster "*et gaole de Flete*" to Simon Fitz Robert, Archdeacon of Wells, for three years, inasmuch as he, the said Robert,[b] had taken the Cross In the Chancery Rolls of this same year (3º John) I find a sum of 15*l.* 10*s.* paid by the city of London "in operacione gaiole Regis de Flete," and a further sum of 10*l.* 12*s.* 10*d.* charged as having been paid "Roberto filio Nathanielis *pro custodia domorum* Regis *de West-*

---

[a] Madox, *Hist. of the Exchequer*, p. 356. (Folio.)

[b] Liberate Rolls, p. 25. *Rot. Lit. Pat. Hardy* p. 4.

minster," and 7*l.* 12*s.* 1*d.* " *pro custodia gaiole de London.*"[a] Three years after this, viz. 25 May, 6" Jo. (1205), Robert de Leveland is back again—if he ever went away—and is excused payment of 10*l.* which he had borrowed, but required to serve " cum equis et armis ultra mare,"[b] he being at the time Keeper of the Fleet. He died some time at the beginning of the reign of Henry III. for in December, 1217, his wife Margaret is granted the same allowances " ad domos nostras ad Westmonasterium custodiendum qualem idem Robertus habere consuevit dum vixit."[c] By which it is plain that *the widow succeeded to the Office of Warden.*

After this the Records contain numerous notices and allusions which throw more or less light upon the early history of the place, and make it appear that in the reigns of King John and Henry III. it was a house of detention for offenders of all kinds, but it was evidently far more commonly used as a debtors' prison, and one in which defaulters to the King's Exchequer were committed, than such as were charged with breaches of the peace, nor does it seem at any time to have been used as a gaol to which *felons* were confined and kept in irons.

Thus in the 18° Ed. I. John Franceys is committed to the Fleet by Thomas Weyland " pro quodam compoto quod Agnes de Valence ab eo exigit," and he is allowed to go forth on bail for settling the affair, and in case he should not succeed in effecting his object he is to return to prison.[d] In the next reign William de Barstove, Chamberlain of Chester, petitions for release from the Fleet—where he had been kept for a year and a day under arrest[e] for a debt to the King's Exchequer. In the 9° Ed. III. Adam de

Rot. Cancell. 3° Jo. f. 100.   [b] Close Rolls, 6° Jo. f. 33.
Close Rolls, 2° Hen. III. f. 346.   [d] Rot. Parl. vol. i. p. 17.
u. s. vol. i p. 401.

Withyford, late Chamberlain of North Wales, presents a similar petition for release, he being a defaulter in the sum of one hundred marks which he acknowledges were due to " Rogier de Mortimer, Count de la Marche ;" but he affirms, in his defence of himself, that his clerk was actually carrying the money to the said Rogier when he was unfortunately drowned in the Severn "au Pount de Mone-ford en Salopshire par crecyn de cawe, e ne poynt estre trove *tan qe il fut desvorre des bestes,* issint qe les dits cent mars furent perdues par fortune."[a] In the 21st Ed. III. (1347), Thomas de Bekering, Sheriff of the counties of Nottingham and Derby, petitions for discharge from the Fleet, where he is detained for a debt to the King's Exchequer;[b] and a similar petition is presented in the same reign in favour of William de Hedersete, who had become liable for " grantz arerages devers nostre Seigneur le Roi," incurred by his late partner, who had died insolvent, in consequence of which the said William de Hedersette "ad demoert en la dite Prison, a grant mischief."

In the 13th Ric. II. (1391), a case occurs where two men, Henry Tebbe and John Grenclowe, are committed[c] for creating a riot in the church of Whitwick, in Leicestershire. Here, too, the origin of the disturbance was a question of money said to be due to the Prior of Holand, who was the complainant. After this the place seems to have been used as a prison, to which any one might be sent on anything short of a capital charge.[d]

---

[a] u. s. vol. ii. p. 91.   [b] u. s. p. 196.

[c] u. s. vol. iii. p. 286 B.

[d] Thos. Hardyng, committed for false accusation, 15 Ric. II. and John Shodwell, for slander (vol. iii. p. 288 B.) The Sheriff of Rutland, 5 Hen. IV. for making a false return (u. s. p. 530). In the instance of Sir Henry de Medbourne, who is accused in the 30th Ed. III. of throwing several persons into the Fleet by the mere exercise of oppression, it seems probable that he did so under colour of their being

The first mention of extortion or excessive fees being laid to the
Warden's charge occurs in a petition presented to the Commons in
the second year of Henry IV.[a] (A.D. 1400), when the petitioners
pray that " les fees de Gardien de Flete soient mys en certain;" and
seven years after this we meet with the first allusion to that practice
which to us seems so curious, and yet which to our forefathers
seemed perfectly natural, of allowing a prisoner to leave the gaol by
the permission of the Warden, and without any other legal for-
mality. A prisoner once handed over to the Warden became a
quasi representative of the debt for which judgment had been given,
and the Warden having the debtor in his custody became *ipso facto*
answerable either for the debt or the debtor. Failing to produce
the latter when called upon, he became liable for the former; but as
long as he kept his hold upon the debtor, to the extent of being
able to produce him in court upon notice given, he seems to have
been allowed to grant almost any liberty he pleased, he himself
taking good care to make his profit out of any indulgence afforded
to his prisoner. It was inevitable that the debtor gave his keeper
the slip now and then, and when he did so the creditor must have
some redress. Accordingly it was enacted, in the 7° and 8° Henry IV.
(A.D. 1406): " . . . qe si ascun Gaoler lesscroit tiel Prisoner aler a
large par mainprise ou en baile, qe adonqes le persone envers qi le
dit Prisoner estoit condempne aucroit sa action et recoverir envers
le dit Gaoler." [b] Notwithstanding this resolution the practice of
letting prisoners have a certain limited liberty seems to have gone

---

his debtors (u.s. vol. ii. p. 329). The committal of William de Buret, in 1214, seems
to have been for contempt of court (*Rot. Lit. Pat.* p. 123). John de Beauney, in
1207, was evidently in the Fleet already for debt, and removed therefrom when the
capital charge was brought against him (u. s. p. 68 n.)

    [a] Rolls of Parl. vol. iii. p. 469.   [b] Rolls of Parl. vol. iii. p. 593 A.

on increasing rather than diminishing; and there are many instances
of actions being brought against the Wardens, and large sums
recovered from them, for their negligence in allowing escapes to be
made from the custody of the " Bastons" or officers of the prison,
whose duty it was to keep an eye upon the prisoner when he had
obtained leave to be at large.[a]

The truth is that the Wardenship of the Fleet Prison was from
the earliest times a kind of adjunct to another office, which included
the safe custody of the Palace at Westminster. The Guardian of
the King's Palace was responsible for its safe keeping, that no
intrusion of unfit persons might be allowed within its sacred
inclosure. He was supposed to keep an eye upon all who wished
to be admitted into the royal presence, and, if it was needful that
defaulters or other delinquents should be retained in durance ready

[a] The curious practice of giving leave of absence to prisoners seems to date from
very early times. In the 1° Ric. II. we meet with a complaint that the Warden of
the Fleet, "sometimes by mainprise or by bail, and sometimes without any mainprise, with a Baston of the Fleet," had been in the habit of suffering his prisoners
to go at large, "even into the country." (Stat. at Large, 1° Ric. II. c. 12.) Notwithstanding the legislation mentioned in the text, and a great deal more of the
same kind, it is quite clear that the practice went on for centuries, and was not
finally abolished till 1697, when it was enacted that "every such going or being out
of the said rules should be adjudged and be deemed, and is hereby declared to be, an
escape." (Stat. at Large, 8° and 9° Will. III. c. 27.) In Harris's time things must
have got almost to their worst point. He says that the Warden had about twenty
officials whose sole duty was to attend upon prisoners on leave of absence (p. 77,
103-105). These men were allowed to remain with their prisoners in the country
for a month at a time (p. 52, l. 10), being in the meantime responsible for their safe
custody. Of course the Warden had taken care to protect himself against the possibility of a prisoner giving him the slip, by obtaining security to the amount of the
judgment debt from relatives and friends. The extent to which the system of giving
leave of absence was carried is very surprising. The Warden (p. 77, l. 28) estimates
the cost to him at 80*l.* a year, which at 20*d.* a day would give an aggregate of nearly
1000 absences, or—assuming that there were even 100 of the prisoners who could
afford to pay for the luxury of occasional 'exeats'—an *average* to this privileged
class *of ten days' absence annually.*

at hand to be produced at call, he too was the official who had to answer for their appearance. For the Palace, without the Warden's licence, none might *go in*; for the Fleet Prison, without his release, none might *go out*. He made his profit by the fees levied and by exactions imposed upon ingress and egress; but it is certain that the Wardenship of the Prison was the more profitable office. From the miserable more can be wrung than from the prosperous.

In common with other offices of trust about the Court, the Wardenship of the Fleet was an office held in *Serjeantry*,[a] and as such it was regarded as a post handed down from father to son as an inheritance, precisely in the same way as a manor. It was not only a saleable property but one on which a mortgage could be raised, and from time to time mortgages were actually levied upon it. The prison with its inclosure, the buildings upon it, and the appurtenances, constituted a kind of huge caravansary kept by a landlord who was the "life tenant" of the estate and whose livelihood was made by preying upon all the inmates, while he gave them absolutely nothing in the shape of bed or board for which they were not compelled to pay and pay exorbitantly.

The English law made no provision for the insolvent debtor who had once fallen into his creditors' power. He was in a far worse condition than the *addictus* under the Roman law, for in this case the insolvent, though handed over to his creditor *to work out his debt* as a slave to his master, yet was protected from the violence of that master[b]; and while at work was labouring for his own deliverance

---

[a] By the *Abbrev. Rot. Orig.* Ed. III. it appears that the service imposed was that "custodiendi omnes prisones ibidem et eciam ad *repurandum pontem de Flete* quotiescunque necesse fuerit," f. 130.

[b] Gaius, i. 141.

and receiving maintenance at his creditor's hands. With us a debtor was simply shut up in gaol and became literally a *lost man;* his release from custody was *ipso facto* a cancelling of his debt, and the creditor who had any hope of recovering his money would never give up his claim upon his debtor's *person,* lest by so doing he should lose all claim upon the *debt.* The prisoner, on the other hand, had a claim for support upon no one: he was not a pauper; he was not a criminal; he was in worse case; he was an insolvent bankrupt; he owed money which he could not pay, and for such as him there was only one punishment—perpetual imprisonment till he had discharged his liabilities. How many unhappy creatures died of slow starvation within the precincts of that same Fleet prison—of slow starvation, I say, not to mention such as turned their faces to the wall and perished silently, the victims of disease or dull despair—it is impossible to estimate and too saddening to conjecture; but the glimpses we get now and then of the condition of such of the prisoners as were literally penniless and destitute of relations or friends or any who could at all contribute to their necessities, recals a state of affairs piteous and shocking beyond description, beyond belief, beyond imagining. Happily the horrors that were going on inside the gaols appealed to the compassion of the charitable, and from the earliest times the duty of contributing to the necessities of " poor prisoners" was acknowledged by all people who had the means, and liberally responded to.[a] The wills of the fifteenth century contain innumerable bequests for the relief of these unfortunates, and many of the London Companies still

---

[a] The earliest instance I have met with is in the *Cal. Rot. Patent,* 31° Ed. III. " Rex in auxilium pauperum prisonorum en le Flete concessit eis denarios vocatos Godspence collecturos de certis custumiis." F. 167A.

enjoy estates of some value which were left in the first instance to
provide funds for the benefit of the poor prisoners who were lan-
guishing in their dismal wards.[a]

Perhaps the bare sustenance of this pauper class of debtors was
always provided for; the alms-box at the gate rarely lacked contri-
butions, but inside these dreadful walls there were scenes and asso-
ciations which to any man or woman who had once had experience
of a peaceful home would appear incomparably more terrible than
the possibility of occasional scanty fare. At the best of times and
under the least rapacious warden the Fleet must have been a
dreadfully wicked place; under a cruel and brutal gaoler it must
have been a pandemonium. When Mr. Pickwick found himself an
inmate of the prison it was after Howard's reforms had been carried
into effect; but even then the picture, which is in no sense an
exaggeration, is repulsive enough. We must go back to Fielding's
days to find in *Amelia* a description of what it was before Howard's
time; and what a description it is! The grossest vice and profligacy
are assumed to be rampant; the gaoler panders to the lusts of his
prisoners, sponges upon their resources as long as they have a guinea
left. connives at the robbing of the new comers by the hardened
habitués, makes his profit out of all that goes on. Drunken prosti-
tutes fight and blaspheme; bullies cheat and plunder and howl and
gamble; the place is a Hell where squalor and ribaldry, coarseness
and violence, are rioting absolutely without reproof and almost
without restraint. Fielding's *Amelia* was published in 1751, just
five years before Howard's imprisonment in France first led him to

<hr>

[a] The Leather-sellers' Company alone still enjoys no less than *ten* such benefac-
tions, which were left to the Company in trust for the relief of poor prisoners between
1470 and 1638.

devote his life to the amelioration of the prisons in his own country. The account which he gives of them[a] in his first work, published in 1774, could not but cause a profound sensation. In it he has set forth a careful account of the Fleet as it existed in 1771, which is the more valuable because the building was burnt down in 1780 by the rioters under Lord George Gordon.[b]

Horrible as the general atmosphere of the Fleet was at all times, yet in the sixteenth century there were vast differences in the accommodation offered to the different classes of prisoners. In a letter from Lord Henry Howard, dated Lambeth, 26 April, 1572,[c] *he begs to be sent to the Fleet* rather than be kept in "close keeping" in the Archbishop's palace. Harris describes Newgate and the Compter as "doleful places" compared with his own more privileged retreat. Elsewhere men were kept in irons as a rule: here they could not legally be subjected to such indignity, and could not even be fastened in the stocks unless they had been exceptionally violent and refractory.[d] Where a man was so situated that he could manage to withhold from his creditors any considerable part of his income—and the state of the law, as then established, made this easy for any fraudulent or obstinate debtor[e]—such an one could live

[a] *The State of the Prisons in England and Wales, with Preliminary Observations, and an Account of some Foreign Prisons and Hospitals.* 4to.

[b] But the eighteenth-century building was very unlike that which the following pages tell us of. As Howard's work is by no means rare, it will suffice here to refer to it without troubling the reader with quotations.

[c] Dom. Eliz. vol. lxxxv. n. 25.

[d] See p. 56, l. 30 *et seq.* In the fifteenth century delinquents who were confined in the other London prisons were in the habit of practising a *ruse* for getting removed into the Fleet. By a legal fiction they confessed themselves *debtors to the King*, and on this pretence they were transferred to what was regarded as the prison for King's debtors. This practice was restrained by statute of 1° Ric. II. c. 12.

[e] See p. 36, l. 34, *et seq.*

in the Fleet in comparative comfort. After some years of confinement men got accustomed to the place: they had dropt out of society, lost their friends, contracted new habits, had become unfitted to mix with their equals in rank, the blight of gaol life had passed upon them; and cases are not infrequent of such as had actually got their discharge refusing to avail themselves of it, and continuing to occupy their old quarters.[a]

The Warden's freehold consisted of the prison strictly so called, and comprehended, besides, an inclosure precisely similar to that which surrounds many of our cathedrals.[b] In this close several " messuages " had been built from time to time by successive Wardens at their own cost. The " messuages " appear to have been blocks of buildings like those in the Temple or Lincoln's Inn, and were like them divided into chambers and let out to such as could pay for them, almost precisely as in the Inns of Court. It appears that there was even some competition for these chambers, and that as long as the occupant paid his rent he could not—or believed he could not—be ejected from them. When he went out he locked his door, and for the Warden to force an entrance was regarded as a trespass—outrageous and illegal.[c] Sir Francis Englefield had three " chambers," in which, says Harris, he received as many as *sixty visitors in a day.* Mr. Chamberlayne seems to have kept up quite an establishment.[d] Ashburnham Peck had his sons to live with him. Others had their wives and families. Francis Tregian had collected a large library during his long incarceration, and when he died in the Fleet there were " many hundred volumes " in his chamber which he had accumulated.[e]

[a] Pp. 9, 27, 65, 66. [b] MS. A. [c] P. 73, l. 18; p. 102, l. 10.
[d] P. 62, l. 15. [e] Pp. 84, 93, 59, 72, 111.

A great inducement to the erection of these blocks of chambers seems to have been given by the legislation of Queen Elizabeth against the Catholics, and the consequent imprisonment of a new class of prisoners,[a] viz. : the Recusant Gentry, whose obstinate non-conformity subjected them to heavy fines, and the Priests who were hunted down by the Pursuivants. This class were prepared to pay for any indulgence, and the profits derived from such prisoners were so large that it became well worth the Warden's while to enter into an extensive building speculation whereby the " chambers " were increased in number fivefold.[b] For this privileged class too there were "gardens and places of recreation"— such as they were—and for others who could hardly afford such luxuries as these there was yet the privilege, not to be enjoyed without the inevitable fee, of taking exercise " on the leads."

But the occupants of the chambers were the aristocracy of the Fleet, who held themselves aloof from the motley rabble, who bawled and swore, and robbed and drank, and fought and gambled in the prison strictly so called. This in Harris's time seems to have been substantially the same as it had been for centuries.[c] It consisted of "six great rooms and a court-yard, with the Tower Chambers and Bolton's Wards." The Tower Chambers appear to have been only recently set apart by the Warden as second-class chambers, the occupants of which were charged less than in the " Parlour Chambers," but more than the tenants considered the Warden had any legal right to claim. They could have been but small rooms, and were three in number.[d] And Harris says they could without crowding hold eight beds. In other words the Tower Chambers were chambers where two or three men at least had one room

[a] P. 86.   [b] P. 17, l. 10.   [c] P. 86.   [d] P. 89.

amongst them. Of the other wards one was appropriated to women; one was called the Twopenny Ward, because the prisoners there paid 2d. a night; and one was the Beggars' Ward, where the prisoners paid nothing and received nothing. Though the Warden mentions Bolton's Wards frequently, it is difficult to make out anything about them, or that they differed in any respect from the ordinary wards where the rank and file of the prisoners were confined.

There was a depth lower than the wards, viz., the Dungeon,[a] for refractory prisoners. Harris tries to make the best of it, but even so his account exhibits to us a very ugly picture: that a culprit once shut up there could be kept in irons and fastened in the stocks was no more than was to be expected; but that the dungeon could on occasion be converted into a place of torture and persecution of a very dreadful kind we learn from more sources than one in the course of its black history.[b]

It did not suit Harris's purpose to reveal to us much about the Dungeon, nor do the complainants in the case seem to have troubled themselves much with that. Nobody would get into the Dungeon if he could help it; but if he did get there—well, naturally, all the worse for him! Nor do the petitioners concern themselves with the Beggars' Ward; that was beneath their notice; and Harris accordingly scarcely does more than allude to it. When poor creatures got there, they were past caring for. We have to trust to an inmate of the Beggars' Ward, more than a century after Harris's time, to get some insight into the horrors of the place; and, revolting as the details are, they apply with certainly not *less* fidelity to the Prison as it existed in Harris's time.[c]

---

[a] P. 88, 89.   [b] MS. (B) and Bainbridge.
[c] "Cry of the Oppressed," p. 89; copy, pp. 130-35.

In the Beggars' Ward an insolvent debtor—who may have been arrested for a few shillings—was left to his fate. For fire, food, clothing, bedding, he had to trust to the commiseration of the outside world, who had never perhaps heard of his name, and only darkly suspected that there was a ghastly sweltering mass of misery inside the prison walls which it was well to alleviate if it could do so. But in the course of those long centuries hundreds must have fallen victims to cold and want and squalor, dying literally like dogs in their corner, mouldy straw beneath them, and foul rags scantily spread over their shivering and emaciated forms. The condition of the prisoners in the Common Wards was only a shade better than that of the occupants of the Beggars' Ward, and for this no thanks were due to the Warden, but to the friends of the prisoner, who still contributed some pittance to his support, and who took care that the rigour of his imprisonment should be lessened as far as might be. These poor creatures had to find their own bed and bedding—as every one else had—but they paid fees for the privilege of lying upon it without some one or more of their fellow prisoners being told off to share it with them.[a] How frightfully crowded the wards sometimes were may be inferred from the incidental allusion of Harris to one occasion when the Tower Chambers, in which it was considered hard that eight beds should be placed, had contained[b] "above 20 beds of the Wardens, and prisoners lodged there *to the number of* 56!" The filth and vermin are mentioned and alluded to *without complaint*—it was taken for granted, and looked upon as inevitable. Harris even mentions it as an instance of his own extraordinary humanity and regard for the prisoners' welfare (!) that " *at the*

---

[a] Two in a bed was the *best* accommodation that a prisoner could expect, p. 82, l. 7. p. 84, l. 10.   [b] P. 90, l. 14.

beginning" of his entering upon his office some of the prisoners
"were *permitted* to come out and fetch water to cleanse the
wards." Nay! "sometimes" the beds were actually aired![a]
The moral degradation corresponded to the physical. "You must
have been most miserable to be so cruel," was Aurora Leigh's retort
to the hag who was hurling curses at her. And those Fleet prisoners
who were "most miserable" in their abject wretchedness were con-
sistently merciless and cruel. In mere wanton mischief men howled
like maniacs through the night, and blew horns while the sick were
gasping out their last breath.[b] Women of the town came in and out
freely; pickpockets took refuge within the "liberties"; the blackleg
and the sharper were safe there; ingress and egress for any one not
actually under arrest was almost incredibly lax; and much more de-
pendence was placed upon such bonds and securities as the lawyers
drew up than upon any bolts and bars which the smith or carpenter
could contrive. We hear of prisoners being robbed of every far-
thing upon their persons by their fellow-prisoners, of brawls and fights
as too frequent to deserve notice, of its being the ordinary thing for
the prisoners to be ready with their sword or dagger. If now and
then the Warden's servant got stabbed, or a riotous ruffian got his
head broken with a candlestick, or some one else got "slain by
misadventure," the occurrence called for very little comment, and
by-and-by things went on as before.

Meanwhile the rations furnished to such as were able to pay their
way to one of the "Hall Commons" appear to have been no better
than we should have expected. The Warden must live, and his
income was derived not only from the rents of the chambers but
from the profits that accrued from the supply of food, drink, and

[a] P. 88.   [b] Pp. 73, 74, 151, l. 36.

fuel. The prisoners said the quality was abominable and the charges extortionate. Some rough attempts were made to remedy the evils complained of, but practically there was no redress. Sir Francis Englefield set up a sort of ordinary in his chambers[a] at which certain prisoners dined; others followed his example. The Warden began to be afraid that his own gains would be diminished. He objected, and took measures to put a stop to this poaching upon his prerogative. The mutiny which broke out at last, and of which we hear so much in the following pages, seems to have been caused by Harris's attempt to force all prisoners to content themselves with such purveyance as he was ready to afford. But it is evident that he abused his monopoly. Even by his own admission some prisoners actually paid for their rations and paid an *additional fee for liberty to find themselves.*[b] Even so the Warden had not done with them; for after they had obtained their provisions from outside they were again charged a fee for licence to cook at the Warden's kitchen.[c] Surely, pleads the Warden, this could be no hardship! Twenty years before, one man " paid 20*l.* per annum for licence to fetch his diet from abroad."[d] That any temperament or any constitution could support long years of imprisonment like this —aggravated as it was by all that goes to make life weary, hateful, and hopeless—is to us, in our luxurious days, almost unintelligible. And yet the denizens of the Fleet lived on. " Many of them," says Harris, " have been prisoners for 30 years, some 25, and downwards."[e] They did die, however, and they died frequently. And what ghastly death-beds they must have been! Even when a poor wretch had got his last discharge and the broken heart had made an end of beating, even then the dead body of the debtor was the

[a] Pp. 93-95.   [b] P. 119.   [c] P. 93.   [d] P. 92.   [e] Pp. 43, 65, 72, 94.

Warden's property, and could not be recovered by the relations without the payment of the fees due or demanded.[a] The cases mentioned by Moses Pitt as occurring in his own experience can hardly have been fabrications, and, if they were not, they can hardly have been without precedent or even unusual.

Amid all this turmoil of violence, lawlessness, and vice, it will perhaps surprise the modern reader most of all to find that not only were the forms of religious worship kept up,[b] but that inside this chamber of horrors the religious dissension and feuds of the outside world were repeating themselves in grim parody. In Marston's " Eastward Hoe "[c] Wolfe the Jailor says, " I have had of all sorts of men i' the kingdom under my keys, and almost all religions i' the land, as Papist, Protestant, Puritan, Brownist, Anabaptist, Millenary, Family o' Love, Jew, Turk, Infidell, Atheist, Good Fellow, &c." He might have been speaking of the Fleet instead of the Counter, for in the Fleet the clamour of conflicting zealots was confusing enough. Popish Recusants, themselves suffering for their religious opinions, stubbornly refuse to attend the Protestant service and treat it with mockery and derision, " drumming " at the doors

---

[a] A long list of complaints against the Wardens of the Fleet for extortion, persecution, and actual torture, might be made out from the Records in the State Paper Office if it were worth while to pursue so painful a subject. In the Appendix will be found the case of Joachim Newton, Warden (or Deputy Warden?), in 1597; and the barbarities of Richard Manlove, Warden in 1690, became the subject of judicial inquiry (Cry of the Oppressed, p. 81). The case of Thomas Bainbridge, dismissed from the Wardenship in 1729, may be read in the Statutes at Large, 2° Geo. II. c. 32, and in the State Trials. It is certain that if matters did not much improve between the sixteenth and eighteenth centuries they could not have got worse. Harris's summary of the past history of the Fleet, at p. 9, l. 21, &c. speaks for itself.

[b] Down to Howard's days, and long after, the fees for the *chaplain* charged to the prisoners are conspicuous. [c] The play was acted in 1605.

while it is going on.[a] Another set of fanatics elect a preacher of
their own, make a contribution for him at the end of his sermon, and
are marvellously edified by his discourse.[b] A crazy enthusiast who
had rendered himself notorious by his extravagant notions and the
energy which he had displayed in trying to propagate them, though
thrown into the Fleet to cure him of his delusions, does his best
to proselytise there, and appears to have had some success. But it
was inside the walls just as it was outside: Men were fighting for
religion without it; and for any influence that their professions
exercised upon their daily conduct, or for any wholesome effect
which these produced upon their lives, they might almost more
profitably have been playing at bowls or working problems in
algebra than belabouring one another with the bludgeons of contro-
versial theology.

The two most notable incidents with which Harris's Apology has
to do are the mutinous outbreak among the prisoners, which
ocurred in July 1619,[c] and the stabbing of Sir John Whitbrooke
by Broughton in the following October.

We should probably have heard little or nothing of either
occurrence if it had not chanced that, two years later, some of the
prisoners contrived to get a formal complaint lodged against the
Warden. As to the stabbing of Sir John Whitbrooke it attracted
very little attention at the time; the event is just mentioned in the
news-letters, and it seems as if the rumours that were circulated
about it by the *quidnuncs* provoked a faint sentiment of displeasure
in certain quarters, but it was a nine-days' wonder, and was soon
forgotten. As for the mutiny, I have not once met with any notice
of or allusion to it in any of the many diaries or letters which have

---

[a] P. 136.   [b] Pp. 48, 50, l. 32.   [c] P. 43.

been preserved. Such things had been and such things would be again. The silence is more suggestive than any comments could have been ; nor is that silence less suggestive because, just about a year after the prisoners in the Fleet barricaded the wards—smashing the furniture, forcing the bolts, and assaulting their gaolers—a precisely similar *emeute* broke out in the King's Bench, and of so violent a character as to need the interference of the High Sheriff of the county with something approaching an armed force.[a] There is no reason to believe that there was any concerted action between the inmates of the two prisons. Both cases appear to have been sudden and spontaneous explosions of passion among a crowd of desperate men, whose condition was past all bearing, and whose misery and irritation had driven them at last to phrenzy.

It would be out of place to continue the history of the Fleet for the two centuries after Harris's time, during which it continued to be used as a debtors' prison. The same abuses and abominations went on unchecked and unreformed for 150 years. At last the "Moral Genius" arose who denounced the iniquities that were so scandalous, and, though it took another 70 years to get rid of the vile system, it succumbed at last. Even towards the end of the seventeenth century some feeble palliation to the barbaric laws affecting imprisonment for debt were from time to time introduced into the statutes; but the very frequency of these enactments shows too plainly how partial such measures were in their operation, and how much they were needed. The men who framed and draughted the remarkable petition and Act which is printed in the Appendix V.

[a] See Appendix III.

were men who were very much in advance of their age. Two hundred years were to pass away before the legislature of this country could entertain such views as those set forth, and before the abolition of punishment for debt was finally determined on. It was not till the 22nd December 1844, that the Fleet Prison and the ground on which it stood was brought to the hammer.[a]

[a] In the Guildhall Library the printed plans and specifications, &c. of the sale may still be seen. In the same collection is a " Plan and Section of the Interior, and Perspective views of the Fleet Prison, by Rotaldé;" it has no date, but it must represent the Fleet as it appeared *after* the fire in 1755.

The Œconomy of the Fleete,

OR

An Apologeticall Answeare of Alexander Harris [late Warden there] unto xix Articles sett forth against him by the Prisoners

Thus say the Prisoners.

A breife Collection of some part of the Exactions, Extortions. Oppressions, Tyrannies, and Excesses towardes the Lives, Bodies. and Goods of Prisoners, done by *Alexander Harris*, Warden of the
5 Fleete, in his fower yeares misgovernement, ready to be proved by Oath and other Testimonyes.

		Answeare. Page	
After knowne quarrells and fightings betweene two prisoners, lodging them in 10 one chamber, where quarrelling and fighting againe, and notice to him thereof given, and of likelye further mischeife, this notwithstanding continuance of them together untill the one murdered the other.		32	1. Murder.
15 Removeing a prisoner out of his chamber, having 51*li*. 1*s*. hidd under his bedd, which the prisoner required he might goe to his chamber to dispose off, which was denyed, and he thrust up in another roome 20 close prisoner until the warden and some of his servants rifled his bedd of that money.		43.	2. Felonie.
11*li*. 6*s*. taken out of the trunck and by violence from the person of a close prisoner 25 sick in his bedd, by the Warden and his servants.		47.	3. Robberie.
After engagement of faith soule and all under hand and seale, contrary thereto, detayneing a prisoner have[ing] libertye by 30 his Majesty's writt, to his great prejudice.		52.	4. Infidelitie.

Answeare.

False imprisonment of men discharged offering to pay all due fees for divers moneths. — 55. — 5. False imprisonment.

5

Close imprisonment of many without order, warrant, or lawe, by moneths and yeares. — 58. — 6. Close imprisonment.

Close and cruel imprisonment, chaineing, manacling, and bolting of them with irons, some of the degree of knighthood, without cause or warrant. — 58. — 7. Cruel imprisonment.   10

Starving of men close imprisoned, guarding them from meate, drinke, &c. and that after command of authoritie to the contrary. — 67. — 8. Starveing close prisoners.

15

Breaking of prisoners chambers, haveing first removed them, opening their truncks, seizeing their goods, and still detayneing them. — 71. — 9. Seizeing and detaineing prisoners goods.

20

Where an order gives upon every dayes goeing abroad by one that is not in execution 8d. to the wardes box, the orders exemplified under the great scale hath a dash over the word *wardes* to make it *Warden's box*, by which practise and under coullor thereof he continually robbeth the poore of that 8d. a day, which is yearely a great matter. — 76. — 10. Robbing the poore men's box.

25

Where the same order gives 12d. a day to the keeper that goeth abroad with such prisoner he robbeth his servante of that alsoe, forcing the prisoner besides to content his keeper. — 77. — 11. Robbing his 30 poore servants of their dues.

Answeare.
Page

He hath warrant dormants under some
of the counsell's hands, not nameing any
particular person, by which continually in
5 all countryes he seizeth upon his Majesties
subjects forceth them to give bonds to be
his prisoners, exacteth intollerable fees and
compositions, &c. where theis apprehen-
sions ought to be by the sherriffs of the
10 shires without such vexation or charge to
the subject.

12. Abusing the
councell's war-
rant dormant.

80.

Where by orders noe man ought to pay
for any chamber (the Warden alloweing
bedd and beding) above 2s. 4d. a weeke
15 he exacteth 8s., 10s., 13s. 4d., and of some
20s. a weeke without beding.

13. Excessive
rates of cham-
bers.

82.

Where before his tyme nothing was
paid for lodging in comon wards, he exacteth as if they lay in private chambers
20 upon his bedding, yea, for the dungeon alsoe.

14. Exacting for
lodging in com-
mon wardes and
dungeon.

86.

He exacteth after those high rates chamber rents of men haveing noe chambers,
but lyeing abroad by the King's writt or
otherwise.

15. Exaction for
chambers, not
having any.

91.

25 He exacteth for dyett whole commons
of men that take none of his meate or
drinke, a thing never demaunded before
his tyme.

16. Exactions of
dyett, takeing
none.

92.

He layeth impositions upon meat and
30 fewell, and forceth prisoners to pay them,
as 2d. a joynt, 3s. 4d. for a loade of billets,
&c. and forceth prisoners to pay 12d.
a bushell for charcoale which are to be
bought for 12d. a sack.

17. Impositions
upon Meate and
Fuell.

98.

	Answeare. Page
Where men be whole vacations abroad by *habeas corpus* he forceth them to pay him 20d. a day for outgoeings, their chamber rent and dyett, horrible exactions never had or demaunded by former Wardens. } 101.	18 Horrible exactions upon such as goe 5 abroad by the King's Writs.
Of men haveing the King's writts to goe about their businesse, he exacteth of them for his leave, of some 40s. 3li. 5li. 10li. or more in money or other bribes, a daylie trade never done by any before, and without yeilding theis fowle exactions they are staied and loose their occasions. } 104.	19. Excessive exactions for his 10 favour to goe upon the King's Writts.

Their fowle exactions, extortions, and base usages towards prisoners 15 by *Robert Holmes* the clarke, *Henry Cooke* the porter, *Richard Mansell*, and other Mr Warden's worthy instruments, servants, and affidavit men, would aske a volume, and is reserved for a longer discourse.

There be many other great greivances which for brevity are 20 omitted, all which will directly be proved and most of theis above be in the particular accusations deliverd in Parliament with the witnesses names annexed, ready to be verified upon oath as they have already been verbally attested before the honourable comittee at fower severall meeteings in the Fleete.   25

Thus saieth the Warden :

The Nyneteene Articles sett forth against the Warden are such, as if he should not answeare, it weare a tacite confession of guilt; and to answeare in this elaborate and tedious manner may be irksome to read. But as he hath undergon the reproach of the 30

accusation, soe he hath presumed to hazard the rebuke of his un-
pollished writeing rather than to leave his innocency unremembred
to the world. And therefore *Non ad forum judicii sed ad infor
mandum conscientiam.*

5 The Warden hath also answeared unto divers particuler men's
complaints which were made against him. And for better cleareing
thereof hath mentioned theis followeing, viz.:

		Answeare. Page	
	The orders and constitutions renewed		
10	and made Anno 3° Elizabeth for governe-		
	ment of the Fleete and the prisoners		
	there.	110.	
	The explanations of those constitutions and ratification.	115.	
15	A particuler answeare to Mr. Edward Rookwood.	128.	Romishe.
	A particuler answeare to Mr. Nicholas Rookwood	128.	Romishe.
	George Lee.	134.	
20	Sir Francis Englefeild, Barronett.	139.	
	Sir John Whitbrook's Lady.	32.	
	Ashburnham Peck.	71.	
	Sir William Price, Knt.		Romishe.
	Mr. John Warren.		
25	Edward Beare.		In generall.
	John Sherley.		In generall.
	John Segar.		In generall.
	Mr. Edward Chamberlayne.	120.	
	The Lady Amy Blunt.	143.	
30	Edmond Sharpe.	147.	
	William Harvey.	151.	
	Edward Coppin.	43.	
	Richard [Christopher] Kennell.	55.	

A particular Answeare to—

The Warden saith :

Though in courts of comon justice it is not admitted to answeare
any mans plea or complaint with recrimination, yet it is to be
hoped that this answeare may be made in such manner of recrimination with great reason and equitie. For men are seldome sent 5
to prison for vertue, but for delinquencie, soe come they to prison
as to the center of justice.   At which place if they presume in
contempt of former judiciall proceedings to abuse themselves and
the place, there is reason they should be stricktlie dealt with all.
And why doe they in Bedlam binde men, in Newgate iron them, in 10
other prisons shutt them up ?   But because some are madd or
crackt braynd, some are full of villany, others drunken and refractory.   And doth there not come to the Fleete (on other occasions)
men that be touched with all theis vices? Yes, surelie, and with
many more. So that it must alwayes be left in the keeper's discretion 15
to act his part according to the persons whom he meeteth withall.
But for such a keeper to putt madd and desperate men together,
irons on the civell persons, restrayne the comformable, exact or
extort money or goods from them that owe nothing or from such
as ought to possess them, is noe way (without doubt) tollerable.   To 20
rayse newe customes, inflict newe punishments, to betray men's
liberty in takeing or letting men goe are things unsufferable.   But
there are degrees of punishment in the fleete and in all prisons.
As for dungeon, shackles, and stocks, they doe differ as much from
ordinary imprisonment as imprisonment doth from freedome.   And 25
lett a true consideracon be made of the persons or prisoners that
have complayned agaynst the Warden, and it will be found that
their complaints are more fraught with mallice and for their owne
ends, then for true cause.   And their endeavour is to turn their
particuler to a comon example and (forsooth) doe good to other 30
prisoners, when they themselves doe wrong to all men that have
had former dealeing with them, and they would that out of the

brests of a fewe outlawed banckrupts, forgerers, perjurers, conspirators, libellors, schismaticks, and opponents of our religion
should yssue a lawe to guide and direct Justice and Judges themselves.

5   If there hath been such great cause of reformation or redressing
of wrongs to prisoners, howe hath it come to passe that soe many
clamours, heretofore made, have beene answeared and avoyded?
Are prisoners men that solely be obedient? Noe surely, for this
difference there is betweene them and their keeper, that he is
10 bound to obey all comands and directions of superiors, but the
prisoners *non habent unde eadant.* They are in prison, and whatsoever they doe they can but be in prison; and as for some, nothing
can comand, nothing persuade or induce them, nothing rule them,
they are men sould and bought soe to their wills, as *stat pro ratione*
15 *voluntas.* And it is a greevious thing to have to doe with them
who, having practized all shifts abroad in the world, doe now come
to exercise their shifts and practizes upon their keeper. As the last
refuge of a forlorne hope, where some, though they are or may be
discharged, will not goe away, others (discharged) will not forsake
20 the place, but still have recesse and dependance. Yea, if a vaga-
bound man or woeman (for there are of both sorts frequent in that
place) once sett foote there he shall find one or other to owne him
as his servant and cover all villanyes.

It is noe novell thing for prisoners to contend and oppose their
25 gardians. In *Babington's* tyme it was soe; *Carlton* was slayne; in
Mr. Anslowe's tyme were insurrections, slaughter of servants, and
prisoners irons and stocks inflicted; Soe was it [in] *Mr. Tirrells* tyme,
in *Newton's* tyme, in *Mr. Reynolds,* in *Trenche's* tyme, in *Mr.*
Phillips, and soe downewards, which, being to many unknowne or
30 forgotten, may lay the more aspertion upon this warden that now is.

But in this tyme are there not more noted and waightie constrac-
tions [*sic*] and oppositions daylie practized in the King's Bench,
Newgate, and other prisons where the prisoners band themselves, not
onely against the keepers and marshall, but against the Citty and

Country, and *posse comitatus*, wherein, if some prevention be not
used hereafter, it shall be better for any that is now a keeper of a
prison to sit downe by the losse, and rather heare then see what
will followe in the prison and commonwealth, whereof some part in
the ensueing answeares will appeare, and this hoped to be allowed 5
to every gardian that he doe rather prevent escapes, breach of
prison, murthering of himselfe and his, then remitt [*sic*] to complaint
when it is done, for if he doe it not soe he shall rather be an Accuser
then a keeper.

The first of the prisoners' plott to overthrowe the governement 10
of the Fleete, was, by impeaching the constitutions for perpetuall
governement there, exemplified in Queen Elizabeth's tyme, by consent
and subscription of the Secretary of State, the Chiefe Justices of
both benches, and all the puisne judges, the Lord Chauncellor and
Treasurer, explayned and confirmed before the Lords of the Privy 15
Councell, the prisoners saying that those constitutions are but
personall and bind noe more but such prisoners as were then in the
Fleete about sixty years past; that they were gotten by falshood
and corruption; That the warden durst not avouch them; soe that
the Warden's power being extenuated in such fashion, the conspiracie 20
to kill him was put in practize, and to breake upp the prison was
alsoe acted, and he and his servants greviously wounded.

After which the Warden, thinking and receiveing direction, that
it was more fitt for him to governe and make good the King's prison
then to complayne on men already imprisoned, some fewe of the 25
prisoners tooke upp the complaint first (abuseing the name of the
whole), yet were then never soe stedfast in their complaints as that
the Warden could knowe who or for what they complayned, being
assuredly perswaded that he had done so much right unto the honest
and better soarte, that (amongst hundreds) he was ever able to pro- 30
duce all the best knights, gentrie, and civell poore to approve his
doeings, and soe should still have been but that he was comanded
the contrarie.

As for a fewe malecontents, they will ever clamour when men of

worth will contayne themselves, knowing they be in prison and
ought to be ruled.

Yet notwithstanding the complaints tending not soe much to have
anything reformed in the Warden or the Governement there, as to
5 make all things uncertayne, whereby neither Governement nor payments might be had; Therefore the lords and others of his
Majestie's Privie Counsell commanded expresly that they should
pay somewhat in the interim, and referred the difficultyes and
differences to be considered by committees of that most honourable
10 board and to the cheife justices of both benches. But the prisoners
(perceiveing it made not for their purpose) became informers in
their own name against the Warden, thinkeing to evade those
orders and constitutions by the strickt lettre of the lawe and condempne the Warden in great penaltyes for practizeing those con-
15 stitutions.

Upon which occasion the Warden made his suite unto the lords
for stay of those Informations, whereupon the comittees came to the
Fleet, heard the greevances, comanded payment to be made to the
Warden, and that the Information should cease untill they had taken
20 further Orders. But the Warden could gett neither quietnes nor
payment, for two prisoners then petitioned his Majestie that the
tryall might goe forward.

They came into the Courts of Justice alledgeing that the Lawe
was their patrimony, the judges bound by oath to yield it them,
25 that it ought not to stopp upon any occasion of Great Seale or
Privy Seale. The Warden then, perceaveing that the cause was noe
longer properly his, but whether the King's Majestie or his royall
progenitors could (by their prerogative) give power to execute an
office of special trust, and finding that neither the comittee's comand
30 nor the King's attorney's *Nolle prosequi* could appease them, and
makeing this knowne to the Lord Chauncellor and judges, some of
the prisoners were sent for and much rated for their insolencie, and
withall the Lord Chauncellor promiseing that things should be

ordered by Comission from the King, the most insolent submitted thereunto.

Soe the Lord Chauncellor moved his Majesty for such a comission, which was graunted, sealed, and directed to him the Lord Chauncellor, to the honourable Treasurer and Comptroller of his howshould, to the Master of the Rolls Sir Edward Cooke, the Cheife Justices of both Benches, and the Cheife Baron, most whereof satt upon that Comission and gave heareing. But the prisoners (then also thinking that they had such advantage by lawe as would overcome the Warden) pressed still to have the benefitt of lawe. The Comissioners therefore, seeing nothing would appease them, gave way for proceedings at lawe. And upon yssue joyned and evidence given on both sides touching the rate of chambers, the promooter for extortion in chambers and lodgings durst not stand to the verdict, but became *nonsuited* and paied costs, never since dareing to goe forward in the like suite.

A suite in lawe about the rent of chambers passed on the warden's side.

The other point touching payment for dyett was alsoe brought to tryall, in which that Promooter himselfe was a cheife witnes, yet was the pursuer of that action overthrowne in lawe; by the words of the statute, by custome, by prescription in eight wardens tymes, and by the constitutions. Soe that a verdict passed for that alsoe on the Warden's side and might have appeased any man whom right or Justice can conteyne. But noe marvaile if theis still contend, for outlawes and jesuites are (almost) all that complayne, and besides that the cheife of them for sowle matters was in the xith yeare of His Majestie's raigne censured in Starrchamber, they all (in a manner) are now defendents there att the King's attorneys suite for their intollerable routs, riotts, conspiracyes, &c. done in the Fleete, which cause is soe farre proceeded in as that matter enough is confessed upon record by the defendants themselves, and witnesses are now examineing to fortifie the same. But theis prisoners, being very sensible what will be the yssue of that suite (to their punishment), have premeditated and boasted that they will

Another verdict in lawe about takeing money for dyett where they had none.

5

10

15

20

25

30

by their clamours make the Warden run away or confound him
before that tyme come; some of them have since that resolved, and
provoked others to resolve, to detayne the fees and duties that
accrewe to him and soe to disable him in his meanes, nay, they
5 have incyted one another to kill him, and besides the one that did
attempt it another hath confessed that he afterwards was resolved
to finish it, they further knowing that touching a fact done in the
Fleete, the Warden might either produce witnesses from amongst the
prisoners or his owne servants; therefore as to the prisoners they
10 except against their testimonyes as banished persons, not remembring
that they be their own Christned [sic] bretheren and have signes and
marks common with themselves, and as for the servants they attempt
to persuade them and the world that their master (the Warden)
hath robbed them, and therefore they have noe cause to adhere to
15 their master but to the prisoners, who stand for their good; and yet
(by their leave) they scofflinglie terme them worthy instruments of
their maisters and *Affidavit men*. In which they blowe hott and
could and sayle two wayes with one wynd, a thing not improper to
men in the Fleete. Yet touching them servants they are the
20 Warden's and noe further then they doe well.

This then is the further drift and scope of their Nyneteene
Articles published against the Warden, viz. to overthrowe him, to
outstand justice, to shun their owne chastisements in the Starrchamber and to have soe many immunities as is possible. To
25 which immunities by way of contrarie every of theis nyneteen
artic[l]es have a secret pointing, and yet those Nyneteene be not
ynough, soe that herein (like *Hydra*) they meane to have heads of
contentions fower or five yeares more (as formerly they have had
already), that in the meane tyme the Warden may have no payment,
30 [as none he hath had], and their owne land and revenues may be
inlarged, and their meanes swell to pay creditors, but it shall be
noe more then ij. iij. or iiijs. in the pound of their debts; reserveing
and keepeing the surplusage for their posteritie. And this reso-
lutely they determyne to obtayne or else lett their creditors take

their carkasses when they dye, soe that it is an hazard counterpoysed
whether the creditor or the debtor beareth the greater, for if the
one dye in prison the other looseth the debt, and if charrity can not
move the creditor lett the hazard doe it.

The prisoner should be the subject of charity, but as the tyme 5
now is, the creditor is the object of scorne, for the one hath said
Loe, thus we lodge, thus we feed, drinke, and bowle, and the other
thinketh he suffereth in the meane tyme; but, saith the prisoner, if
you descend to our conditions so it is, if not, adieu, you shall seeke
us before we seeke you.   10

Surely a modest and temperate governor of a prison should much
availe the comon wealth and be a good medium between the
creditor and the delinquent. The Warden for his part shall submitt
himselfe and stand neither for revenge or gaine, onely for the
reputation of a faithfull subject, a sinceare officer, and a Christian 15
man. But such hath been the malignity of a sonne of Symonie
residing in that place, as to add unto the Nyneteene Articles and
peirce above the flesh into the very soule by alledgeing before
great persons and boasting of it afterwards that the Warden is cir-
cumcized; but he (falsely) spake the truth, for it is true in the 20
spiritt but not in the letter, in the heart but not in his flesh, who
haveing conversed with most Chistians in the world, yea with most
nations Jewes, or Turks, attributed ever in the better sense somewhat
to them that were religious and did hope for good of such men;
but in the Fleete, finding seared consciences, stupid myndes, and 25
carnall desires, he prayeth the Lord to visitt them in mercy and
make their affliction convert them, not onely releiving the prisoner
but him also that is their governor, who is and shall be at all tymes
more a prisoner thorough care and oversight than the prisoners
themselves, and may well take upp the saycing of the holy Prophett 30
David, " Who [sic] is to me that I remayne in Meshech and dwell
in the tents of Kedar, my soule hath too long dwelt with him that
hateth peace."

One thing hath stuck much in the mynds of men, which is that

the Warden payeth a great rent for the place, and some conclude
that therefore he must take or exact much, and that it were necessary the rent were abated, whereby the prisoners may pay lesse.

Surely such reason and consequence is utterly to be eschewed,
5 for first *caveat emptor*, if he had overfarmed it (as men have farmes
in theis days) att his perrill be it, that is noe rule or reason why he
should extort, but rather leave it or undergoe the losse.

But to prove that he hath not overrented it, it shall appeare that
it is better cheape to him then to any other Warden in 30 yeares
10 before, soe much can be made manifest; and about 30 yeares hereafter it will be better by many hundreds when leases determyne
which now are of small value, and also when that the Warden
should be disposed to build (as he may) upon the freehould and
lett it to prisoners or strangers as formerly hath been done, when
15 it was devided in dowrie and to coheires, for a freehould is a
seperate thing to the prison; the freehold [being] held in graund serjeancie, vizt. *custodiendi prisonam*. Therefore it is the building and
confluence of prisoners that hath increased the rent, for as to the
warden he hath not inhaunced either rents or flees, or restrayned
20 usage and custome. Besides the rent is not chargeable onelie for
the Fleete, but for keepeing of, *ballicam custodiendi*, the King's
pallace at Westminster, which hath great fees and emoluments,
sometymes in two dayes worth 400*li*. and if duties might be freely
claymed there, it is noe lesse worth then the Fleete, and the office
25 of Guardian hath had fees in large nature, both as a pecuniarie
paine to deterre men from being committed, as alsoe in regard of
the great hazard of life, lymme, and goods which the Warden
undergoeth by receiveing and answearing each waighty prisoner
in his kind, whereby in one hower he may be undone, for what
30 prison keeper in England (like him) hath had at one tyme the
King's prisoners for two hundred thowsand pounds debt, besides
the affayres of State. And therefore, if he hath beene carefull to
suppresse daunger when a generall breach of prison was attempted
and in part acted by theis that nowe complayne and himselfe and

servantes treacherouslie wounded almost to death, hath he not
merritted his fees and duties, and to be protected against reproches?
Lett the thing judge and such as know what a prison is where the
confusion of Babell doth dwell. Lett them judge or else *acqui-
escere* in them that daylie take accompt of the accidents there, for 5
it is noe smale difficultie now, long after things are done, to give
a reason of every circumstance and fact, which discretion might
then move a Warden or his under officers to doe this or that which
now may be forgotten, the proofes not remembred, or witnesses
dead, after three or fower yeares past since they were don, as most 10
of theis were, and were then [not?] controverted while they were
fresh in mynde.

But to come nearer to the matter of theis 19 Articles which are
published against the Warden. To 14 of them, which about two
yeares past the prisoners did exhibite against him before those 15
Comissioners appointed by his Majestie to heare and determyne

Anno 1° R. 1. the variances, they made their *Exordium* that because Anno 1
R 1 (who gave the keepeing of the Fleete), he gave alsoe a freehold and a fee of vjd. per diem for doeing the service, therefore it
is a free prison and noe continued duties are to be paid by prisoners. 20

Answeare.   Which is as much as if a man came to London and aske an
hoast or innkeeper whether the howse be his owne, or that he pay
rent, and thereupon conclude that if it be his owne the guest is to
have his lodging and attendance for nothing; but if the hoast
should say he hath lettres pattents under the great seale of England 25
that the same guest might lye there, and noe where ells, and pay
such and such duties, what reply can the guest make? Soe it is
with the prisoners and the Warden, so is it also with the leive-
tennants of the Tower, with keepers of castles and others. It is
called a free prison in regard the warden holdeth it *absque aliquo* 30
inde [sic] *reddendo* to the King and not free to the prisoners.

2 Allegation.   They likewise alledge that 1° Elizabeth it was purchased by
Tirrell at the rate of 160*li* per annum, and that long after it was
held at 100*li*. per annum and refused for 200*li*. But now that

(thorough extortion) there is made 4,000*li.* per annum by the relation delivered to one *Mr. Shotbolt.*

To which is answeared, that the purchase paid by *Tirrell* (as appears by the deed inrolled) was 6,060 markes, or 4,000*li.* which if
5 it be devided at tenne or twelve yeares purchase, being more then an office of that nature was worth in those dayes (which is above three score yeares past), it will bring out 400*li.* per annum, tenne yeares purchase, and therefore here is *sutor ultra crepidam,* for 160*li.* at that rate would yeild but 1,600*li.* in money, and there was
10 not then the fift part of the buildings and lodgings which now are.

Mr. Anslowe (as is crediblie informed) held it by fyne (and otherwise) at 600*li.* per annum, and had but some part of the benefitts of the prison, nothing of the pallace at Westminster. And as for this Warden's valuation of it at 4000*li.* per annum, it might be,
15 supposeing that if the benefitts of the pallace were had, &c. But what if the one with the other cost in expences 4,000*li.* per annum, what will be then advanced? And as to *Mr. Shotbolt,* for all the great shewe was made to him (if any such be), he was to give the warden but 133*li.* 6s 8d. *de claro* per annum for it, and perhapps the
20 Warden had beene better to have contracted for halfe that, soe it had been with a man that would have paid it. What prejudice then has fallen to this Warden, who (as appeares by his bookes) hath not in all manner of shewe above 2,200*li.* comeing in per annum, and spendeth and looseth more then the same, thorough
25 such good guests as prisoners are. Whereof one doth boast that he hath spent 300*li.* in suite against the Warden to catch him upon informations, and yet never paid the warden a penny in the tyme he hath beene Warden; what should become of the office if all prisoners did soe? Especially if a warden had had it which had been
30 able to loose nothing by it? Such a one might (as now this is likely) either become a beggar or lie in prison by defeature as these doe.

Alsoe they alledged that before Tirrell's tyme there was never taken but ijs. iiijd. for the fyne or fee of the commissioners, and

CAMD. SOC. D

(marginal notes:) Answeare.

3 Allegation. Quer of this fee in the *quo*

warranto, it is
the fee of the
barr at West-
minster.

that when in 3° Elizabeth it was referred to Commissioners to sett
downe orders for perpetuall government there, the Commissioners
would not doe it without approbation of the prisoners.

Answeare.

Howe false this is lett it appeare bye the constitutions 3° Eliz.
for then all the prisoners and Warden did mutually joyne in peti-   5
tion that Commissioners might be appointed to erect good and
necessary orders of newe, and to establish all such orders as should
be proved to have continued tyme out of the remembrance of men,
and that there might be a register or record thereof, whereby they
might be certayne.   10

Which Comission being graunted and great scrutinye made by
certiorari to the Warden and other officers of record to bring in all
writeings that did concerne the old usages, orders, and customes
there, the Comissioners did conclude without any opinion or approbation of the prisoners or of the Warden according as in their wis- 15
dome they thought fitt, and did sett downe all rates of fees and
governement of prisoners.

But because in matter of dyett (which is arbitrarie) how a man
will be fedd and what ordinary he will goe unto; wherefore to that
point onely the prisoners were called, and to nothing ells, to make 20
choyse and to sett downe what they thought fitt.   For in reason
they were to be fedd as they would pay, but it doth not thereof
followe that their fynes, fees, restraynts, libertyes, &c. sould be as
they themselves would agree unto, for the lawe, *ab origine*, hath
determyned that;   And moreover this assertion receaveth a further 25
evasion, for of all those that did agree to the rate of dyett, there
was neither archbishop, duke, earl, &c. baron, or knight, that was
then in custodie to value the bounty of such persons, and yet there
was a rate sett downe for them, which rates (for their honors be it
spoken) in point of dyett, they have not onely paid (takeing nothing 30
for it), but yet further have exhibited to the warden and his while
they have beene there.   What a goodly coulor and glosse had
these men to move for new constitutions if the inferior prisoners
had not then asked the question, but now they be unexcusable.

And whereas further they collect the reason why the Warden
should have but ij*s*. and iiij*d*. fee *de quolibet homine comisso* from a This was the fee in court at Westminster and at Fleete.
graunt made almost 500 yeares past, and from diverse inquisitions
made upon former Wardens' death, and the wardship of the heire,
5 wherein his Majesty is interressed by the tenure, and therefore
would conclude that as Adam began in innocency and simplicitie,
soe the Warden's fee should still be the same to the world's end,
and that, howsoever banckrupts and delinquents are growen more
cuning in their generations, yet neither fees nor tymes should
10 meete with them, for they would have the old lawe on foote that
nullus liber homo imprisonetur, &c.

Yet lett them nowe give the warden leave to think that in 3º
Elizabeth those grands and sages which reviewed and established
the orders for government of the Fleete did not by confederacie
15 and conspiracie increase the fees of ij*s*. and iiij*d*. in a praecipitous
manner to 21*li*. 10*s*. for a prisoner of one degree to 14*li*. 15*s*. for
another degree, to 10*li*. 6*s*. 8*d*. for another, and soe downe to 7*s*. 4*d*.
and this in such fractions and broken somes; but rather that they
found a president or reason for it before *Tirrell* purchased the
20 Fleete, who was well knowne to be a gentleman that neither aspired
or was like to be countenanced in obteyncing soe excessive increase
and varyation of fees, and that it was long before done, and ordered
to the end that the meanest man whose ij*s*. iiij*d*. was as good silver
as the best man's might not looke for the like observance and
25 attendance in the Fleete as the Nobles had, and it doth appeare
long before *Tirrell's* purchase, that a certayne reverend bishopp of
our Church being persecuted and sent to the Fleete did there pay
such fee as a baron now paieth, whereof he would not have thought
much and complayned if barons had paid but ij*s*. and iiij*d*. a
30 peece; and therefore if theis clamorers doe think themselves injured
they shall doe well to endeavour (as they beginne) to have muni-
cipall lawes of their owne within the walls of the Fleete erect
consistorie, and under the generall and indefinite name of prisoners

corporations or bodyes politique call the Warden and others to
answeare, at which tyme, if their court have any type of justice,
the very name of those graunds and sages will be not onely a good
plea in barr of theis unsavoury arguments, but alsoe patronage enough
for the Warden himselfe, when he shall be admitted to answeare   5
any prisoner hand to hand, the Accusers may thinke that the Warden
doth mock them (truely if he doe not, he well may, for their
fabulous and arrogant proceedings, where there are lawes, statutes,
historie, prerogative, custome, verdicts, and evidences against them).

4.   They conclude very honestly and reasonably that according to 10
the true meaning thereof they may have a coppie hung upp in the
Hall of the Fleete that the prisoners may knowe them to avoyd
controversies hereafter.

Answeare.   This their conclusion that hath the shewe of concord is yet like
Sampson's foxes, whose heads are turned another way, for in the 15
end, whereas the constitutions and customs were, that the Warden
might shewe and the prisoner enjoy ease for his money, all their
23 H. 6.   ayme was to punish the Warden on the stattute of 23 H. 6 in xlli.
toties quoties, he shewed them any case, and they try the orders of
3ᵉ Elizabeth, but they will not be guided by them, soe that they 20
which succeede this Warden have great cause to take heed that they
shewe them noe case: a strange thing it is that prisoners complayne of ease.

And as for hanging upp of a table of the ordinances for governement, there never wanted one in the Hall of the Fleete, which the 25
prisoners understanding in a sense most beneficiall for themselves, a
table was alsoe hanged by it, howe the sense was explayned by the
judges and corroborated by the lords of the privy councell. But the
table which had the sence hath been from tyme to tyme taken (if
not to say stolne) away, to the end that prisoners would be still 30
sencelesse, or ells (surely) theis constitutions had never growne to
the point that now they be, to the troubling of the Lords, the
Judges, his Majestie himselfe, yea the wisdome and state of the

whole kingdome, and men which comonly looke on the first table
may perhapps blame the Warden whom the second table will
acquite in all men's judgements which be indifferent.

And although a tender hart may soone be sensible of a fault that
5 is committed, yet for two reasons it would be hard for the Warden
of the Fleete to answeare.

First, because most of those articles are generall, as if he had used 1.
all or many of the prisoner according as is sett forth.

Secondly, because they have not sett downe the tyme when the 2.
10 fact was done, neither the circumstances, reasons, or occasions of
doeing such as were done. Many whereof shall be avoyded for
just and good, but God, whose proper work is onely to turn that
unto good (which they meant for hurt) did (as is before declared)
bring this to passe in some measure when the prisoners were heard
15 before the commissioners, for then they delivered in wryteing those
14 Articles (the same in substance that 14 of theis 19 now are), to *And a coppie*
which the Warden not onely by word but by wryteing made *given to the*
answeare, which is extante to be seene in some of the Commissioners *Warden.*
hands; whereupon and upon the verdicts aforesaid the prisoners did
20 desist and the most held themselves convinced.

But the malignitie and unreconcileable hatred of some banckrupts
is such, that, thinkeing those 14 Articles would be reputed unworthy
to be iterated without some notorious additions, therefor to them
are added five more, and those of noe lesse consequence, then first
25 murther, secondly fellony, 3ly robbery, fourthly infidelity, a fift of
a forgery by altering the constitutions under the Great Scale of
England, made for the perpetuall governement of the Fleete, and
theise be things in the prisoners opinions soe haynous as the very
nameing of them is able to quell a man at once.

30 Theis with the rest came forth at such a tyme as that most
honourable assembly was to be dissolved and noe tyme for answeare,
soe as the Warden was for that present outwardly left with a brand
or tincture, but such is the power of God in a cleare conscience
that inwardlie it made his hart to leape and rejoyce when he sawe

there was nothing but theis of mallice without matter to taint him
withall, and tooke it as a testimony that they, knoweing if they
should (as they might if they durst) bring every or any of this five
into ordinary course of justice, by indictment or otherwise, would
not doe it for feare that if they fayled in their proofes it would   5
revert on their owne heads by like ordinary course of justice, and
the Warden might impleade them for it.

Therefore to avoyd such impleading this was by their Fleete oracle
thought a sure and sound course how to calumpniate or libell, and
not to be subject to punishment for it. Notwithstanding which,   10
it is to be hoped that wise and judicious persons will for their
mallice reject or little esteeme their matter, and conceive that if the
Warden had been soe fowle and exorbitant, he could not soe long
tyme and in so excellent a comonwealth have found protection, remission, or connivance after soe many heareings as have passed at   15
councell board at comittees, then att and before the judges and
justices in particuler and in generall, unto all which in his daylie
attendance he rendreth accompt of his actions, and answereth such
complaints as arise, unto which comonwealth and to every power
that standeth for it (who can best judge the quallitie and nature of   20
a prison and prisoners), he most humbly submitteth himselfe with
this further prayer; that the extent and continuance of his office, soe
long as it keepeth within the due lymitts may not be held ob-
noxious either thorough the greatnes or frequency of the persons
that are comitted thither, by reason of whom it must needs be an   25
object of the father's hate for his sonnes sake, of the sonne for the
father's sake, of kindred for their allyes, of maisters for their
servants' sake, of the neighbour for the neighbour's sake, of the
countryman for his countryman's sake, of the friend for his friend's
sake, of officers for officers; yea, the late prisoner for the present 30
prisoners' sake. All which noe doubt doe readily consider what a
prisoner doth suffer, but not soe readily consider what comand is
layde on the Warden to inflict, what cause in Justice there is to
comand it, or what vicious quallitye there is in the prisoner to

induce it. Whereby it followeth that most often some of theis
fathers, children, friends, &c. doe sue for favour and importune the
Warden to use kindness to the prisoner, yea, oftentymes to hazard
his creditt and estate for them; but never shall it be seene that
5 any man will persuade the prisoners to deale kindlie or reciprocally
with the warden, or retorne to witnes what good the warden hath
done to many under his custodie.

Soe that the warden is like to a white in the butt for all estates to
shoote att, and can neither hope of retribution for those good offices
10 which he doth as Warden, or as a civell freind; and the reason is
that, though prisoners and their keepers be relatives, yet there is
such an innate and prejudicate opinion on the prisoner's part as that
(rarely) he can love his keeper.

And therefore the keeper for his first ground hath to doe his
15 dutie with all care and circumspection (without idle jealousy or
foolish passion) in obeying the King, the Lords, the Judges, the
Lawes, and Constitutions; and soe he shall become an absolute and
independant officer, without awe of detractors or backbiters, for, as
the Fleete is the King's owne proper prison next in trust to his
20 Tower of London, and as that is his fort in the east, soe was this
one in the west of the citty and chamber of his kingdome; therefore fidelity and discretion concurring in his officer there, it will
noe doubt be a motive to his sacred Majestie to lett his protection
reflect upon it, and upon them that mannage it, maugre all the
25 stratagems and pollicyes of such prisoners as now affront it, or
rather justice and the execution thereof.

For if they which accuse the Warden of that which he or his
servants have indeed and necessarily acted, as takeing money from
Mr. Leccester and Thraske, causeing Chamberlayne to be wrapt in
30 his gowne when he would not by any intreaty put on his clothes,
takeing Rookwood alsoe in his shirt when he likewise refused to
put on his cloaths, breakeing open Peck's trunk to take out stolne
goods, putting irons on a crewe of Romish affected and factious,
who stabbed, wounded, meant to kill, and to make generall breach

of prison, keeping in his chamber a second and third plotter of his
death, endeavoreing to keepe meate from them that immured and
shutt up themselves of theire owne accord, suffering some to lye
without a bedd who had none of their owne, neither would pay
for one to the Warden; if they had therewith all sett downe the 5
occasion, circumstances, and tymes, why and when the Warden did
theis things, and to whom they were done, he would have spared
them the labour to seeke out witnesses, for he doth confesse and
avowe it to be done lawfully, justly, and reasonably; nay that he
could do noe lesse in regard of his service to his King and country, 10
forsake keeping the King's prison and prisoners, and preserveing
himselfe and servants from being slaughtered. The Warden's passage,
dwelling, and conversation being in the same howse and under the
same roofe against them, soe as he cannot soe much as personally
shunn any man, except he lock them upp in one warde or other or 15
in their chamber, and therefore they which complayne and diverse
more which complayne not, did urge him to theis things and heaped
coles on their owne heads thorough their nifarious doeings in that
place.

It hath alsoe beene urged that the fees and duties which the 20
Warden doth demaund of his prisoners are soe great as that in a
little tyme which the prisoner lyeth there and payeth them, he is
brought further behind hand and disabled in satisficing his debts or
performeing that for which he is comitted, and this is (seemeingly)
a great burthen; but where the practise of the Fleete to meete with 25
the practise of the prisoner is knowne, the fees doe neither make
or marr, except (as is said) the Fleete should be made an hospitall
for delinquents, who, if they possesse a thousand, or thousands of
other men's, doe by keepeing that and makeing their accord with
the creditor drawe the charge of the imprisonment out of the 30
creditors pursse.

But howsoever when a man is comitted, whether he be gentleman or yeoman *revera*, yet at his comeing thither it is in his owne
election to be of the gentleman's comons or of the yeoman's comons.

or of neither, and accordingly he is lodged and dietted at soe lowe
a rate as he pleaseth.   But if he, which best knows his owne meanes,
will be lodged and fedd with the best, and after he hath begotten
trust for a yeare or two yeares' lodgings, &c. (upon pretence of
5 livelyhood and possibillity to pay) in the end pretendeth poverty,
though in truth he hath (by lyeing there) better his estate [sic]; if
this plea doe nothing at all move the Warden de jure it is not to be
wondred att, or he to be thought blame worthy; neither can it be
thought much that sometymes the Warden contendeth with the
10 beggars of the charitie upon such points, for he findeth that when
some gentleman or yeoman have lyen long there and runne in his
debt, then at such tymes as they have weryed their creditors and
made their owne easy conditions, and doe resolve to ridd themselves
from the Fleete, after long keepeing their discharges in their pocketts
15 they doe labour earnestly to be admitted to the charity (amongst
the beggars) and (either by bribeing the beggars or inportunate
clamor, and sometymes false certificates) obteyne it; which once had
then cometh their discharge forth of their pocketts, and looke we
are beggars, and *in forma pauperis*, from whome there is nothing
20 due to the warden but vijs. iiijd. att our departure, and yet he
demaunds 20, 30, or 40li. and here is our discharge (dated a yeare
past), and we are kept for our fees, and in such a case most of the
prisoners will be their seconds, though when this gentleman or
beggar is gotten out, then he is *Mr. Dives* at his fayre house ac-
25 complished with all things, and can dispend a hundred pounds or
two per annum; for it is mayntayned there in the Fleete (as a holy
maxime) that the man is cursed that selleth his patrimony or his
possessions (though bought with other men's money) to pay debts
withall.   And as for such money as is taken upp at use, it is
30 a justifiable and pious deed to keepe the userer without it, he
being a man worthy to be punished; and that if God hath given
one man witt and capacitie to goe beyond another, it is reason
that such a man should use his tallent of witt by circumventing
another man in his land, money, or goods.   Yea, if a man have a

reversion which may presently be sold for many hundreds ready
money, yet that man shall keepe his reversion, and in the interim
that it fall he ought to be admitted on the charitie of the Fleete, by
which prophane pollicyes and reasons they defeate all estates and
conditions of men, and put the Warden's discretion soe much to the 5
touchstone as he is often condempned of hard hartednes by such as
little descend into consideration of the nature of the prison and
prisoners.

What calumpnies hath beene raysed agaynst the Warden in the
point of halfe comons (as if all men paied it) though it be a meere 10
embrion without shape or rule, and is ever varyed and applyed to
the quallity and abillity of the prisoner to give somewhat (and that
very little, as hath beene shewed) for license to take his victuall
where he pleaseth! For if the porter of the Fleete be bound to attend
the comeing in and out of their servants of meate and company, 15
and the Warden to afford them roome, Yea even scavedge for their
ordure and sweepeings, surely it is more then they can have abroad
for nothing.

What a slaunder is it to say, the Warden alloweth but six days to
the weeke, because perhapps his clarke in recconning with a 20
prisoner hath mistaken first or last a day, and left but six days in
one weeke, with which and a thousand such other solæcismes and
Fleete doctrynes they rather shewe what may be said then what is
just and fitt to say, soe that if there be once but xij*d*. casually taken
nay but ij*d*. out steppeth an information for extortion, as from *Mr.* 25
Rookwood and *Chamberlayne*, but if the Warden loose a 100*li*. or
two by death or non solvencie of a prisoner, a thousand pounds
more or lesse by an escape, noe man will contribute to his losse,
naie the prisoners will rather take a president or oportunitie to doe
the like, then take any pitty on the Warden.   30

There is a greate hope and expectation that order will be taken
for the more ease and lesse fees of prisoners. By collour whereof
they pay not a penny in the meane tyme, and that the Warden
shall hereafter take his fees for the tyme past, as (if it may be pre-

sumed soe to say) by predestination; but if such soares be bound
upp and easye plaisters applyed, creditors will be the next suitors
to have the cankers and wormes of commerce and entercourse
smoaked in a more bitter fashion then they be, ells the good must
5 suffer for the badds' sake, for lett a viewe of the prison be taken
(man by man) and it will be perceaved that one hath sold, Naie
doth now sell, his libertie to feed his belly, another to cloath the
back, another to maintain his punck, another to lett his lands
descend to his yssue, others to sport and play, others to keepe
10 money by them and putt it out to use, and rarely shall be found a
poore man, who by accident or visitation hath beene occasioned to
come to prison, for (thanks be given to God) there is a great deale
more pietye in this kingdome and commonwealth derived from
the creditor to the debtor, then prayers or humilitie from the
15 debtor or prisoner towards the creditor; Naie, if it were not to
speake against charitie, there might much more be said of that
likewise, onelie this, that if a legacy be given to discharge some
poore men which lye for smale matters, themselves will mutiny to
have it shared amongst all rather then take the benefitt aloane, soe
20 little suffering and soe good a desire to tarry have the poorest
there.

The rich are of the same mynd, not remembring that the best
way to revenge themselves of a badd Warden were that in dispight
of him they would gett out and be free, yet there ayme is to be
25 comended if either they can avoyd the ould fees by driveing
away their Wardens, or procure lesse fees hereafter thorough their
great hypochrysie.

It had not beene fitt here to particularize or name men were it
not of necessity, and to sett out an answeare to theis Nyneteene
30 Articles by some of them published against their Warden before he
be convict of offence, which if it be lett goe unpunished, *gaudeant
boni fortuna*, for if they had libelled before they were prisoners
they should surely have beene subject to punishment. If the prison
free them from this and others it will surely be a seminary of that

and more fowle enormityes; but some prisoners must be named for
cleareing of the things in question, yet soe as to deliver the Warden
of bad men and matter with good words, least otherwise there
should be noe difference betweene him and the prisoners saveing
that they rayled first, and least that he should seeme to be of that 5
orator's opinion who said, that if men had taken pleasure in
speakeing evill, it was fitt that they should loose that pleasure by
heareing evill, and howsoever he wryteth in the third person, yet
he is the first whome it concerneth; and if the stile or method be
badd, it is that which he could and what the tyme would permitt, 10
his place being rather for action then meditation or wryteing in
this kind.

If any offence be taken at that which is here written (as the
Warden hopeth none shall be) it is his burthen and he must beare
it (though with much sorrowe), for God is his witnes he did never 15
affect the being Warden, but haveing been first brought upp in the
rudiments of lawe, and next in voluntary travaile beyond sea, and
lastly in great ymployment there, he resolved (if soe it had pleased
God) after his travaile to have rested under his vyne and fig-tree,
with remembrance of what was past.   20

But when necessary and unlookt for occasion drewe him to this
place, he first conceived that there was *turpe lucrum;* afterwards
being more urged he examyned the justness and value of the fees
and duties.

And lastly when there was noe remedy but he must be warden, 25
he besought of God to give him an heart answeareable to serve the
commonwealth and doe poore men good.

But his conflict and troble in that place hath beene such as
hitherto he hath come short in both; soe that, his glasse being
runne, a new man must come to the helme, and he shall carry noe 30
substance, noe creditt, noe comiseration, yet here is the inward
glory, that howsoever he may be accused he can never be convinced of such grose crymes or a mynd and purpose to doe evill;
for with many men he contended for example sake, but whosoever

submitted himselfe there was alwayes an end, and loveing reconciliation without respect of gaine, and this he was constrayned to
stick unto. Because if the prisoners thorough contention did once
obteyne any thing against right, then by tradition it became a
5 custome authenticall.

Here is noe storie or discourse of art to attract any man to read
it, but an humble defence is here of an innocent man, written to
satisfie such persons as thorough the clamour of factious prisoners
have apprehended worse of the Warden then there is cause; unto
10 them therefore he addresseth himselfe with prayer that if any thing
stick in their mynds then they would take soe much paines to read
it, and favourably to judge him, who in his owne nature is myld
and gentle, as in his extreames of daunger with *Whitbrooke* doth
appeare.

15 For it shall be mayntened for a truth that *Sir John Whitbrooke* (thorough a plott and confederacy with others touched in
this answeare) came into the Warden's studdy where the Warden
(in his gowne) was wryteing, and fashioned his speech, sayeing
that he came to speake with the Warden about his lodging, who
20 answeared that he would willingly speake about that and money
for it, whereupon the Warden putting dust upon the wryteings and
turneing his back to lay them aside *Sir John Whitbrooke* strook
him on the head with the sharpe end of a hammer, whereof one
cleft was before broken off and the other cleft newly whett,
25 giveing fower wounds to the scull and some bruses before the
Warden could close with him; but then the Warden, thrusting him
out of the studdy, did throwe *Whitbrooke* on the back and took
away the hammer, *Whitbrooke* (being undermost) did hould the
forepart of the Warden's gowne soe as he could not rise, att which
30 tyme the Warden's blood abundantly gushed downe upon *Whitbrooke*, and the Warden could have beaten out *Whitbrooke's* braynes
with the hammer but that he was neither wrothfull nor daunted.

Then after two maydes servants (heareing the noyse) came into the
roome, and one loosed *Whitbrooke's* hands from the Warden's gowne,

or ells the Warden must have killed him to acquitt himselfe. Soe
soone as the maydes came the Warden shewed them the hammer
all bloody, telling them that *Whitbrooke* had wounded him therewith; the butler of the howse then alsoe comeing upp to cover
the table the Warden bidd him and others (which followed) to laye 5
hands upon *Whitbrooke*, &c. but to take heed they hurt him not;
soe they letting him rise and rest himselfe he tooke a stilletto out
of his pockett and stabbed the Warden's deputie cleane through the
middle of his hand which (notwithstanding it was presently dressed
by a good chirurgion) did rankle upp to his shoulder, and was like 10
to have killed him; he also stabbed the porter of the howse directly
against the heart and drewe blood, but it pe'reed not; he stabbed
the goaler into the hand and twice through the sleeve of his dublett,
soe as then they lay violent hands upon him, put on irons and
carryed him to the strongest warde of the prison (called *Bolton's* 15
warde).   And howsoever false suggestions are made (to obscure this
fact) by many persons concurrent in it, yet there is such apparant
proofe where and how the hammer was provided, the stilletto or
Scottish dagger purloyned to doe this deed withall, and that *Whitbrooke* himselfe confest the haveing and bringing of them to that 20
purpose, with a multitude of witnesses truely testifieing one and the
same, as noething can be more pregnant.

   Therefore it was high tyme for the Warden to looke to the
governement, and to the suppression of theis things, or ells his
executors might too late implore Justice, when he were breathlesse 25
in his grave, and creditors might seeke their debtors at large with
losse when they were once gone; for though the office of the Fleete
be of a great value and may be a pledge to answeare such prisoners
or suffer for them (if they escape), yet if a generall escape had
beene made, what office is of value to satisfie for it? and therefore 30
he which keepeth a prison in a peaceable comonwealth must discharge noe lesse fidelity then he that keepeth a fort in tyme of
warr, or ells irreguler persons will make devastation upon all
estates, and the prison will be but a sinagogg of Jewish ceremony,

where the trybes of the wicked will plant themselves, and suck the
milke and honny from the true chariteable and religious of the
kingdome; and, although the Warden hath not to doe with the
merritts of prisoners causes for which they are comitted, yet, touch-
5 ing their conversation, he hath to oppose the badd (whome alone
this answeare doth intend to convince), and to be observant to the
honourable, generous, and well affected (whom this answeare
neither toucheth nor soe much as pointeth att), but with their due
respects.
10   Some things for the Warden's defence will be found to be repeated
often to severall accusations, which could not conveniently be
avoyded, because, though many prisoners joyned in one conspiracy,
yet their facts were diverse, and the Warden's defence is but one to
those severall facts and persons, and therefore hopeth to be pardoned
15 for that repetition.

The First Article.

Accusation of
murther.

After knowne quarrells and fightings betweene two prisoners
lodging them in one chamber, where quarrelling and fighting againe
and notice to him thereof given, and of likelie further mischiefe,
this notwithstanding continuance of them together until the one 5
murthered the other.

And the *Lady Whitbrooke* in her petition to the King's Majestie
alledgeth inveterate malice betweene *Whitbrooke* and the Warden.

Answeare.

By these which point at two prisoners (whereof the one slewe the 10
other) is meant *Sir John Whitbrooke*, concerneing whose death
and how farr the Warden may be touched with murthering of him,
being suddenly slayne by his fellowe prisoner (whom he first
wounded in the forehead and strooke downe with a candlestick),
lett the ensueing answeare, true, and to be proved in all points, 15
leave the reader to judge; especially if it were fitt to sett forth how
farr *Sir John Whitbrooke* in his life tyme was tainted judicially
with other matters, which (according to charity) shall be here
omitted, saveing what perteynes to answeare this allegation.

Court of
Requests.
Court of
Chancery.

In July 1618, the Warden haveing order out of two courts to 20
keepe *Sir John Whitbrooke* close prisoner, he (the Warden) labored
an atonement thereof with his adversary; yet in the meane tyme
Sir John gott out, assaulted the Warden in his studdy, wounded
him fower blowes in the head with a hammer, and stabbed three
servants with a stilletto, 10 July 1618.   And upon this some three 25
score prisoners breake upp all the strongest prisons and dores of the
wards and Tower chamber, assaulting the Warden and his servants
with weapons, &c. according to a plott and purpose before resolved
upon, as appeares by depositions; and the Warden did rather governe
then maligne, for he can give good evidence that he tendred *Whit-* 30
brooke's estate and affayres, although he endeavoured to hold his
lodgings in despight of the Warden, and without payment.

The Lady further alledgeth that the like inveterate mallice was betweene *Whitbrooke* and *Boughton.*

The warden answeareth that he neither newe or heard what was betweene *Whitbrooke* and *Boughton,* for amongst soe many prisoners 5 many variances fall out which he knows not of.

The Lady allsoe alledgeth that the like mallice was betweene the Warden and *Boughton.*

The Warden answeareth that there was never any quarrell be- When this tweene him and *Boughton*; perhapps *Boughton* held himselfe injured Warden came 10 for being kept in prison, therefore would pay noe dutyes, soe that *Boughton* in he was put into the Comon Prison. the Fleete
After which the Warden, perceaveing him to be phantasticall, lodged in the offered him liberty, wished him to converse freely with the gentle- bers or Comon men there, Yea, kept him from his retyrednes, thinkeing thereby to Prison. 15 quallifie his humor, which was that he would not come out of his chamber till he were freed out of prison by Parliament.

The Lady likewise alledgeth that *Whitbrooke* was wounded by the Warden and his servants.

The Warden answeareth that *Whitbrooke* was not wounded, and 20 it is deposed by diverse, that the Warden tooke great care, and gave comand that they should not hurt him, onely to bereave him of his stilletto above said, they strooke downe his stabbing arme with a firefork, and soe tooke away the stilletto. It was but a silly bruse on the arme that he had, and lesse then he might have had, if the 25 Warden's care had not prevented it.

The lady alledgeth that in September the quarrell betweene the Warden and *Whitbrooke* was renewed.

CAMD. SOC. F

The Warden answereth that in July 1619, *Whitbrooke* and *Boughton* with six others (being lodged in a great chamber), they and six more shutt out thirtie of their companie and fortefied the gaole against the Warden, refused all perswasions of the Warden, constables, and Alderman's Deputie, the comands of the Lord Cheife 5 Justice, of the Lord Chauncellor and his Serjeant at Armes; yet yeilded to the clarke of the councell sent from the Lords, *Whitbrooke* and *Boughton* being then in one humour; and upon un-blocking the prison *Whitbrooke* desired liberty, it was offered him upon security, he would give none, then he made question where 10 to lye, to which was answeared there were five other roomes he might make his election of which he would; but he said he would none other but where he formerly laye (it being indeed the fayrest). They fortified those roomes againe when the Warden was out of towne, soe as dureing *Whitbrooke's* life and *Boughton's* being there with 15 their adherents the Warden had noe comand in that part of the prison.

The lady alledgeth that the Warden (for revenge) resolved and reported he would send *Whitbrooke* to *Boulton* to keepe.

The Warden answeareth that he for governement sake and to suppresse misdemeanours doth thretten to putt prisoners (offending) 20 into *Boulton's* [*sic*] Wards (many yeares familiarlie soe called as he thinketh of bolts or irons put on them), where *Whitbrooke* was put when he wounded the Warden and his servants; he continued there but a small tyme, and was removed to a roome called the Tower Chamber (where *Henry Boughton* and many others did lye), thence 25 *Boughton* was removed into the comon prison in December, 1618, and *Whitbrooke* was removed thither 16 June, 1619; soe as to that tyme they lay five moneths within one lodging, and six moneths severed in other lodgings and noe quarrell stirred.

A strong place in the prison called *Bolton's* Wards.

The Lady alledgeth that presently at their comeing together 30 *Boughton* suddenly stabbed and wounded *Whitbrooke*, whereof he dyed.

The Warden answereth that over and above the eleaven moneths aforesaid, yet from June 16th untill September 16th, 1619, being 3 moneths, they two combyned in their exploits against the Warden without falling out (for ought the Warden knewe), but 16 September 5 *Boughton* fell out with *Harvey* (one of his chamber fellowes), whome *Boughton* assayled with his teeth, and bitt him by the thombe, whereof *Whitbrooke*, *Willis*, *Harvey* and others there lodged, advised the Warden, wishing him to take some course. The Warden sent diverse messags by the gaoler to *Whitbrooke*, to 10 remove thence and to lye elsewhere; he would not, sayeing, none should remove him but by violence, and they were soe strong there as the Warden could doe nothing, none ells durst come amongst them. *Holmes* and *Maunsell* offered him libertie amongst other gentlemen upon bonds.

15   The Warden acquainted the Lord Chauncellor of theis fortications, of some other stabbing there, of this particuler brawle, and besought his lordshipp to send them to Newgate. The Lord Chauncellor comanded such motion to be made at the tyme of a seale; it was moved by *Mr. Woomelayson*, as appeares by his breife, 20 then his lordshipp wished oath to be made of this offence and called for presidents to remove them, in which meane tyme *Boughton* (being provoked and wounded by *Whitbrooke*) did stabb him, whereof he dyed within 13 dayes, and it was about 14 moneths after he wounded the Warden and stabbed his 3 servants as appeareth 25 by the generall lodgeings and places where they laye, sometymes together and sometymes severed, ensueing to be seene in the end of this answeare to this Article, and if the testimony (which was long after delivered to the Warden by a prisoner in the Fleete) be true, then the same *Harvey* and one *Tymothy Willis* and *Sir John* 30 *Whitbrooke* himselfe did (of sett purpose) whett on *Boughton* to anger and quarrell, because they scorned *Boughton* and meant to assayle him.

When *Whitbrooke*, *Boughton*, &c. ymured themselves upp in

the wards as aforesaid, a view or survey of the roomes was given
the Lords of the Councell and they satisfied.

After the tyme of the supposed quarrell (which was about *Whitbrooke's* and *Boughton's* forteficing the house) they contynued
lyeing where they were before, amongst others.   5

Wheresoever they had lyen they might quarrell when they mett,
as *Whitbrooke* many moneths before broke *Willis* his head with
a pott or candlestick.

The Lords of the Councell had *Whitbrooke's* liberty to consideration and would graunt him none without bonds.   10

Boughton, being not in execution, was offered what liberty he
would.

Whitbrooke did never informe the Lords of any quarrell or doubt
he made of his safety touching *Boughton*, &c.

Whitbrooke confest he strooke and provoked *Boughton* first, 15
before *Boughton* stabbed him.

The falling out which was notified to the Warden was betweene
Boughton and *Harvey*, not *Whitbrooke*.

When *Boughton* had wounded *Whitbrooke*, then *Whitbrooke*
went (of his owne accord) to lye out of the roome where *Boughton* 20
was, and soe he might freely have done at any tyme before and
left Broughton's company (if it had not pleased him), for diverse
other roomes were readye at hand for him and open.

Allegation.   It is alsoe alledged by some, that after *Sir John Whitbrooke* was
dead, the Warden would not suffer armes or scutchions to be put on 25
his herss when it was to goe out of the Fleete.

Answeare.   The Warden, perceaveing that a number of people of that Romish
sect would come to the Fleete at his buryall, and others to gaze,
commanded his porter to be carefull that prisoners went not out;
then (said the porter) it will not be fitt to putt on the scutchions 30
until he be out of the gates; whereto the Warden said, he hath

indeed left his armes, because I tooke from him by single hand the
hammer and stilletto wherewith he wounded and would have
slayne me, but I regard it not. This speech the porter uttered againe,
yet bidd them put on the sentchions, which they refused to doe,
5 as those that would take an occasion of unkindnes and to traduce
the Warden of mallice.

Wherein *Sir John Meeres* and others can witnes, that while *Sir
John Whitbrooke* was liveing the Warden prayed them to visite
Whitbrooke on the Warden's behalf, and to move a conference and
10 Christian reconciliation, and that truth might be confessed; to
which *Sir John Whitbrooke* did condiscend, but as *Sir John Meeres*
was comeing to fetch the warden for that purpose *Mr. Edward
Rookwood* (who calleth himselfe and is termed the *Vicarr Generall*
of the Romish in the Fleete) followed and said that *Sir John Whit-
15 brooke's* mynd was altered, and soe nothing was done; but *Rookwood*
and another jesuited person (while *Whitbrooke* was lyeing and
dead) did soe accompany him as noe Protestant had accesse to him,
which jesuited person was after (by the Warden's discovery) apprehended and comitted as a factor to pervert and send beyond sea
20 the children of the Gentrie of this Kingdome and persons of quallitie.

It is alsoe alledged that *Boughton* did provide a sword, and it Allegation.
was brought him by a woeman from whom the porter of the Fleete
tooke it and delivered it to the Warden (as he did indeed), and
therefore say theis accusers that the Warden knewe the same sword
25 was to kill *Whitbrooke*.

The Warden had it about a yeare and a halfe before this accident Answeare.
(of *Whitbrooke's* death) happened, and delivered it back againe to
the woeman that brought it, with charge not to bring any thither
whatsoever.
30 It was avouched that the sword was *Boughton's* and put to dressing to a cutler, who sent it home againe, so as *Boughton* might
have killed *Whitbrooke* with it before it went to dressing if he had

intended any such thing; Nay, *Boughton* had alwayes in his trunck
(as appeared afterwards) a stilletto so keene, so cleane and ready, as
would soone have done such a fact if he had meant it; Yea, swords
and other weapons want not in the Fleete, and the Warden cannot
prevent it.   This fact was meere accidentall, and not precogitate   5
as the lawe hath found it, which acquitted *Boughton* of manslaughter upon his arraignement.

The Warden gave noe abettment, had noe intelligence, provoked
neither party, strock noe blowe, was not present.   How can he be
charged with the murther?   10

Surely theis accusers are in their soules more guilty of murther
by reason of this false accusation, in which they would kill the body
and creditt of the Warden, then he any way accessary to the fact of
Boughton.

But, say they, the warden should have put them into severall 15
chambers.   Why?   He knewe nothing of any unkindnes but betweene *Harrey* and *Boughton*.   But if he had, he could not keepe
200 persons from meeteing one another, or lodge them sevrally.

Nay (say the prisoners) he ought not to comand any man to his
chamber upon likelyhood of murther or ought ells.   20

And *Sir Francis Inglefeilds* complainte against the Warden inty-
mateth (in his owne case) soe much, though by their leave the
Warden will doe it, until he be comanded the contrary; but it is a
comon thing for prisoners to find fault one with anothers conversation, sometymes as not wholesome, not cleanely, not temperate, not 25
peaceable, and many other respects, because they would either lye
alone, have a chamber aloane, be private and without contradiction
in their mirth and solaces; and when it comes to consideration there
is neither wholesome, cleanely, temperate, or peaceable of the one
that complayneth or the other that is complayned off.   30

Allegation. But say they further that the Warden put *Sir John Whitbrooke*
out of his chamber into the Tower Chamber or the comon prison
keepeing away his bedding, soe that he lay either on another man's

bedd or none at all.　And this was the first occasion of *Whitbrooke's* fact.

When *Whitbrooke* did growe not onely factious but (according ᴬⁿˢʷᵉʳᵉ.
to his nature) quarrelsome with divers men (strikeing some of them)
5 and that his former dangerous courses to stabb and pistoll men, for
which he was censured (in Starr Chamber) was considered, together
with the orders of court to keep him close prisoner and his designe
to make a president in the house for all men to lye in their
lodgings without payment, and besides that he being charged with
10 many executions of great waight could not give bond for true imprisonment or payment, Nay, noe man would be bound for soe
desperate a person, therefore he was put into the Tower Chamber;
but as for his bedding and goods the Warden sent two men to offer
them to him, as appears by the message sett under their hands at
15 that instant; he then standing upon it that he would perforce
retorne and possesse his chamber, did not deliver his key or take
his goods, and in the meanetyme lyeing on some other man's
bedding, the Warden opened the chamber and putt *Whitbrooke's*
goods in safety.

20　It seemeth that afterwards he (on whose bedd *Whitbrooke* lay)
tooke away the bedd, which was more then the Warden knewe or
had any motive thereof.

Afterwards when *Whitbrooke* had wounded the Warden (this
comeing in question at Councell Table) the Lords appointed him to
25 pay, and the Warden to lodge him in a chamber and lett him have
his bedd, &c. the Warden for his part obeyed, but of *Whitbrooke*
nothing was had (all being lost by his death) which by his life
might have beene saved.

They say that *Whitbrooke* hurt the Warden with his owne sworde,
30 but of *Whitbrooke's* provideing (and confessing) the hammer and
stilletto which did it, good proofe can be made and that allegation
disproved, as is before declared.

A note of the severall places and tymes where and when Boughton and Whitbrooke lodged together or severed one from the other.

Sir John Whitbrooke lodged.   *Mr. Boughton lodged.*

1617.	**1617.**	5
15 May, in the Greene Yard.	In the Tower Chambers.	
12 June, in the Greene Yard.	In the Tower Chambers.	
7 Aug. in the Greene Yard.	In the Tower Chambers.	10
4 Sept. in the Greene Yard.	In the Tower Chambers.	
2 Octob. in the Greene Yard.	In the Tower Chambers.	
30 Octob. in the Greene Yard.	In the Tower Chambers.	25
20 Nov. in the Greene Yard.	In the Tower Chambers.	
If at any tyme they did fall out it was at this tyme. 25 Dec. in the Tower Chambers.	In the Tower Chambers.	20
22 Jan. in the Tower Chambers.	In the Tower Chambers.	
19 Feb. in the Wards.	In the Tower Chambers.	
19 March, in the Wards.	In the Tower Chambers.	25
1618.	**1618.**	
16 April, in the Wards.	In the Tower Chambers.	
14 May, in the Wards.	In the Tower Chambers.	30

Sir John Whitbrooke lodged.	*Mr. Boughton* lodged.	
11 June, in the Wards.	In the Tower Chambers.	
10 July, in the Wards.	In the Tower Chambers.	1618. Note, 10 July, he wounded the Warden and his 3 servants.
16 July, in Bolton's Ward or Bolts on Wards.	In the Tower Chambers.	
3 Aug. in a chamber by the Warden, and then put into the Tower Chambers.	In the Tower Chambers.	
3 Sept. in the Tower Chambers.	In the Tower Chambers.	
1 Oct. in the Tower Chambers.	In the Tower Chambers.	*Whitbrooke* and *Boughton* theis 5 moneths lay together in a roome amongst others after the Warden was wounded.
29 Oct. in the Tower Chambers.	In the Tower Chambers.	
26th Novemb. in the Tower Chambers.	In the Tower Chambers.	
24 Dec. in the Tower Chambers.	In the Tower Chambers till 28 December.	
21 Jan. in the Tower Chambers.	In the Wards.	Theis 6 moneths they wer severed, for that *Boughton* and others claymed to have the use of the leads and for that cause *Bough-ton* was put into the Wards.
18 Feb. in the Tower Chambers.	In the Wards.	
18 March, in the Tower Chambers.	In the Wards.	
1619.	1619.	
15 April, in the Tower Chambers.	In the Wards.	
13 May, in the Tower Chambers.	In the Wards.	

CAMD. SOC. 6

<table>
<tr><td>

June 8, 1619, and after the complainte of *Whitbrooke* the Warden procured a Comission to have all things examined, and the Comissioners and prisoners opened their greifes.

</td><td>

10 June, in the Tower Chambers and there continued till 16th January, 1619.

</td><td>

In the Wards.

</td></tr>
<tr><td>

This 4 moneths together none more freinds then they joyneing to fortefie the wards and keepe them, soe as it came before the Lords of the Councell and was ordered there.

</td><td>

8 July, in the Wards.

</td><td>

In the Wards.

</td><td>5</td></tr>
<tr><td></td><td>

5 Aug. in the Wards.

</td><td>

In the Wards.

</td></tr>
<tr><td></td><td>

2 Septemb. in the Wards.

</td><td>

In the Wards.

</td></tr>
<tr><td></td><td>

30 Septemb. in the Wards.

</td><td>

In the Wards.

</td><td>10</td></tr>
<tr><td>

1619.
Dyed of the stabb which *Boughton* did give him, 7th of October.

</td><td>

7 October, in the Wards.

</td><td>

And now Sir John dyed.

</td></tr>
</table>

Being stabbed by *Boughton* with an ordinary knife upon an 15 accidentall justling, in which *Whitbrooke* (as is said) did strike downe *Boughton* with a blowe in the forehead with a candlestick, and this was 15 moneths after the tyme that *Whitbrooke* wounded the Warden and his servants.

Boughton in his lettre to *Coppin* setteth downe two reasons of the 20 fact why *Boughton* did stabb him.

First, to gett himselfe removed from the Fleete.

Secondly, because there were three upon *Boughton*, therefore he made of sure of *Whitbrooke* by killing him.

The Second Article.

Removeing a prisoner out of his chamber, haveing 51*li*. 1*s*. hid Accusation of felonye.
under his bedd, which the prisoner required he might goe to his
chamber to dispose off, which was denyed, and he thrust upp in
5 another roome close prisoner until the Warden and some of his
servants rifled his bedd of that money.

By this is pretended that one *Coppin* (who ever did beare the Answeare.
name of a poore fellowe) lost 51*li*. with takeing whereof if he dare
charge any person or persons, the Lawe is and hath beene open for
10 him theis two yeares past. But his abettors have putt it here rather
to infame then that they can think it true, as by the ensueing
answeare appeares.

For *Edward Coppin*, lived as a poore prisoner in the Fleete
for breach of a decree, and continueing above six yeares, would
15 never be drawen to pay the Warden one penny for meate, drinke,
lodging, or attendance: but at last he ran away, and was upon the
Warden's pursuite taken againe, but before he ran away he was
sometymes restrayned of the libertye of the Fleete yards and walks
(as is the custome of all prisons in England); and he lodging in
20 the three Tower Chambers with sixteene persons, they often thretned
their keeper to stabb him, to take away the keyes of the prison, to
bind him, to hang him; lastlie they fortefied that prison, soe as the
Warden could not dispose or order them. And with two malletts
and steele chissells they had cutt the stone workes of the dore, soe
25 as noe locks or bolts could shutt them; and while they were thus
doeinge *Coppin* came downe to fetch a mallett, wherewith he was
taken beneath, and presentlie put into another warde aparte from
his fellowes, about three a clocke in the afternoone, 15 July, 1619,
not speakeing of any money.
30 Att 8 a clocke that night the Warden sent upp some 10 or 12 of

his servants into the Tower Chamber to bring downe those prisoners.
before which tyme *Coppin* sent upp word by *Elizabeth Lane* (*Mr.*
Chamberlayne's woeman) that *Mr. Chamberlayne* should take *Cop-*
pins trunck into his studdy, which he did.

Att the goeing upp of the Warden's servants they were resisted ⁵
with a stilletto, beddposts, and faggot sticks, and a servant of the
Warden's wounded by one *John Aborne*, who (with some others)
retyred into the Inner Chambers (shutting themselves inn), yet the
Warden's men brought downe some of those sixteene, leaveing the
least offensive behind.   Then after this the Warden went upp him- ¹⁰
selfe, and by perswasion caused *Aborne* and company to open their
dores, and soe takeing away things that might serve as weapons,
locked upp the prisoners in other wards untill he might repayre
those broken.

July 16.   One *Fletcher* the gaoler (in that interim) often tymes asked ¹⁵
Coppin how he did, and what he wanted, who said he was well, not
adding any other words of note.

July 17.   Another of the Warden's servants goeing along, *Coppin* called to
him out of the windowe and shaked a bagg sayeing, Ah, you, here
is that which your fellowes would have had.   ²⁰

July 18 or 19. A rumour was spredd in the Fleete that *Coppin* had lost 50*li.*
The Warden heareing thereof, sent for *Coppin* and asked him; he
said he would say nothing except *Sir Francis Inglefield* were
present.   Then the Warden said, Nay, *Coppin*, if you have nothing
to say to me you may depart againe.   ²⁵

Then the warden was informed by *Mr. Boughton* and *Wall* that
the day before it happened that *Coppin* was removed they had
made meanes to borrowe some money upon a pawne, and *Coppin*
professed and swore he had not soe much (being fower (4) pounds)
as they demanded.   Then the warden caused *Coppin's* trunck (being ³⁰
new and well locked) to be opened in *Coppin's* presence, and delivered it to him, in which Trunck within a Bagg put in a Box (as
they said) there was about xxixs.; and then was sett on foote this
rumour when *Coppin* had advised with *Mr. Rookwood* to doe it.

About January, 1620, *Edward Coppin* confessed that he never receaved any money since he came to Prison.

Mr. Williams saith that he hath heard that *Coppin* hath confessed he lost noe money.

5   *Mr. Wray* testifieth most materiallye in this point, that he questioned *Coppin* why he should say he had lost soe much money in that manner, who answeared it is noe matter, for it is a good deed to hang the Warden's servants.

Edmond Sharpe was bedfellowe with *Coppin* when it is supposed
10 that the money was lost, and he hath beene detected of fowle crymes.

George Wheatley doth testifie that at the tyme *Edward Coppin* was removed from the Tower Chamber into Bolton's Wards, he did see the said *Coppin's* Bedding removed and was there present at that tyme, and to his knowledge there was noe money or any
15 likelyhood of any Bagg of money there to be seene or found, and he verily thinketh the said *Coppin* lost not one penny, for *Coppin* being in Bolton's Wards with his Beding, he at that tyme never complayned that he lost one penny or any other thing.

Elizabeth Lane saith, that when *Coppin* was removed she asked
20 him if he would have ought and he missed nothing, But prayed her to speake to *Mr. Chamberlayne* to take *Coppin's* Trunck into his custodie, which she did accordinglie, and afterwards when it was voyced that *Coppin* had lost money, she said to *Coppin* he might as well have bidd her looke to the money as to the truncke.

25   *Sir Edward Cleare* doth testifie that *Coppin* said unto him, that he (the said *Coppin*) could not charge the Warden or his servants with such money, but sure he was he lost soe much.

The afore named *Henry Boughton* being in Newgate and convict Anno 1620, for slaughtering *Sir John Whitbrooke* delivered a Message in the January 20.
30 heareing of one *Cooke* a keeper of Newgate to *Boughton's Nurse* that she should goe and demaund certeyne goods of the Warden which if he sent not he would cutt the Warden's throate wheresoever he mett him, But the Warden answeared that he had by the Lord Cheife Justice his order delivered the goods to certeyne

Gentlemen who claymed them, and then, perceaveing that *Coppin*
held intelligence with *Boughton*, the Warden suspected that *Coppin*
would doe some hurt, for discovery whereof the Warden sent to
Coppin to remove out of Boulton's Wards, but he ernestly entreated
to continue there, and offered to pay a weekely rate to be permitted   5
to lye there; yet the warden removed him and all his goods (save
a Trunck) which (warned by the last stratagem) he attached in
forme of Lawe, and after (unknowne to the Warden) the Serjeants of
London opened and praysed the goods, and therein found *Boughton's* letter insinuating stabbing of the Lord Chauncellor and the   10
Warden, with scurrilous rayleing on the Lord Chauncellor, &c. as
by the coppie of that letter appeares.

In this Trunck *Coppin* said (before it was opened) that he had
about tenne pounds, but there was found onely xxis. which was permitted to him to take with all the rest.   15

How much cause soever *Coppin* hath to complayne, yet if the
Warden would have lett him passe when he ran away it is to be
thought that he would not easily have beene found to prosecute his
complainte, but the Warden hath prevented that and made him
tarry to shewe both his skill and his greivance, if he have any.   20

That *Coppin* might (as is alledged) desire to returne to his
Chamber it need not be doubted but that it was to dispose of his
money; it might be a mentall reservation, but was not uttered, for if
it had beene uttered the money could not have beene lost or rifled
away by the Warden or his servants, because xviij prisoners were in   25
the roome five howers after *Coppin's* restrainte, and before the
Warden's servants went upp, and those servants which went upp
surprised and devided the prisoners a long tyme before the Warden
came there, who came onely to view the breaches made in his
walls and dores.   30

The Third Article.

Eleaven pounds six shillings taken out of the Trunck, and by violence from the person, of a close prisoner sick in his bedd by the Warden and his servants.

Accusation of robbery.

5 This toucheth money taken from one *Thraske* then a Jewdaiser or halfe Jewe, comitted close prisoner by the Lords of the Councell, from whome and such like though in the Gatehowse, King's Bench, Fleete, &c. it hath beene used to take away and keepe their money, yet the Warden tooke not his untill he abused it very dangerouslie, 10 and whether this takeing away may be said Robbery, let the answeare followeing decide.

Answeare.

And although the complainte be used with a Circumstance, as if the Prisoner were sick, thereby to make a shewe as if the Warden gaped at his death and money; that was most untrue, for *Thraske* 15 was in perfect health.

Who after he came to the Fleete upon such straite comand, censured to Pillory, Whiping, and Branding, and a roome (where eight persons laye) being fitted for him aloane, and one appointed to take charge of him and carry him victuall, &c. within a 20 weeke after he sent the Warden two lettres, the one directed to his Majesty, the other to the Lord Chauncellor, and both superscribed to be delivered upon perrill of allegiance. The Warden blamed the keeper for medling therewith, but, dareing neither to send them back nor keepeing them, charged the messenger to say 25 the Warden was out of the way and not to be found, and imediately the Warden went to the court and tould the Lord Archbishopp's Grace of the lettres, who (angerly) asked how a close prisoner could write lettres, and would heare noe more.

Next him the Lord Chauncellor comeing forth from the King, 30 the Warden shewed the lettres, who breaking open that directed to

himselfe said, this lettre hath some good tracts or passages if they
be cinscare, and so retorned to the King to whome the other lettre
was directed.

After this the Lord Archbishopp and others at Councell Table
much blamed the Warden touching those lettres, and comanded the 5
Warden to looke narrowly to *Thraske*, for that he sent abroad
manuscripts to his pupills, did read allowed and as it were preached
in his Chamber to be heard of prisoners and others of his owne
sect.

Then happened one oportunitie whereby the Warden hoped to 10
discover *Thraske's* purveyance and intelligence, which was that one
Mr. Prickett (then a prisoner in the King's Bench) preaching in
the Fleete and *Thraske* present at it, after sermon *Thraske* (being .
beneath the Chauncell) came towards *Prickett* sayeing, he thanked
God for *Prickett's* doctryne and for his owne edification and slightly 15
gave money to him, whereof the Warden being advised (*Mr.
Prickett* himselfe affirmeing it) said it was xvijs. vjd. a some taken
and given at all adventures as it seemeth.

For theis reasons the Warden sundry tymes serched *Thraske's*
roome, but could find nothing, after which the Warden, thinkeing 20
that perhapps the keeper was not trustie, or partly seduced to
Thraske's doctryne (as appeared afterwards by *Thraske's* booke),
late in a night the Warden called the keeper, sayeing, I will goe
see *Thraske*; the keeper said, Sir I will goe before and open the
dores (which indeed were three); but the Warden permitted him 25
not to goe aloane, but accompaned him with servants and others
desireous to see *Thraske* and that roome, who altogether went to
Thraske, then in bedd, and serching found his Penns, Inck, and
paper, and in a Trunck and about him xjli. vjs. whereof some vjli.
was white money (made upp xxs. in a kowle bound about with 30
browne thred as donatives), and serching *Thraske's* cloathes (which
he did much withstand) the Warden found betweene the outside
and lyneing of his hose a paper booke in octavo almost written
through conteyneing all the proces of *Thraske's* first lettre to the

Eight in
number went
to *Thraske's*
lodging with
the Warden.

King. In which he traduced the King's Majesty and the State (for which he was censured in Starrchamber), his lettres to the Archbishopp, his sentence, &c. and soe continued therein a diary of intelligence touching Spaine and England and the Fleete, with his 5 dreams and interpretations, his repasts, fastings, disputes with prisoners, converting of them, how he had his money and lettres conveyed to and fro. Other things the Warden discovered touching the hole made under the trunck thorough the planchers of the chamber, and a bagg with a coard to drawe upp or lett downe any-10 thing at the windowe, all which money, inck, wryteings, and bookes the Warden carryed away, acquainteing the Lord Chauncellor therewith, who directed him to attend *Mr. Secretary Naunton*, who delivered the booke to his Majestie (the Warden being present). In that booke one *Edward Rookwood* was very often named to be 15 an agent or intelligencer, a disciple, and to have reported to *Thraske* diverse dangerous things of the King, the Lords, &c. and forreigne reports prohibited, and menconed his sonne *Nicholas* to some ends, for all which the said *Edward* and *Nicholas Rookwood* were by the Lord Chauncellor, *Mr. Secretary Naunton*, and the 20 *Lord Cooke* comitted close prisoners, and *Thraske* more close if it might be.

Now, whereas it is layed as an assertion, Yea, robbery, to the warden's charge, for takeing this money, it is to be observed the sect of *Thrasks* increaseing (wherewith our Nation and Religion was 25 taxed by Popish wryters), the charge laye heavy upon the Warden to prevent *Thrasks* wryteings and his means of supporte, whereby he corrupted his keeper and perhapps others. Therefore the Warden tooke away the money in the presence of many witnesses, and writt in his Cash booke the day, the quantitie and quallitye thereof. 30 The Warden's servant (a clarke) did coppie out that booke into another (which robbers use not to doe), and the Warden did shewe the money publiquely in the Fleete to divers gent. who doe witnes it.

Robbery is to take anything felonious-ly or by force or by thretts, where the taker hath neither lawful power or custome, and intends to conceale it.

At that tyme of takeing the money he tould *Thraske* in the presence of many then present, that it was ready to be bestowed for his necessary use, and then left him some part thereof.

He also acquainted the Lord Archbishopp, Lord Chauncellor, and *Mr. Secretary Naunton*, of that money, though he cannot 5 charge their memoryes further then it extendeth.

When *Thraske* had worne out his cloathes and desired other, the Lord Chauncellor bidd the Warden buy for *Thraske* some cloathes, which was done accordingly, even soe much as *Thraske* desired; the Warden alsoe gave him money to buy wyne for his comforte at 10 tymes.

The Warden delivered likewise of that money to him which was *Thraske's* keeper to provide divers weekes dyett for Thraske, when he refused the Warden's meate, because porke, connyes, ducks, and such like uncleane meates (as he held opinion) were dressed with it. 15

The Warden with all affablenes found dyett and lodging to *Thraske* and his keeper dureing his close imprisonment, and dyett at the Warden's own table after he was comfortable, being in all by the space of fore score weekes, and hitherto could never gett payment or allowance of him or elswhere, for, in tyne, while the war- 20 den did expostulate to be paid of his Majestie, *Thraske* tould the warden that if any of that xjl. rested unlayed out in cloathes it was fitt it should rest in the Warden's hands till he could make better satisfaction. And dureing this fayre pretence he gott away and sent the Warden a bond sealed and subscribed to pay when he 25 should be able and as should be fitt, soe that the Warden doth suffer forbeareance of lxxxl. or thereabouts.

The practise of the Fleete, King's Bench, Gatehowse, and all such prisons, is not to permitt close prisoners to have money, knives, penn, inck, and such like, whereby to attayne their ends to the 30 prejudice of the service. And *Thraske* did never thinke himselfe injured, but retorned loveingly to the Warden and was preacher in the Fleete a long tyme, but the malignant there (not he) broched this complaint.

Thraske's close imprisonment occasioned the takeing of his money and booke.

Which booke discovered *Rookwood's* ill accertion to the King. Whereupon *Rookwood* was comitted close prisoner, broke and cutt 5 the prison dores, and (with others) made a fowle tumult, which occasioned putting on of irons.

That Tumult occasioned the Warden to send upp his servantes to suppresse and bestowe them.

This suppressing occasioned Coppin (who was one of them) to 10 accuse those servantes of theft and now lastly the warden of starveing his prisoners.

How farr such conspiracye of sectaryes may infringe the service of his Majestie and endanger all wardens or keepers, it is humbly left to Consideration.

The Fowerth Article.

After engagement of faith, soule, and all under hand and seale,
contrary thereto detayneing a prisoner haveing liberty by his Majestie's writt, to his great prejudice.

This if it be truely understood touching one *Mr. Hayne* a   5
prisoner in execution in the Fleete, it is rather a suggestion of
infidells then that it hath any ground of truth, as appeareth in this
answeare followeing.

One *Thomas Hayne* a prisoner in execution for xvc*li.* or thereabouts besides actions, obteyned by a petition (to the Lord Chaun- 10
cellor) an *habeas corpus,* and leave to goe into the Country untill
the end of the next terme followeing; when he shewed the Warden
the peticon, the Warden tould him it was unlawfull and unmeete
that a prisoner should be out of London in the terme tyme, because
the Warden was to produce him in any of the courts soe often 15
as he should be called for or ells he should be fyned; wherefore *Hayne* had libertie and direction onely to tarry till the
begining of the terme, and then if he came he was to move
againe for a new writt to endure for that terme; but when *Hayne*
was gotten into the Country he came not againe untill 13 dayes 20
within the terme, and lodged himselfe in Milford Lane, and his
keeper came to the Warden at Westminster, sayeing first to the
Warden and after to the clarke of the Fleete, that *Hayne* said he
was noe prisoner and would not retorne to the Fleete, which words
(noe prisoner, &c.) were true in stricktness of Lawe, though his 25
keeper knewe not *Hayne's* drift, for *Hayne* being failed in his
tyme it was an escape in Lawe, and the Warden bound to pay the
debt, with which misterie the Warden did not acquaint *Hayne's*
keeper, but bidd him bring him inn, yet in fower dayes after the
Warden neither sawe keeper nor prisoner.   30

Then *Hayne* wrott a lettre to the warden sheweing that though
he had absented himselfe from his keeper yet he would come inn
if the Warden would have it soe. The warden answeared by wryteing
and protested by oath that if he came inn then he would permitt
5 him to goe out againe, and therefore praied him to come, &c.
But *Hayne* nor his keeper came at the Warden in fower dayes
after, att which tyme there came a writt which had often beene
offered to the clarke of the Fleete before (and still suspended by
intreaty), comaunding the Warden to bring *Hayne* to the King's
10 Bench Barre on the next day in court, being the last day of the
terme, to be charged with a new execution, whereupon the clarke
appointed one *Thompson*, a servant of the wardens, to bring in
Hayne if he mett him.

Thompson, attending another prisoner abroad, met *Hayne* and
15 tould him he had order to bring him in, but because he had
another prisoner in custodie praied *Hayne* to come aloane, but he
did not come in.

After which the Warden, consulting with his clarke and servants
whether *Hayne* meant honestly, and urged by new necessity of the
20 last writt, they resolved that the Warden and some of his servants
should goe one way and the clarke with others another way to
seeke *Hayne*, and seekeing him the warden mett *Hayne* in the
Temple, whence draweing him out by discourse and telling him of
the new writt, fower or five of the Warden's men seeing him offer
25 to goe another way, did (by their master's direction) carry him to
the Fleete, and he was there kept for more suerty of his being the
next court day in the King's Bench.

At which tyme he was taken from the Fleete and sent to the
King's Bench prison, where meeteing one which was formerly a
30 prisoner in the Fleete and departed indebted 150*l.* to the Warden, a
man that accused his grandfather and endangered his hanging to
have his estate. This man, getting the said lettre which the Warden
wrott to *Hayne*, tooke notice that the warden had restrayned
Hayne, and so he accused the warden of infidelity, and divulged it

The warden
had enlarged
the warrant
for the whole
terme, though
Haines knewe
it not.

to the world without informeing them that *Hayne* did not come
inn voluntarilie, but by compulsion and serch (by which the
Warden's promise and protestation was disolved), and soe noe cryme
is on the Warden.

A signe that there is a great sprirritt of mallice rageing, when 5
men will calumpniate a man for an infidell (if a promise had beene
broke indeed as here was noe breach), before they knewe the
reasons of his doeings or enquired of the circumstances, tymes, or
occasions; but when it is considered how they doe the like in other
matters it is to be hoped they shall be the lesse creditted.   10

The Fift Article.

False imprisonment of men discharged, offering to pay all due fees for divers moneths

Accusation of false imprisonment.

This is deduced from the Warden's keepeing of men after they be discharged untill they pay their fees and duties, a thing ever mainteyned by Lawe, custome, and direction, especially in this *Christopher Kennell's* case, who sett this reproach on foote.

Answeare.

For if a banckrupt or other doe by pretence move his creditors to compound on new security and soe free him from imprisonment, if the Warden lett him goe without payment or security, he cannot afterwards sue him, whom he needed not to have trusted in prison, but put him into the hole if he fayled in his weekely dutyes, and this clamor against the Warden doth sildome happen more then where he useth most curtesye to men of evill hearts, as appeares by this perticuler answeare to the said *Kennell*, which may serve to all of that kind, and other kind there is none.

For the Warden dareth not to bring a man to prison without warrant. If he should he makes himselfe subject to great damage by accion of false imprisonment.

But *Kennell*, when he was discharged refused to pay the ordinary dutyes, or to compound for them in any reasonable manner; whereupon the warden by suite to the Lord Chauncellor obteyned a reference unto two persons without exception (as appeares), and they ordered the busines; which done, and *Kennell* (not observeing) complayned to one of the Secretaries of State, where the Warden answeared it Then he complayned to the Lords of the Councell, there alsoe the Warden made answeare; then he complayned to the Lords Comis-sioners from the King for the busines of the Fleete, who tould him directly that they would not give other order, but he should pay it

before he went. Then he betooke himselfe to the factions in the
Fleete, and opposed the quietnes and governement there, soe that
the Warden was constrayned to keepe him for president sake, for
such prisoners as would not pay their fees have beene detayned by
order of the King's Bench, by order of the Comon Pleas, by order 5
of Chauncery. If the question arise of what is due, then the Warden takeing any more is subject to action of false imprisonment
for detayneing them, or extortion in takeing too much. And this
hath beene the directions of the Judges, Lords, &c. from tyme to
tyme, soe as this clamor needeth not, if they would lett things be 10
judged. And there is not any collour to charge the Warden with
other false imprisonment, saveing keepeing them after discharge
untill they pay their duties, which is a custome throughout all the
kingdome; and when this or any other difficultie of the like nature
hath happened, the Warden (or often tymes the prisoner) have beene 15
suitors to the Lords and Judges to have it referred, whereupon both
sides have quietted themselves and obeyed, except some one more
refractory then other (as *Mr. Kennell* is) who (for want of other
imployment and mayntenance) is the general agent (for hier) against
the Warden, though (of all men) he hath least reason in regard of 20
the Warden's usage towards him in point of fees and duties, where
the Warden accepted of him 80*li.* in lieu of a 160*li.* allotted by the
referrees for nyne yeares imprisonment, and yet he hath not paid
that by tenne pounds.

The Warden hath observed that fees and dutyes are, as it were, 25
created three manner of wayes, viz.:

By Act of Parliament.

By Custome.

By tolleration of the State and Judges of Courts.

Then, to reason from the substance to the effect, it may be said 30
that custome and tolleration hath been to keepe a prisoner after
his discharge untill he pay his dutyes; and auncyently all discharges
had a clause (payeing their fees and duties). If this then be abro-
gated, the Warden must be excused if he give noe trust nor ease,

Rep fo. 10.

but put them into the meanest places, which would be very bitter
unto a number of well descended gentlemen, who purposely remove
thither, whome (as may appeare) the Warden hath more comforted,
releeved, and trusted then any officer of his quallitie in the realme
5 of England.

The Sixth and Seaventh Articles.

Accusation of close imprisonment.

6. Close imprisonment of many without Order, Warrant, or Lawe, by moneths and yeares.

Accusation of cruell imprisonment.

7. Close and cruell imprisonment, chayneing, manacling, and bolting of them with irons, some of the degree of knighthood, without cause or warrant.   5

Answeare.

The answeares followeing will cleare theis accusations, for close imprisonment is of diverse natures, viz.:

Close in their chambers for matters of State, which is never done without warrant, and with such noe man may speake or bring them victuall; but the Warden is specially to provide for them, and soe 10 he doth.

9 Rep. fo. 87.
3 Rep. fo. 44.

1 B. 2. cap. 12.
Dyer Pasche,
8 E.
Camera Stellata. 24 h. 8.

Alsoe close prisoners by order out of the Courts of Chauncery and Starr Chamber &c. the use whereof is comonly that they goe not abroad, and sometymes are kept in their chambers, but doe speake with many about their busines, unlesse order be given to 15 the contrary, as in *Inglefeild*, *Beare*, *Oliver*, and *Jennyson's* case, some for heynous contempts, and some for conspiracyes to be discovered, for which purpose the Fleete is the Kings ymmediate and proper prison.

For execution and trespasse they must be close without conference with others or intelligence of things abroad.

Ut per m ad pœnas metus ad omnes.

Other closenes there is none but restraint of dangerous prisoners, 20 badd debtors for great somes, perjurers, forgerors, conspirators, and such like censured persons, by whome the Warden or his servants may be undone or slayne thorough violence to his person or office, as by *Whitbrooke*, *Rookwood*, *Inglefeild*, *Chamberlayne*, *Lee*, *Sharpe*, and a great many more, whose cause is by the Warden['s] 25 relaters [*sic*] almost ready for heareing in Starr Chamber and the fact confessed by some defendants and ready to be proved by witnesses without exception.

If the warden doe keepe such within their owne precinct, wardes,

walls, and yards, where yet there are many prisoners and chambers, can it be termed close imprisonment when they speake with all men which will come to them, victuall themselves, and those that will may come to church (whereof many doe not, and therefore
5 doe evade it with a glosse upon their close imprisonment, they being indeed Popish, whereof the faction is (in a manner) wholie compacted.)

The resolucion of all the Judges to the K. councell in Star-chamber, 12⁰ Reg. Jac. is, That Prisoners in Execucion ought not to goe at libertie in prison.

All prisons in England doe restrayne such as thus demeane themselves, and such as pay not their fees, for their is noe other meanes
10 to constrayne them to pay their fees and duties; for if they may be well lodged and fetch their dyet from abroad, they will not onely never pay creditor, but defeate justice, and lett the Warden have nothing to mainteyne him in his attendance.

Sir Francis Inglefeild's restraint which he calleth (false) close
15 imprisonment, was but within his warde, where were five chambers, and gentlemen lodged; and it was upon *Sir Francis* not payment of fee for his liberty, for mutinyes and [mutinous] provocation to stabb or pistoll the Warden, [and] receaveing a dangerous and murtherous prisoner into his lodging whome the Warden could not
20 lodge or bestowe in safety because of *Sir Francis* his abettments, which were infinit, against the Warden and his office. And this imprisonment was done but two dayes with a keeper to open and shut at all tymes for all comers, which were above three score in a day, as the keeper saith.

By a warde or wards is meant a place that hath many chambers, which, beside their generall dores, hath another enter dore to locke up all that lye there.

25 And if this be not tollerable for the Warden to doe (which all Wardens have ever done) who on misdemeanours have put prisoners to keepe their chambers, how can one Warden governe 200 persons, of whom if any escape, fire the house, kill, or wound, it is too late afterwards to complayne, because noe seate of justice can give the
30 Warden remedy when once such matters are happened and passed? for which considerations, if the Warden be jealous of the King's debtors and others, he hopeth it will not be taken an offence, but a service to the comon wealth.

And every prisoner is to give bond for true imprisonment, good

As appeares by the 1st article of the Constitutions.

behaviour, and payment of duties, or ells he is to have noe benefitt
of libertye, and this being the first dutye of a prisoner, if he fayle
therein the Warden may faile in ministring bedd, meate, liberty, or
chamber, and may put irons on such as be in execution, according
as the Lawe doth appointe and tollerate. 5

It is an exceeding troble, charge, and care to the Warden to
keepe any man close prisoner, and when it hath been imposed in
matters not touching the state he hath made humble suite against
it, and obteyned sometyme remission, sometyme release.

The cruelty here meant was putting a payre of hand irons upon 10
one Mr. Chamberlayne for machinations to distroy the Warden and
office, bolts on Sir John Whitbrooke for wounding the Warden and
attempting to beate out his braynes with a hammer and stabbing
three officers of speciall trust with a stilletto, bolts on Lee for concurring in theis, and bolts on Mr. Nicholas Rookwood for cutting 15
open the prison dores, and demeanours odious to all his fellow
prisoners, for which the Lords of the Councell sent him to Newgate, as was Lee, Mynors, and divers others, soe that the Warden's
fact in that point was but a begining of that correction which
justice it selfe did second by sending them to Newgate for further 20
punishment and quieting the King's prison. If a knight be a
murtherer he must suffer as inferior men doe.

And as for Sir John Whitbrooke; The Warden hath direccon to
put other manner of irons then were put on and in another fashion,
but (it being the Warden's owne case) he did the lesse, and such 25
as were put on were complayned off at the Councell Table, yet
there was noe comand to take them off untill a second complainte,
and upon a suggestion that Whitbrooke was wounded, whereas he
had noe wounds but a little bruse or contusion in his arme.

And it might seeme a crueltie to bring porters to carry Mr. 30
Chamberlayne upp into his chamber, but who shall consider what
Chamberlayne had done before, and that it is a custome in the
Fleete when men will not be ruled they are sett in a chayre for
avoyding hurt and soe carryed to Westminster (as proces of the

court doe comand or other where at such tymes as they be obstinate
and perverse) will excuse the Warden, for in just and necessary
things they must be ruled and overcome, or ells such confusion will
followe as noe justice shall be prosecuted, touching whom there shall
5 be more at large sett forth a perticuler answeare, when the Warden
shall see his perticuler allegations, which, though they have heretofore been very peremptorelie and clamarouslie sett forth, yet when
the Warden rendred the reasons and cause of using him after that
manner. the Warden was dismissed with (*sic*) blame in highest
10 and lowest places of ordinarie justice.

Therefore as in the stattute of Westminster 2 the lawe saith that
manucipenter in jerris, soe the Warden hath done but his dutie on
theis persons, who are all (except one *Mynors*) that have been ironed,
and he is soe honest as to confesse that both himselfe and the rest
15 have deserved them, and *Mr. Bellingham* may as well witnes for
irons in the Fleete, as he did weare them in the sherriff's prison
before he came to the Fleete, and as is accustomed thoroughout the
kingdome, which many more (now in the Fleete) doe by suffering
in other prisons well knowe to be true.

20   The irons which be in the Fleete have beene of most auncyent
continuance, and therefore likely to have beene used there; the
payeing a fyne for to be freed of them proveth the use, and there
are some knights (farr above *Whitbrooke* in rank) now prisoners
that did weare irons 30 years past for misdemeanors after they had
25 fyned to be free of them in the Fleete.

And all the ancyent servants in the Fleete of 30 yeares standing
doe testifie that upon misdemeanors prisoners have had irons put
upon them, as in the discretion of the Warden seemed good.

Also about 23 yeares past, when theis (amongst many other
30 matters) was in question before referrees from the Lord Chauncellor,
the Honorouble Master of the Rolls delivered his opinion that if
the use of irons were abridged the howse would be subverted.

The Warden did never shewe spleene or passion in the putting
irons on prisoners for private revenge, as appeared by *Mr. Copeman*,

Gough, Thompson, Agleworth, Coppin, and others, that being in
execution for great somes have run away and escaped, whom when
they have beene apprehended with great charges, and the Warden
(for some) compelled to pay their debts, yet he never put irons on
any of them, because the offence was but dampnification of the 5
Warden in his goods.

But who doth mutiny, conspire, or breake the prison, it is an
offence against the King, the State, and the Office, and they have
ever beene put in irons, as may be maynteyned both by Lawe,
custome, and discretion in the one soart and the other, and as most 10
of the prisoners in execution have removed themselves from other
prisons to the Fleete for their owne case, soe if they like not their
usage there they may remove againe to the King's Bench, &c.

By the accusation for cruelty is alsoe further meant the bring [sic]
of prisoners perforce out of their lodgings, and that hath beene when 15
they will not remove with often intreaty by appointment and by
promise haveing other lodgings offered, as Mr. Chamberlayne, who
had not soe much as paid for two chambers, a studdy, and other
roomes for himselfe, his wife, and familie, where they lived in the
Warden's owne private bedchambers divers years, and yet said he 20
would lie there in the Warden's dispight; whereupon the Warden did
cause him to be carryed to another good chamber where formerly
he had lyen, and there was his bedd made, fyer, wyne, &c. put
ready for him by the warden's appointment.

As for Sir Francis Inglefeild, who alsoe was fetched or carryed 25
out of his chamber, he had not paid his fee or fyne for liberty
and irons, he held three roomes, had the walkes on the leads many
moneths, and when the Warden had two noblemen comitted on the
suddayne, and noe chamber to bestowe them in, Sir Francis was
desired to give place and another chamber made ready for him, 30
where he had formerly lyen, but he said he would not remove
without violence, whereupon he was fayrely carried out of his
chamber after many intreatyes to goe of his owne accord, as in a
particuler defence against him shall appeare, for after many howers

discourses he yeilded to be carryed because he would thereby take
advantage.

If prisoners may lye where they will, soe long as they will and
not give place to noblemen (who are their betters), and if such as
5 Sir Francis Inglefeild (being in faction) begin a president in that
kind, then all prisoners in their place will doe the like, and liveing
where they list the Warden must lett them rule, till all be out of
rule.

There are not severall lodgings in the Fleete for every severall
10 prisoner, and therefore of necessity some must be removed at the
discretion of the Warden to place others, especially they that did
deny the constitutions of governement there, and said, they were
gotten by bribery and falshood, and that the Warden durst not
avouch the constitutions, which (inter alia) say the Warden should
15 appoint the prisoners their bedd and chamber; wherefore it cannot
be doubted in any comon understanding but that it is the Warden's
part and not the prisoners to appoint it themselves.

A scantling of the Warden's crueltye or lenitye may be taken by
the great tolleration and trust that the Warden hath given to the
20 number of viij or ix^xx prisoners; a multitude whereof have never
paied him in all the yeares and tyme that he hath had the charge
and custodye of that place (though they be very sufficient) who
by their practises are become indebted to him some 200l. some
100l. and some downewards, as appeares by bills, bonds, bookes, and
25 accompts subscribed.

Himselfe never layed violent hands on any man, never conspired
there detention or used circumvention in their comitting thither,
but indeed this trust given to them and kindnes shewed them is
the cause why the generall for the most part doe connive if not
30 sett on the fewe which complayne, thinking that if the Warden fayle
in his place and credit, then there will be none to call them to
accompt for what they owe him. And they have now soe tasted
the benefitt of contention, still disputeing what is due, and never
paying, as that the ablest and honest seemeing men thinke it worth

the labour and cost to contend still, and the poorest, being once gotten behind by mispending what otherwise should pay the Warden, will never be able to pay what is arrere.

I shall crave leave heare to answeare the objection which asketh " Why doth the Warden trust them soe long, and not call for his 5 money at the weeke, the moneth, or quarter?" Suppose he doe, and that he pay him not. What, then? Shall he put them from the liberty of the howse, and restrayne them in the straitest prison, as all the prisons in the kingdome doe? Why, then, they have taken upp a comon sayeing, and it hath beene much harkened unto, that the 10 Warden doth keepe them close prisoners; a thing not onely above his power, but the power of superiors. But let it be considered whether it be not of congrewence that as a debtor or delinquent is sent to prison for none payment or performance, and soe his liberty is taken away, whether there be not the same equity during his 15 being in prison that he shall not have liberty of all the prison and walkes, except he pay the Warden's dutyes and performe orders of the prison.

The question then is who shall lay this on him, the Warden or the Judge? Answeare, they whome neither civell or ecclesiasticall 20 judge, the King's prerogative, or comand can rule; yet this Warden must rule him *ex officio*, or ells justice never cometh to his period, but the Judge shall have as much to doe about ordering the imprisoned as about convicting him before imprisonment.

Soe that it is a paradox whether a fewe Insolvent Banckrupts 25 and Scismatiques were not better undergoe too much coertion then revell in a prison, contempne, traduce, and declyne justice, judges, and justicers, without end or measure, yet to the Fleete they will bring their wives, children, and servants to cohabite, woemen are brought in bedd there (but the children baptised fewe can tell 30 where), and noe other breeding have some then there; they infect the place with diseases incident to youth, and fill it with stinck and noysomnes not to be named; they exempt themselves from howserent, parishe dutyes, and all taxations in the comonwealth; they en-

Have indicted the Lord Chancellor of old and late times.

deavoured to have a chamber in the Fleete, with gardens, yards, places
of pleasure, at the third or fowerth part that it would cost abroad,
soe that by excesse of familyes there are two or three mesniall
servants to one prisoner in the Fleete, and by exemption of payment
5 it is better then an hospitall, for to an hospitall none shall be admitted that hath livelyhood abroad, none can there have his wife
or his leman, none can put his money at interest, deale on brokage
or pawnes, none have protection to walke the citty but that his
creditors will arrest him, and carry him to the doleful places of
10 Newgate or the Compter.

In an hospitall he shall be conformable in religion or detected for,
it, and perhapps be expulsed.

In the Fleete all this may be done, and from the Fleete many
will not goe though they be cleared or you would force them,
15 because they can lye there, pay nothing, be abetted and cherished
by factious prisoners and others of their owne tribe, followe and
sollicite Lawe suites, and troble all men in words and deeds, and
with a little Fleete reading become counsellors, attorneyes, doctors,
chirurgions, scribes, cookes, and all manner of handycrafts to that
20 precinct, where sometymes are plotted robberyes abroad, cutting of
purses in towne, to steale and bring in by the hands of their setters
and versers, and noe hew and cry, constable, or officer can followe;
for the Fleete is a priviledged place, which should keepe all goods
howsoever ill gotten as the prisoners would have it; but if the
25 Warden oppose them, they can touch him with murther, felony,
robbery, and infynite enormityes, and by the multitude of clamours
(though untrue) bereave him of protection or continuance; for
many of them have beene prisoners 30 yeares, some 25 and downewards, and have had the practise of all or most gaoles in the king-
30 dome, and therefore are graduates in their profession, to the great
edifieing of their proselits and detering the Warden, and they keepe
themselves loaden with a multitude of actions and executions which
are or might be discharged, to the end that if a creditor would
remove them, the number of causes draweth a great charge of 5,

10, 15, or 20*l.* soe as the creditor is not willing to undergoe it, though with them more restraint in another place or prison of the King's Bench, where if they be they shall speedily in body or goods undergoe execution; but the priviledge of the Fleete (subordinate to the Court of Comon Pleas) is such, as a man going   5
there called to the barr for debt may refuse to appeare, whereof there followeth nothing but an outlawry, which theis freebooters doe soe little esteeme as they accompt it a happie transgression to come from the King's Bench prison to the Fleete, where they can be but outlawed reversable at pleasure.   10

The Eighth Article.

Starveing of men, close imprisonment, guarding them from meate, *Accusation of* drinke, &c. and that after comand of authority to the contrary. *starveing.*

The allegation of starveing close prisoners is soe fabulous and false *Answeare.* as it hath no colour, for lett all prisoners that have beene close and
5 their keepers [be] examyned and the contrarie will manifestly appeare, this imputation being causleslie forged by one *Mr. Edward Rookwood*, who being comited and ordered close for matter of state, the Warden (knoweing whom he had to doe with all) did at his owne costs (which is yet unpaid for) cause his dyet to be provided and
10 brought unto him, and likewise appointed that what he had every meale should be written downe. And, although some part of that wryteing (by length of tyme) is lost or mislayed, yet some part remayneth justifieing that his ordinary meales cost the Warden xij*d*. xiiij*d*. and xvj*d*. a meale, and sometymes a joynt of meate of
15 iij*s*. at once, or whatsoever he would with reason call for.

But at last, when he had beene many weekes there and meant to bereave the Warden of payment, the keeper of his meate, drinke, and attendance (which he ought to allowe), and to endanger them with some stratagem, he faigned himselfe sick, refused the Warden's
20 provision, endeavoured to corrupt his keeper, and lastly called for a Doctor of Physick, which (by the Lords order) being admitted, and *Doctor Fryer* comeing thither late in the forenoone, *Rookwood* (amongst other fictions) retorned to lye downe and groaned (as his keeper saith) and alledged that he was starved, whereupon the
25 Doctor (seeing in his windowe the most part of a roasted pullett which was left of the meale before) asked how he could starve haveing such meate, and then after being permitted to take meate from his owne howse (which was a continuall troble to have it overseene), he contented himselfe with the tenth part of soe much as he

had before, and yet first and last was in health good enough, as
the Doctor very justly and truely related to the Warden.

Another or lesse occassion of such allegation of starveing was that
in July, 1619; after that the said *Rookwood* and his sonne *Nicholas*
(who alsoe had beene a close prisoner in that kind) were permitted   5
liberty of the Fleete, and *Nicholas Rookwood* (for revenge sake)
behaveing himselfe rather as a Bedlam frantick then a gentleman, to
the utter dislike and greife of all others in the prison, and with
steele chissells, malletts, and hammers, cutting all the stone workes
of the dores of the Tower Chambers (where they then laye) into 10
which the bolts and locks did shutt, soe as noe dores could be
fastened upon eighteene prisoners of great waight. The Warden
therefore (not without danger and bloodshedd of his servants,
Rookwood and the rest useing stilletto, long bedstaves, bedposts,
and faggot sticks for resistance), as aforesaid, removed them into the 15
strongest wards of the prison, where further the said *Rookwood*,
Sir John Whitbrooke, *Boughton*, *Coppin*, and *Seager*, with seaven
others in an evening did combyne together, when 32 other prisoners
(which lay in those wards) were abroad in the walks of the howse,
and did shutt and block upp the dores of that warde, forteficing 20
themselves within, and not permitting their fellowes to retorne to
their lodgings, where soe houlding it (to the Warden's extreame
danger) they would by noe intreaty of him or other officers of the
citty or comand of some Privy Counncellors open it, and lett in their
fellowes; whereupon the Warden, being advised to keepe them from 25
victuall untill they rendred themselves and the place, he did for
one day (like as in Newgate a while before had been done) put it
in practise; but being advertized that those fewe had seized the
salted beefe, bacon, cheese, &c. of the other 32, shutt out, and by
that meanes with what was given them at the beging place and 30
elswhere they did abound, the Warden gave over that designe and
made his recourse to the Lord Chauncellor then out of towne.

In which tyme those voluntary immured persons clamoured to the
Lord Cheife Justice, whose first answeare was, that it being in their

owne power to come forth (as others did) he sawe noe cause to
releeve them with meate, yet thorough further Clamour he at last
Comanded that the(y) should have victuall, And victuall thay had
both before and after soe plentifully that when, the Lord Chaun-
5 cellor's ancthoritye not prevayleing, the Lords of the Councell
soe prevayled as they rendred themselves and opened the dores,
some one man of them sent out of the prison above two dozen of
Bread. If it were needfull the Warden could prove *Sir Francis Inglefield* and others carryed to them with their owne hands Joints of
10 Roast Mutton and Lambe; But the effect of this supposed starveing
was never seene by any man's face, by any man's sicknes, infirmity,
or death, and is onely sett out to abuse the hearers, As yf hunger
had made them breake stone walls, who brake stone walls before
they were hungry and immured themselves in all things abounding,
15 as some whome they inclosed with them by constraint did then
informe the Warden, and are ready still to justifie.

And further to unmaske this imputation the more and to shewe
the Warden's care in that kind it may be remembred (as it standeth
proved upon record) that when *Sir John Whitbrooke* by his
20 murtherous attempt had brought the Prison into an uprore, soe
that it touched the Warden (as all others before him by the like) to
secure the Prison and shutt up the Wards where the most dangerous
prisoners were, untill things might be setled, He then came unto
such as he had shutt upp, and fayrely tould them he would victuall
25 them if they needed, And accordingly did send both roast and
boyled meate in a plentifull manner, which they did receave, And
yet for all that they broke upp three strong dores one within
another, and came forth when they had beene shutt in but from
morneing till two in the afternoone.

30 In all which circumstances opened at the Counsell Board and
before Comissioners and Comittees, the Warden cleared himselfe from
tyme to tyme soe farr as a man may which hath to doe with such
tainted persons, On whose falcityes the Murther [of] *Whitbrooke*,
the Felony of *Coppin's* Money, the Robbery of *Throske*. &c. are all

like a Chayne (whose links they made and forged) fastened upon
the Warden.

Mr. *Jennyson* of the same tribe, being a close prisoner, did one
meale complayne of his Dyett, Whereupon it was viewed by Gentlemen, and vallewed that the Warden could allowe him none such 5
after the rate of viij*d.* to the meale (which is the ordinary Comons
of the howse), yet the Warden is still unpaid for what he and many
others in that kind have had, which is but a meane incouragement
to the Warden for keepeing close Prisoners.

The Nynth Article.

Breaking of Prisoners Chambers haveing first removed them, opening their Truncks, seizeing their goods, and still detayncing them. Accusation of Seizeing Prisoners Goods.

5   Although this be a generall charge or Accusation, yet for that Answeare.
onely one hath complayned punctually according to this whole
charge, which noe other hath collour to doe in the whole, though
perhapps in part or parts their evill will be much; Therefore it may
be understood that this trencheth on the Warden's putting or shutt-
10 ing a Prisoner out of his chamber for none Payment on the Prisoners
Part, or want of roome for other Prisoners on the Warden's part;
Which Prisoner having goods or stuffe in his Chamber, presently
taketh occasion to desire retorne to his Chamber, whither if he once
gett he maketh it his Castle against any remove, soe that it is not
15 safe at all tymes and that all men have warneing that they shalbe
removed, lest fortifications and tumults be made. What then, shall
not the Prisoner have his goods? Yes, verily, though perhapps an
hoast abroad or any man that taketh lodgers would scarce suffer it;
He shall have his goods. But put case he will not take them.
20 Why, then they shall be inventoryed and offered him, and that is
soe much as may be done, and it was done, as appeares by good
proofe in *Peck's* case. *Mr. Chamberlayne* cannot complayne in
this kind, For upon his first remove he had all his goods save that
he fableth of the losse of a Bond of vij M. *li.* (surely a great value,
25 and such at the rate of iiijs. in the pound (as he offereth his creditors)
would pay all his debts), And halfe a dozen of silver spoones he
lost too, untill he found them againe lockt upp in his owne cubbord,
whereof he kept the keyes. In his second remove, when he was
putt into the Comon Prison that was no place for his many Truncks,

and to fitt and place his owne and other men's evidence, As in his
oath in the Exchequer he gallantly setteth forth; And it is to be
hoped that the bond of vij M. *li.* was safe layed amongst those
evidences. Therefore the Warden bidd him carry those Truncks
and things back out of the Prison, and detayned some meane 5
howshould things untill opportunitie of disposeing them or makeing some accord with *Mr. Chamberlayne;* But afterwards, upon
the Lords Comittees being at the Fleete, the Warden was comanded
to deliver him his things and he to pay the Warden. All which
things *Mr. Chamberlayne* had, even to a Sawcer and a Mustard- 10
pott, except an ould peece of a curtayne valued at vj*d.* For which
if the Warden happen to be either a Wilfull or cuning Banckrupt
(as *Chamberlayne* hath often called him) it is to be hoped that
Chamberlayne will (according to his owne rule and offer) take a
penny and a fift part of a penny for the debt, which is after the 15
rate of iiij*s.* in the pound. Though yet for all the Lords Comands
and other Comands since, the Warden can neither gett the fift part
nor any part of a penny that is due to him for theis six yeares.

As for *Mr. Sharpe's* complainte, though it be of noe Collour or
Substance, he shall have an answeare at large and for his creditt. 20

But one *Mr. Ashburnham Peck* is the man to be Answeared here.
For the *Lady Amy* her goods are staied and held in another nature,
and she sueth the Warden at the Comon Lawe.

Rookwood had all his goods delivered him by Order at Councell
Table upon payment of 15*li.* to the Warden by the same Order. 25

Peck therefore a prisoner 19 yeares hath a good estate of 80*l.*
per annum besides leaves; very small somes would discharge him,
but he payeth noe man. He was lodged by the Warden 8 yeares
in a good Chamber of the Warden's owne Roomes, he often promised
and vowed payment at quarter dayes, but never paied penny; But 30
then he would urge how his Children robbed him of his money, and
sometymes of his gold lace from his Cloathes, yet they were still
entertayned at the Fleete; And (though reputed cutpurses) hidd
themselves in the Fleete, untill at last the Gallowes had one from

Newgate, the other escaped by Naturall death after twice imprisonment for cutting of purses.

Himselfe purloyned the Warden's pullen, the lathes from the
walls of the howse to roast them, feasting and ryotting, One while
5 as if with his servants, other while on pretence of marriage, and
would not lett them be kept out by the Warden (though *Peck's* own
Daughter which attended him hath besought it of the Warden with
teares). He used to sett on foote Daungers and then reveale them,
By which and like shifts he protracted payment of his fees, and
10 therefore was put out of his chamber into the Wards; before which
tyme, *Peck* haveing taken away the Beding of one *Rith*, a Prisoner
and Bedfellowe in his Chamber, who dyed, *Rith's* Mother claymed
the same; And upon theis occasions the Warden kept it when *Peck*
was removed untill with a knife drawne *Peck* came thorough all the
15 Prison and tooke per force from that Chamber all save the very Bedd,
and the Warden had nought but the Bedd in the behalfe of *Rith*.

Peck had the rest of all kinds, or he might have had it, for it
was inventoryed and offered him; But he, claimeing a lease of his
chamber, said He would retorne and possesse it, As appeares by
20 Testimonye.

As for breakeing open prisoners chambers, opening Truncks,
and seizeing their goods, this *Peck* purloyned goods of *Sir John
Whitbrooke*, which being often enquired for and demaunded of him
he denyed them, and was further detected (as followeth) proved
25 on record.

Peck with his Accomplices came into the gaoler's lodge (which is
keeper of the Wards) and thrust him out with his aged wife, and
in resisting greeviously brused the Gaoler, Takeing away his keyes
of the Prison and offering to stabb the man that was under the
30 goaler, when he endeavoured to come and rescue him. He bruised
the Goaler soe soare as he languished thereof. *Peck* and others said
that by detayneing their dutyes they would hould the Warden
soe hard to it as he should be forced to run away.

He annymated prisoners not to pay, and wonne the prisoners in

the wards to breake fower of the Prison dores there at the tyme
when the others were to be broken in another part of the Prison.

Peck was the spokesmen for them all when the Warden entreated
them to be quiet, And with a hatchet and a chissell broke open a
dore and lett out others.   5

Peck bought the hatchet to doe it that day it was done, and the
chissell was *Thurmans* (*Peck's* wife's Father), who lent it volun-
tarily to doe the deed. In cutting open the dores he was called
King Peck for conquerring the Warden.

Peck and *Rookwood* discourseing of a Warden slayne, he said 10
it were noe matter if *Harris* were used in that kind.

Peck used words of incouragement to attempt the like on this
Warden.

He incouraged *Lee* to rayle att and slaunder the Warden to bring
him in hatred.   15

Peck said (after the Warden had wounded) he was sorry *Whitbrooke* had not killed him.

Peck thretned to cut the throats of all that should give advise
of the conspiracy.

Peck brought the Engines to breake the locks and dores with 20
shouts and cryes, while the others in the Tower Chamber broke
that part of the Prison with sword, staves, wheelers, axe, and stones.
They assaulted the Warden soe as with neighbours Armed the Warden was forced to suppresse them.

Peck called by *Rookwood, King Peck.*   25

Peck with others broke through a wall of 5 foote thick, and alsoe
broke a strong Barr of Iron that went round about the dore of the
Prison, to keepe in the stone worke.

For theis fowle abuses *Peck* was by the Lord Cheife Justice removed to Newgate, where after he had a long tyme beene and 30
durst not open his Truncks in regard of the goods that he had stolne
or purloyned, the Warden called in some neighbours and some
Prisoners and after opening them Inventoryed the goods, keepeing
indeed some 40s. worth thereof in liew of a 100l. debt due by *Pecks*

one promise and agreement, and sent him the chest wherein the
evidences were, without touching one of them, as appears by good
Testimony.

Soe that this complaint heaped upp without distinction of tymes
5 and occasions doth seeme odious, But being opened with the reasons
cannot but shewe just and moderate dealeing in the Warden, and
the like can be shewed for any other if such be; For when a prisoner
is put out of his Chamber, and will not deliver upp the key, the
Warden must needs breake open the dore or loose the use of his
10 Chamber, And this was the very case with *Sir John Whitbrooke.*

There is a great deale of cuning compacted in this Article of
Accusation, As if the warden had shutt a man out of his Chamber
and presently opened the Truncks and seized the goods, the truth
being that after the putting him out of his Chamber, and that he
15 had refused the goods for the present, yet afterwards he tooke
them at severall tymes, And soe continueing Prisoner untill a yeare
after that, for misdemeanors he was sent to Newgate, left his Truncks
in the Fleete with the purloyned goods in them, whereupon the
Warden (who never permitted Truncks to goe out without seeing
20 what is in them) wished theis to be opened in presence of witnesses
and sent them to Newgate, Retayneing 40*l.* worth of *Peek's* goods in
liew of 8 yeares lodging and duties in the Fleete, and more of *Peeks*
there was not save two pillowes and an ould covering of Darnex,
three Blanquetts, and two Bolsters with the purloyned goods.

25 If the Warden should say that he may take (though he never did
soe take) any man's goods by distresses for rent agreed upon within
his freehold, He conceiveth it would not be much gainesaid by
Lawe or *Catalla felonin.* But let them argue that who have longer
interest in the Mannor or Soake of The Fleete, where there hath
30 beene power of the good behaviour by Lettres Pattents ever allowed,
agreeable to the original graunt S. P. R. F. — " Bene et in pace,
libe, quiete, integre, plenarie et honorifice cū oibȝ libtatibȝ et libos
consuetud ad predict custods ptinen."

The Tenth Article.

Where an order gives upon every dayes goeing abroad by one
that is not in Execution 8*d*. to the Ward's box, The Orders exemplified under the great Seale hath a dash over the word Wards to make
it Warden's box; By which practise and under collour thereof he 5
continually robbeth the poore of that 8*d*. a day, which is yearely a
great matter.

This is a very impudent untruth and set on foote cheifely by *Sir
Francis Inglefield*, for neither hath the orders under the great
seale any such dash over the head, nor the record it selfe, for it is 10
in both written (Warden's) at large, And about 23 yeares past for the
like Calumpniations some prisoners wer censured in Starrchamber
and (with papers on their heads) did in every Court at Westminster
(where the Warden hath his attendance) acknowledge their offence.

It is impossible that any man of Judgment can thinke that the 15
Warden either should or would permitt a prisoner (whose escape
may cause the Warden sometymes to pay thowsands) to goe abroad
at the Warden's perill, And that the poore of the wards should
reape the benefitt of his hazard by haveing the viij*d*. to their box.
Were it not that some men doe tell an untruth soe often that themselves beleeve it in the ende, This might much be wondered at by
all men except theis Prisoners.

The Eleventh Article.

Accusation of
Robbing his
Servants.

Where the same order gives 12d. a day to the keeper that goeth abroad with such prisoner He robbeth his servants of that alsoe, forceing the prisoner besides to content his keeper.

Answeare.

5 This, haveing relation to the former, depends on the sence and meaneing of the orders of the Fleete, whether the Warden hath right to the xij$d$. or his servant, But for eight Warden's tymes it can be proved that the Warden for the tyme being hath had it. Thirty yeares past *Sir Francis Inglefield* himselfe (and divers others nowe
10 prisoners of 3 or 4 Pills) paid it, and about 20 yeares past it was questioned on the Prisoners' complaints to the Lord Chauncellors and Comittees and yet never altered for reasons which followe, as the Warden conceaveth.

For if a Prisoner doe goe abroad, The Warden must send a keeper
15 with him. The day is devided soe that the prisoner payeth 10d. for the fornoon and soe much afternoone.

Then it is to be supposed that they come home to dynner and supper; can the Warden give his man (who must be a man of some quallity and trust) entertaynement and meate for 8d. a day, or for
20 the 12d. when perhapps the prisoner useth him one day and not againe in a yeare after; And the Prisoner premeditateing howe much and many generall Busines he will doe that day on which he will goe abroad.

He goeth out earlie and travelleth not like his keeper, who goeth
25 daylie, but as one not weryed before, and the servant must soe followe of Necessity or loose his Prisoner, till late at night, as noe porter would doe the like for iij$d$. or iiij$d$. a day.

This xx$d$. a day doth amount in the yeare to some iiij^{xx}li. amongst all the prisoners; for which the Warden keepeth almost 20 servants
30 for that service onely, and besides falleth into many losses by escapes

and Runawayes before their fees be paid, who make that goeing out their collour to run away and after send in their discharges. Soe that if it shall be thought fitt let it be concluded that a prisoner which goeth abroad shall give suertyes before he goe, finding a man at his owne charge to attend him, And soe the Warden shall be eased of a multitude of his servants. 5

In other Prisons their Master keepers will not lett them goe for soe little as xx*d.* a day.

And sometyme the Warden to releeve the poore letts many goe for nothing, And to serve the Courts of Justice, the Councell Table, the Chauncellors and Treasurer doth bring out many prisoners at once attended with many servants, for whome he neither hath nor doth ask ought. 10

And sometyme there is occasion for some of theis, being charged with tenn or Twentie Thowsand Pounds, more or lesse, to goe abroad, and at their goeing must have two or three keepers, from whom the Warden's pay is still but one, and the same with that for the meanest, who is charged with lesse somes. 15

And somewhat the better to cleare this point it may be seene and read in the Porter of the Fleete his booke how the Warden hath directed him, and confirmed it under his hand, to take after 20*d.* a day of the Prisoner and appoint him a keeper, Soe that the Prisoner is not bound to give either little or much more to his keeper, for the Warden leaveth it indifferent and in the Prisoner's Choyce. 20

25

Att the tyme that the Constitutions of the Fleete were made, it was then meant and practized that noe prisoner should goe further then Westminster or to his Counsell as he went or came, But late Custome hath inlarged their Walks all over London, and yet they will not inlarge their payments to the Warden or his servants. 30

Soe as respecting the Warden's gaine and pay he wisheth they went not abroad at all, they would be the more vehement to cleare themselves, and should be better stripped of the masked Estates they hould.

To the Court.

An' 1617.

If it be said that the Warden by takeing the xij*d*. of that xx*d*. a day doth robb his servant, surely he robbeth by prescription, and by consent of him who is robbed. And which of the Prisoners that hath paid it is there that doth complayne; As for those that
5 have not paid it (which are those that doth complayne) they complayne by speculation, and not by suffering.

The very words of the fift Article of the Constitutions are that of every such prisoner it may be lawfull for the Warden to take viij*d*. a day to the Warden's box, and for his keeper which shall be
10 with him xii*d*.

The sence of which words doe justly beare that the Warden must have both the 8*d*. and 12*d*. as the practize hath continually shewed.

By which words there is but one to take and that is the Warden, and not the keeper of the prisoner, he must take what the Master
15 pleaseth to give him.

If it be asked now what is meant by Warden's Box, it is soe old the Warden cannot find the Begining of it, but sure he is that when the 8*d*. was first taken the standard of money was such as viij*d*. was more worth by much then the whole xx*d*. is nowe, and all
20 things more cheap then now they be.

Robbery is to take money perforce and with a felonious intent to obscure and hide from the knowledge of justice or Comon persons that which is taken, But whatsoever hath come to the Warden in this kind he hath a tytle to it, he receiveth it of his
25 Porter or Clarke by way of Accompt, or at the prisoner's owne hands, and acknowledgement is made by Acquittance or otherwise; soe as the Accusers should have qualified this terme if they either had sence or charitye.

The Twelfth Article.

Accusation for abuseing the Councell's Warrant Dormant.

He hath warrants Dormant under some of the Councell's hands (not nameing any perticuler person) by which continually in all countries he seizeth upon his Majesties Subjectes, forceth them to give bonds to be his prisoners, Exacteth intolerable ffees and Com- 5 positions, &c. where theis apprehentions ought to be by the Sherriffe of the Shires without such vexation or charge to the subject.

Answeare.

As for the word Dormant they be noe otherwise Dormant but that as the waightines of decrees in Courts doe concerne his Majesties 10 Justice or Revennewes, Soe the warrants be renewed from terme to terme and as occasion requireth.

Whereas they say that the warrants are under some of the Councell's hands and doe not add their most honourable appellation; they seem to disjoint the Councell, as if a Warrant from some of 15 them might the more be excepted against.

The Warden hopeth that Prisoners will not presume (neither will it be admitted) to defyne to the Lords of the Councell what warrants they shall subscribe or allowe the warrant of the Fleete; neither whether he that hath see many hundred yeares attended 20 the service of state, att and about the Royall Pallace and Courts at Westminster, or a sherriffe which is changeable every yeare, shall execute those warrants.

And as to the Warden's fees they are lesse then a pursevant Messenger of the Chamber, or a Serjeant at Armes, and (by useing 25 the Warden) the Subject hath ease rather then burthen; For as to the exaction of intollerable fees there is noe such matter used or the Lords ever trobled with any complaints therein, because there is taken but the meere Dutyes. If any fault hath beene comitted it is for spareing the imedate bringing of the party comitted into the 30 prison where he may make eleccon to place himselfe and accordingly to pay as a Gentleman or a yeoman; And hereby perhapps oft tymes

a gentleman passeth with payment of a yeoman's fee, And sometymes a yeoman will rather pay a Gentleman's fee then be brought
upp presently (and before the terme), whereby he shall be prevented
of agreeing with his Adversarie cr obeying what the Courts Comand;
5 Besides when the Termes have beene kept in other shires and
places of exempt liberties, yet then, by full consent and approbation
of the Judges, the Warden hath carryed the Executing of all Orders
and Services of the Courts.

The Thirteenth Article.

Accusation for
Excessive
Rates of
Chambers.

Where by orders noe man ought to pay for any Chamber, the
Warden alloweing Bedd and Bedding, above ijs. iiijd. a weeke, he
exacteth 8s. 10s. 13s. 4d. and of 20s. a weeke without Bedding.

Answeare.

Touching Chambers and Lodgings the Warden leaveth every man　5
to his eleccon; The Orders of the Prison are, That noe Parlor
Comoners and Hall Comoners must lye two in a Bedd like Prisoners,
They of the Parlor at ijs. iiijd. the weeke, They of the Hall at xiiijd.
If any such will lye in the Prison then there is noe question of
their payment nor any more required.　　　　　　　　　　　　10
But the missery is this that none there will pay att all, but stand
upon it that they should pay nothing, which is contrary to right,
to Custome, and to usage; And the Wardens have ever beene paid
for such who being the most dangerous are still lodged there, And
untill theis fewe yeares there was noe other place or prison for any　15
to lodge in.
An° 1597. the Prisoners then Articling against the Warden sett
forth that one Prisoner paid xxxs. others xxs. xvs. xiis. xs. a weeke
for Chamber without Bedd. The Warden then made his Answeare to
the Comittees that he tooke xs. a Chamber and the rest was for　20
more chambers then one, and in respect of Dyett, though they had
none, but fetched it abroad.
Soe if Prisoners will have more ease then ordinarie, and a
Chamber or two for themselves and theirs in the Warden's howse,
they are by the Orders and Constitutions to Compound with the　25
5 E. 6 Dy. 71,
1 H. 7, 37,
Ple. Com. in
Hill and
Grange's case. Warden for it, it being the warden's freehould and demyseable.
And the Warden hopeth that his freehould Lodgings shall be noe
more subject to a meane valuation, then an escape of a Prisoner,
fireing the howse, or other dangers by desperate Debtors, unto
which the Warden is subject by such as lye there; Or the Fleete,　30
deprived of that which other Prisons doe take, Nay which is taken

for lodgings in the Towne, For men of quallitie (which cheifely come
to the Fleete) will lye alone and have good roomes, as Sir Francis
Inglefield had three and divers others the like, yet when there
turne was served would pay noe more then if they had lyen in the
5 Comon Prison, which is directly contrary to the 10th, 11th, and
12th Articles of the Constitutions, Explayned by the Judges and
ratified by the Lords of the Councell, for takeing away all cavills
betweene the Prisoner and the Warden.

And it is alsoe warrantable by Lawe that the Warden may make
10 the best of his Lodgings within his freehould without contradiction,
yet he taketh onely what former Wardens tooke without inhaunce-
ing them in any soart.

But, say the Prisoners, that if the Warden doe lodge Prisoners in
his freehould (which is none of the Prison) Then those debtors
15 in Execution are noe more in Execution, but the Creditor or the
Debtor may bring an Escape against the Warden, or an *Audita Que-*
rela, and soe the Prisoner cleare himselfe, or the creditor recover
his debt of the Warden; And that if the Warden doe make it his
prison Then they are to pay but as if they lay in the Prison.

20 But to the first point, whether they be out of Execution when
they lye there, It may be considered there was a tyme before the
Stattute of 1 R. 2 and 7 H. 4 was made, that wheresoever a Prisoner
in Execution did goe yet he was not out of execution; Then followed
the Stattute, That if a prison keeper did suffer his prisoner *ad largum*
25 *ire*, the keeper should pay the debt; But it cannot be said that the
prisoner doth *ad largum ire* soe long as he is within the walls and
precinct of the Fleete, where he went before the statute was made;
For as the Tower hath its prison for debtors, and many Castles in
this kingdome hath a prison within it, Noe man can say that the
30 prisoner is at large, soe long as he is either within the Tower or
the Castle walls, And, as every sherriffe of a shire may make his
prison where he pleaseth within the shire, and the prisoner soe long
as he goeth not out of the shire cannot be said to goe at large, Soe

the Warden of the Fleete doth not lett the Prisoner goe at large soe
long as the prisoner is within the walls, rules, or precincts of the
Prison. Noe more then the Marshall of the King's Bench doth
lett those goe at large which lye out of the prison within the rules
and precincts of that prison as to him is allowed and tollerated.   5

And to the second point, That if the Warden doe make the freehould a prison, Then they must pay as if they lay in the Prison,
that is thus answeared, viz.:

They must not have a Chamber or two Chambers for one prisoner
and his wife and famelye to keepe howse in, but lye two in a Bedd 10
like Prisoners, and every Chamber to have a Bedd or two or more
according to the greatnes of the Chamber, as is used in all Prisons,
and then the Warden should make the like rate of one Chamber by
many that lye in it as he doth by one man's lyeing there, and the
prisoners suffer that which they most seek to avoyde, which is being 15
pestered in the prison; And then should it not happen their wives
to be brought a Bedd in their Chambers, a thing both unseemely
and intollerable in a prison.

If when a prisoner bringeth his freind, wife, or child to lye in
his Chamber in the Fleete the Warden should aske money for their 20
lodgings it would seeme a base thing. Surely it seemeth noe other
that a prisoner which will pay but the meanest rate of lodging
should covett such liberty and thinke to pay noe more then if he
lay with another prisoner two in a Bedd according to the Orders of
the Prison.   25

And if such things be tollerated Then must his Majesty must (*sic*)
be sued unto to inlarge and build his prison, as well for the prisoners
that lye in it; As for their frinds, wives, children, and servants
which are noe prisoners, yf not then the prisoner is to yeild the
warden allowance for haveing ease in the Warden's freehould ac- 30
cording as the Constitutions aforesaid doe justly allow; And as the
Warden hath by Lawe and Custome justified it, when the prisoners
have sued him for Extortion in this case.

For the Warden will soone joyne issue with the Prisoners that
if they will quitt and remove out of the freehould they shall not
pay above the rate, For he may and can lett it to strangers.

It hath alsoe beene alledged that the rate of the Chambers
5 (rented as they be) yeild the Warden a masse of benefitt each yeare,
the contrary whereof doth appeare, for prisoners are not the best
payers, and some lye there many yeares and dye without payeing,
and others lye many yeares and then become Insolvent.

To such prisoners as lye two in a Bedd the Warden is to find
10 them Bedd, and for Bedd and Chamber they are to pay. ·

Whether by Bedd is meant all furniture of Bedding that is to be
doubted, for it was never put in practise; but as for those which
lye in the Warden's freehould lodgings by agreement he is not
bound to find them Bedd or Bedding except it be so conditioned;
15 And such will hardlie vouchsafe to lye on the comon Bedding which
passeth from man to man; And the Warden can as hardlie buy a new
Bedd for every new prisoner which cometh, and therefore the
lodgings of ease were provided for men of quallity and not for the
meane soarte of prisoners as the accusation would seeme to inferre,
20 And when *Mr. Chamberlayne* informed against the Warden touching
Chambers All the cheife gentlemen in the Fleete certified under their
hands that they held their Chambers by agreement to have a
Chamber alone to each, and were contented with the rates.

The Fourteenth Article.

Accusation for Exaction for lodging in the Comon Wards. Where before this tyme nothing was paid for lodgings in the Comon Wards, he exacteth as if they lay in private Chambers upon his Beding, Yea for the very Dungeon alsoe.

Answeare. That which they call Comon Wards in the Fleete is not exempt 5 of payment, for the place called the Wards, consisting of six great Roomes and a court yard, with the Tower Chambers and Bolton's Warde, are the King's Auncyent Prison, and for divers hundred yeares men were imprisoned there onely.

All the rest of the Fleete, Close Garden and yards, with certeyne 10 Messuages, were given to the Warden in fee by Grand serjeancy for ever, viz.: for keepeing that prison, which is an Argument that the prisoners lay in that prison and paied their Dutyes for lyeing there; And untill about three score yeares past, when the Accesse of prisoners to the Fleete was increased, All the prisoners lay in those 15 Wards where there is the Baron's Ward(called soe of *Baron Broun-jennell* who lay there), the Woemens Ward (of woemen lyeing there), the Two Penny Warde (of paying ijd. a night), and the Beggars Warde (of payeing nothing). And in some of theis Wards within the memory of man did other persons of great worth and their 20 wives and children lye, and paied good rates as if they had lyen elswhere.

Bishopp of Gloucester, &c. Those Wards were furnished with the Warden's Beding, which was not afforded without pay, Onely the poore that Begged at the Box were exempt from payment if they continued themselves in 25 the Box Warde, But if not, Then (as it appeareth by the Constitutions for Governement of the Fleete) they paied somewhat, for the Constitutions at the Tenth Article hath theis words:

That if any poore man which beggeth will have more ease then for the same is appointed, It shall be lawful for the Warden to 30

appoint such a person a Bedd or Chamber, the partie agreeing with
the Warden for the same as shall be thought reasonable.

The same Constitutions further say:

That if there shall at any tyme a person be comitted that is not
5 able to pay either Hall or Parlour Comons, nor will be of the Box to
take the Charity, The Warden shall appoint a Bedd and Chamber for
such, the partie agreeing with the Warden for it at his reasonable
discretion.

Which points of the Constitutions doe make it cleare, that all
10 persons and places are to yield payment, except those simply
wherein the Beggars lye; and noe man can deny but that the constitutions made touching fees, &c. (which are certeyne) doe relate
onely to the prison; And in fees which are not certeyne they relate
to the Warden's freehould, leaveing it to the discretion of the War-
15 den how to order or use his freehould. Like in all prisons there
is a Maisters side or howse for the keeper, where the better soarte
doe lye at better rates then in the Comon prison, soe is the practize
in the Fleete agreeable to lawe and declaration made by the Judges
confirmed at Councell Board 37 Eliz. as aforesaid.

20 And the Custome of the Fleete is, That if a waighty prisoner for
debt (of what quallity soever) come thither, Which is not able to
countervayle his Execution by security for true imprisonment, Then
he was not to have liberty of the howse, but was put into the said
Wardes; And noe man will thinke that the Warden should take
25 charge of such a man without being paied for him. If he should not
be paid it would followe then, That from all other prisons in England
where they take money of the meanest that lye there, They would (as
it is now already practized) by meanes of this and other absurd im-
putations layd on the Warden, remove themselves to this the King's
30 Prison (a place most proper for his owne debtors and service for the
State), thereby to be exempt of charge. Nay, those prisoners that
have in other prisons been most dangerous for Routs, Ryotts, and
breach of prison, and therefore comitted to Newgate amongst Rogues
and thieves to be punished, doe already by meanes of this discord

in the Fleete so much affect the libertyes there as they have caused
themselves to be removed thither, and doe vindicate liberty to
walk and bowle promiscuously with the Noblest and men of quallity
and will not be restrayned, yea, such as have beene theeves and
branded men doe without distinction and controll clayme the full   5
liberty of the whole Fleete, whereof if they be restrayned in the
prison they noyse and voyce themselves to be kept close prisoners;
As if the Warden should provide gardens, walkes, and places of
Recreation for such, Or ells be taxed of Rigor and Severitye where
indeed it never was permitted to such to have libertie out of their 10
owne wards, untill of late tyme they have gotten it through Clamor
in them, and want of disciplyne in late Wardens, joyned with a
zealous compassion towards prisoners who, if they be meeke, humble, and needy, ought to be comiserated; But otherwise the tolleration of such as are Insolent Banckrupts and such as doe infest a 15
prison is to hurt the comon wealth, makeing the Fleete and London the receptacle of all the scum of the kingdome; For, though in
Christendome there is not a prison of such scope and ymunities as
the Fleete, yet prisoners would still have more liberty and lesse
payment; And in the begining of this Wardens Interest in the office 20
some one or two of the civellest and least waighty prisoners in the
Wards were permitted to come out and fetch water to clense the
Wards and to carry them Bread, Beere, and necessaryes, And sometymes those one weeke and others another weeke were ayred, yet
came not so much as to the chappell to prayers, but had prayers 25
amongst themselves very strictly and orderly used; to the sermon
onely they came and retorned presently to their Warde.

As for the place called the Dungeon it is noe more dungeon then
any roome on the floore or ground of the Fleete, or of the aforesaid
Wards, being without descent, onely somewhat stronger retyred or 30
Boulton's   private, and used for to sett in Stocks, bolts, and Irons such as are
Warde.   unruly.   It hath convenient light, Chimney, and place of Ease,
where (by report) there lay some tyme a great one Dowager to an
ymminent person; And for that the outrages of *Lee*, *Peck*, and

Mynors, with their Confederates, were such as to breake downe the
inward grates of Iron and the Irons that went round the dore in this
place, the Warden therefore put the windowe (at which they receaved Engines) higher out of their reach, and made a hole whereby
5 they which lodged there might take in meate, drinke, &c. And
the Warden is assured that of all which have beene lodged in this
Warde not one hath paied him ought, though something be due
from the meanest which doe not begg.

And in the Tower Chambers, where in lyke manner they clayme
10 priviledge of none payment, it was 30 yeares agoe by the prisoners
themselves alledged to conteyne 8 Bedsteads, of which the Warden
made lxxij*l*. by the yeare; By which it appeareth that the prisoners
then paid soe for that, whereof this Warden should have nothing if
the prisoners may prevayle; And they will first lye 3 or 4 yeares on
15 the Warden's Beding and pay him nothing, when if he put them
from it they exclayme that the Warden doth make them lye on the
boards, as if the Warden's Burthen were above all other prison
keepers to be soe able or Charitable to find Bedds for all men without being paid for it, yea to find it to such as desire noe better
20 purchase then to purloyne or sell it as their owne when he trusteth
them with it, which is not tollerable in any Inne, Ale-howse, or
Barne, much lesse in a prison, where they must either pay or use
what they bring with them; And when the prisoner hath lyen soe
long and payed nothing, oweing perhapps, 5, 10, or 20*l*. and
25 keepeth the Warden from money, It cannot in equity be said that if
thence forward the prisoner provide a Bedd for himselfe therefore
he shall pay the Warden nothing for his chamber, for perhapps the
prisoner doth detayne of the Warden's soe much as would buy 5
or 10 Bedds, By the want whereof the Warden is dampnified more
30 then he is benefited by the prisoner provideing a Bedd for himselfe.

Besides if payment be taken away (because the prisoner provides
his owne Bedd) then all will provide their owne, and the Warden
shall find them roome and attendance for nothing; And the Warden
did use to furnish divers prisoners in the Wards and Tower Chambers

with Bedds untill they spoyled them; And by degrees used the Bed-
steeds sometymes for fire in the winter, and at other tymes to
fortefye the roomes wherein they lay against the Warden and the
Courts of Justice, and some part to annoy and beate downe the
Warden's servants; Upon which occasions the Warden tooke away   5
his Bedds and Beddsteads for a tyme and left them to lye on Pallett
Bedds, if they had any of their owne (as many good men doe
abroad who are at more liberty); In regard whereof the prisoners
alledge that they lye upon the ground because their Bedds lye upon
the Boards or flowers [*sic*, floors].   10

And whereas the prisoners have talked and taxed the Warden
about that Eight Bedd Chamber (being indeed the three Tower
Chambers) it was proved before the Lords Comittees at the Fleete,
that in those Chambers formerly had beene placed above 20 Bedds
of the Warden's, and Prisoners lodged there to the number of 15
56, But it is alledged that this was on an extremity and while the
Wards were in mennding, but yet it proveth that it was done, and
so may be done againe, when the use of the Wards is taken away
(by being full) that noe more can be placed there, And it proveth
alsoe that the Warden had Bedds and allowance for mens lyeing 20
there.

The Fifteenth Article.

He exacteth after those high rates Chamber rents of men haveing noe Chambers, but lyeing abroade by the King's Writt or other-wise.

Accusation for Exacting for Chambers not haveing any.

5　Some men who be sent to prison, being such whome either the Judge which committeth him is pleased to suffer to goe abroad or leaveth it to the discretion of the Warden or to the Custome, doe exceedingly presse to lye without the Fleete, where (within) Chambers be alwayes for them. If then the Chamber stand empty
10 (in the meane while) should not the Warden be allowed for it? A landlord will looke for the like, And he that desireth to lye abroad never requireth whether there be Chambers in the Fleete emptie or full; soe that in his understanding he hath no wrong nor the Warden any benefitt, who can comonly lodge more then he hath,
15 though perhapps not soe well as they would.

Answeare.

The Answeare to such as have noe Chambers is further made in the 10th article of Accusation, touching prisoners that goe abroad on *habeas Corpus*; but add here that many men had rather pay for two Chambers then lye there a night; and this, some for their quiet
20 rests sake and some and for their reputacons sake. They must pay for their ease, Ergo for lyeing abroad, And the Warden is excepted in the stattute of 23ᵗ H. 6 to the end he may shewe case.

The Sixteenth Article.

Accusation for
Exaction of
Dyett, Takeing
none.
He exacteth for Dyett whole Comons of men that take none of
his Meate or Drinke, A thing never demaunded before his tyme.

The Constitutions for Governement of the Fleete renewed
3° Elizabeth are: 5
That noe Prisoner shall buy beere, Ale, wyne, or other victuall
out of the howse soe long as they may have sufficient and good
provided within the howse, &c. att reasonable prices, as within
London (Except the Warden shall give license for any consideracon
as to him shall seeme good).   10

37° Elizabeta
[sic].
The Constitution 30 Aprill, 1598, was, upon the like complaint
of prisoners as is nowe made, referred from the Lords of the Councell to the Cheife Justice of the Comon Pleas, the Queene's learned
Councell at lawe, &c. who explayned the same and certified their
lordshipps touching the orders or Constitutions according to the   15
true sence and meaneing thereof, viz.: that the prisoners shall still
be reckoned and cast upp as in Comons untill they have agreed
with the Warden for it, And this (amongst others) the Lords of the
Privy Councell caused to be entred in the Register of Counsell for
takeing away all cavells and ambiguityes in tyme to come, some   20
one man then paid xx*l.* per Annum for license to fetch his dyett
from abroad.

Soe that upon the sence and explanations of theis Constitutions
under the great Seale and Register of Councell the Warden doth
ground himselfe to have power to cast upp his prisoners as in   25
Comons till he be agreed withall, Or to have Consideration given
him for license to take it elswhere.

The Custome in *Sir George Reynell* and other Wardens' tymes
was to give license for consideration, and the prisoners did not or
could not avoyd it.   30

And the Warden that now is justified himselfe by verdict at Lawe
in this point when that was informed by a promoter, as it was done
about lodgings alsoe.

The practise of the Warden alsoe hath beene to compound with
5 such as would, that they might dresse their meate in the Warden's
Kitchen, by his Cooke and fyer according to the number of the
prisoners' company, giveing (at the most) some 40s. some 30s. some
20s. a quarter, other some little or nothing, and this for such as
are certeyne Prisoners there and not likely to departe.

10 Those that goe and come and for whome the Warden keepeth
standing Tables, doe or may take Dyett according as they be within
or abroad, and doe pay it sometymes in whole and sometymes in
part, as at Inns of Chauncery, &c.

As for *Sir Francis Inglefeild* being a Prisoner he was often
15 desired to come to the Dyett provided for him and others, and told
it should be provided. His answeare was, that the Constitutions and
orders aforesaid were gotten by falshood and bribery or to the like
effect, and that the Warden durst not avouch them; And soe he, not
onely refrayneing the Dyett, but receaving divers of the best prisoners
20 in the howse to Dyett at his table and takeing money for it, the
Warden did try the point of Dyett with *Sir Francis*, and charged
him with soe much as the halfe at that tyme, but never charged
any other in that manner, *Sir Francis* alone by thinkeing to breake
orders was specially urged to keepe them.

25 The equitie of the Prisoners being in Comons, or agree for it, is
pregnant, viz.:

Threescore yeares agoe the Warden was allowed xs. a weeke for
a Gentleman's Dyett, when the Gentleman of the Inns of Court paid
but xxd. or ijs. which is an Argument that the Warden was to gaine
30 much by the Dyett and the Prisoner suffer in his purse.

That of the Inns of Court is now increased to vij or viijs. and
the Wardens is as it was, and the Dyett as good as it was, soe as he
looseth.

The Warden's servants (comonly about 40 in number) who attend

the services and dispatches of the howse, are to be fedd with the
remaynes of the Comons, the poore prisoners releeved, the concord
and the society of the Warden and Prisoners maynetayned, by
which the Warden can judge of the Prisoners affeccon in Religion
in State, [sic] to give accompte thereof (if need be) and the 5
recourse of many unfitting men and woemen is avoyded.

A prison is not to be opened at Dynner tyme or supper tyme as
is the usage of the Tower, King's Bench, Wisbiche, Elye, and all
great howses of the kingdome; for, besides the daunger of losse of
prisoners; goods, pewter, &c. are conveyed out, to the Warden's 10
great charge.

Mr. Mennell [sic] (that made his complaint before the comittees
in the Fleete for vili. taken of him for halfe Comons) was a Prisoner
five yeares in the Gentlemen's side, and tooke many prisoners to
Dyett with him, dressing their meate in the Warden's kitchen, For 15
which he was asked but vili. and paied but iiiili. which is xvis. a
yeare, and upon it they have taken upp the phrayse of halfe
Comons.

To those who are poore this Composition is never obtruded, and
to the rich at xxvili. per Annum for their dyett some gaine would 20
arise to the Warden for the reasons above said.

Kennell cannot justly complayne thereof; For, though the
referrees allowed the Warden iiijli. per Annum Composition, he
paied none, but of lxxli. allotted the warden for 9 yeares Dutyes of
all soartes, there was but lxli. taken, and xli. to be taken, the 25
Warden remitting the rest at Kennells intreatie and loveing accorde,
which Kennell hath since infringed.

The Warden hath two speciall wayes to rayse money from the
Prisoners, which is for their lodging and for their Dyett, But they
evade both in this manner, viz.:   30

First the Prisoner being comitted the Warden of necessity must
lodge and bestowe him somewhere; In which he (the Prisoner) will
make a fayre shewe and promise of payment, soe that he may have
a good Chamber to himselfe; but being once possessed thereof for

[a] yeare or yeares, he will pay nothing, whether he enjoy it or be
put from it; For all the Warden can do is but to put him from a
Chamber into the Prison, and being there he saith nothing is due,
and soe colloureth his none payment.

5   The other point touching Dyett, how able soever the Prisoner is,
he may or doth pretend that he is not able to pay for his Dyett, and
therefore he will fetch that from abroad at the Cookes, and perhapps
feed himselfe and his famelie in good fashion therewith, finding it
more convenient to eate and drinke with his wife and famelye then
10 at the Wardens Comoms. And soe both wayes the Warden shall
have noe benefitt except they compound.   Nay, it is taken as a
comon practize that one Prisoner doth take to Dyett many other
Prisoners, makeing a livelihood amongst themselves and enjoy the
Wardens roomes to doe it in, and yet for that roome would pay but
15 as if they laie in the Comon Prison.

Other Prisoners thorough liberty have meanes to get into their
lodgings the Warden's pewter, linnen, &c. some steale his plate,
intrude into his Battery and Kitchin, and with such impudency use
themselves, that if the Warden may not restrayne them a confusion
20 will followe, and noe civell man will undertake the place.

There is a weekes Dyett included in all Prisoners fees, and noe
prisoner ever denyed the payment thereof, though he never came
to take it; and therefore it is noe newe thing for men to pay or
compound for being out of Comons, which shall be substantially
25 proved to have beene accustomed tyme out of mynd.

The Constitutions which doe give order touching a prisoners
goeing abroad by the day doth distinguish payment for before
noone and for afternoone, whereupon it is to be inferred that he
must eate at the Prison; If at the Prison, then surely the Warden
30 is to provide for him.

About 30 yeares past the Prisoners, being in contention with the
Warden, did (amongst other things) make a Calculation of the
Dyett then allowed to Prisoners, and what the Warden did yearely
gaine thereby, which was 380*li.* 18*s.* per annum; where this Warden

is nowe soe farre from gaineing by the Dyetting of Prisoners as he looseth some yeares 3 or 4 hundred Poundes per Annum, as is to be made apparent by the booke of Accates there, Soe that the case of Dyett is losse to the Warden vij or viij*li.* per annum in regard of tymes past, though all men should pay truely; wherein alsoe there is 5 hundreds losse every yeare partly by inhabillity, and partly through shifts and contentions of Prisoners, yet the Warden cannot avoyd keepeing a Table for Prisoners because the ffees of entrance doe bind him to it besides the reasons aforesaid.

And about that tyme certayne comittees appointed to heare the 10 differences there (amongst other thing) did specially certifie that the allowance of Dyett was to be increased as tymes made it deere, and there is noe way so apt to take away cavelling betweene the Warden and Prisoners about this point as that the prisoner, giveing a Consideration to the Warden, may take the best course he can for 15 himselfe, Soe it be without annoyeing and pestering the Prison with his famelie, which consideration if it were once made certeyne peace would ensue.

It would be somewhat pharisagicall for the Warden to ennumerate how many Prisoners he doth feed and succour in tyme of their 20 sicknes meerely out of Curtesie, which as it is his christian dutye to doe, soe let it be esteemed.

When the Warden came first to attend the office he sent particulerly unto the Gentlemen that were Prisoners in the Fleete to request them to come into comons, or Dyett of the Warden's pro- 25 vision; And alsoe published in wryteing fixed in the Hall and parlor of the Fleete, that he would provide generally, for all, and the[y] should according to the Constitutions of the howse pay for it, or otherwise redeeme it by makeing some accord with the Warden.

Whereupon many of them, being guided by the true sence of the 30 Orders of the Fleete, either came to the Dyet or made some easy conditions to take it elswhere, and thought themselves well used; Soe that (besides the generall rumor made by the factions there who never paid for anything) there is noe particuler man that can justly com-

playne, Except one for a matter of 40s. or 50s. taken by chance
and without direction where the Warden meant it not (and yet is
justifiable in stricktnes of the Orders) because that person might
have taken his dyett, and it was for his owne case that he tooke it
5 not, and thought himselfe happie to be spared, yet for advantage
sake he refused to take his money againe when it was offered him.

The Seventeenth Article.

He layeth ympositions upon meate and fewell, and forceth prisoners to pay them, As ij*d*. a joynt, iijs. iiij*d*. for a load of Billetts, &c. and forceth Prisoners to pay xij*d*. a Bushell for Charcoale, which are to be bought for xij*d*. a sacke.   5

To the point of meate the Answeare is, That the Warden of the Fleete was wont to take of each joynt of meate which was dressed abroad and brought in, ij*d*. in lieu of the benefitt which might arise to him by the prisoner if he dyetted in the Fleete, as he ought, except he agree for it.   10

Mr. Edward Rookwood haveing long lyen in the Fleete and never paied his Fee to the Warden or his Officers, either for his meate or lodging. Therefore the Porter and Gaoler of the howse would not attend to lett in his meate and drinke untill he had paied them ij*d*. a joynt, soe farre as their Fees of ijs. did amount, which 15 they receaved and kept.

Rookwood informed upon the Stattute for this, and *Mr. Chamberlayne* (who likewise informed in another kind) was his witnes amongst others. The Warden proved his custome, avoyded them in point of lawe, and had a verdict on his side, though he never 20 before intended or since tooke any such ymposition upon meate, But such as doe not compound for their dyett they doe allowe ij*d*. a joynt for roast and a j*d*. for boyled, to roast and boyle in the Warden's kitchin, for avoydeing opening of the gates in Dinner and Supper tyme, and this is both reasonable and honest, save theis 25 which live by other mens losses, and would have a free prison to be their freehold for life, because they meane never to lye anywhere ells.

And as to the ymposition on fewell there is as much and as good sold for money in the Fleete as any man can buy abroad by retayle, 30

And it is not meete that prisoners send in and out of the Fleete for
wood soe oft as they please, for the Porter may soe be deceaved
and prisoners escape.   Besides Prisoners ought to have noe stowage
in their chambers for wood or coales by grosse.

5   6 February, 1617.   The Warden published certeyne Articles
and fixed them on a Table in the Fleete, that all things sould there
should be as good and as cheape as abroad, or ells the seller thereof
should be excluded the howse.

If 200 Prisoners (which number is comonly in the Fleete) may
10 cooke the meate, which they, their wives, children, servants, and
freinds doe eate (all wch doe in number double or trible the
Prisoners), then every Chamber must be made a kitchin, which is a
nasty infectious thing in any familie, much more in a prison, able
to infect a Citty or Kingdome; and it would require much roome
15 to stack wood and be dangerous for fireing the howse.

The Chamberlayne of the Fleete hath for many yeares taken
care of the fewell, that it be such as may stand with the safety of
the howse (often endangered to be fired if smale or brushwood be
burnt, or seacole, which is a piercing fire for Chambers or upper
20 roomes), for which attendance he findeth two men and 3 or 4
roomes for stowage to keepe it dry, besides yards, which in a prison
where roome is more scarce then abroad doth meritt that as much
benefitt should arise to him as to others which sell wood by retayle,
And it shall ever be justified soe good and cheape as abroad in
25 that kind.

And as to sale of Charcoale at excessive rates, The Warden
doth Answeare that he never knewe that any was sold or vented
in the Fleete, untill that he perceaveth a prisoner (under collour
of the Warden's servant to the prisoner's gaine) in the great frost
30 last, when the Thames was twice frozen over, and wood and coale
were extreame scarce in the Towne, did onely at that tyme sell
at unreasonable rates, which the Warden for his part did utterly
disavowe and explodd out of the howse.

And as to the Prisoners they never complayned to the Warden

thereof but keepe that and other such things in the deck of the shipp, as may perhapps be propper in the Fleete but not honest to make so great a clamour for a Bushell or a sack of charcoales.

Mr. Rookwood grewe soe thrifty that because the victuallers and others of the Fleete should gaine nothing by him he used to hale 5 upp out of the streetes with a Coard his Bread, Beere, and Coales, soe long that at last there was found in those roomes where he lay, swords, staves, wheelers' Axe, &c. wherewith they brake upp dores and assaulted the Warden and his, Yea he could tell how to send away the feathers of his Bedd in a poake and the Tyke 10 after it, when he was turned over to another prison, and all to bereave the Warden of payment.

And when his man by his Maister's appointment and charge enformed againt them which sould beere in the Fleete, All the prime Gentlemen and others there did testifie under their hands 15 that they had as much and as good for money as they could have abroad.

If a prisoner offer to bring in a cart load of Billett or Faggott, the fore gates of the Fleete must be shutt while the back gates are opened by one and the same porter (for more then one cannot 20 be) and this begetteth daunger and troble, For which reason the porter taketh a small Allowance to gett somewhat for being bereft of the benefit of retayleing which every hoasterie, Inne, or Alehowse hath, where there is noe danger by Escapes or opening of gates, And, upon this strange and exorbitant point (as it would be made to 25 seeme) there is not 40*s.* a yeare gotten, for he that hath money to buy a groats worth of faggotts cannot buy a load, If he send for a groats worth abroad the very fetching will cost him somewhat, and this troble and charge is avoyded by haveing it in the Fleete by retayle as hath ever beene used, And 30 yeares past the prisoners 30 in their exceptions or complaint against the Warden shewed that the Warden gott 40*s.* per ann. by retayle of fewell.

The Eighteenth Article.

Where men be whole vacations abroad by *Habeas Corpus* he
forceth them to pay xxd. a day for outgoeings, their Chamber rent,
and dyett, horrible exactions never had or demanded by former
5 Wardens.

Accusation
of Exacc'on
upon Prisoners
goeing abroad
by Writt.

This Article and Allegation is false in manner and forme thereof, Answeare.
And for Answeare it is to be considered that those that goe abroad
by the King's writt are such prisoners as be in Execution for debt,
And the writt here intended and meant is the extraordinarie writt
10 of *habeas Corpus* graunted by the King's gratious favour out of his
Court of Chauncery, which is obteyned by such Prisoners in
Execution as are likely to perrish in estate of Land, Evidences, or
person for want of liberty (once in many yeares) to goe into the
Country for view of his Evidence, sale of his Estate, and Compound
15 with his Creditors, Of which writt (omitting to shewe here the
good it procureth to the Prisoner and to the Creditor, who often
concurreth in obteyning it) There shall be onely touched the
manner of the Warden's usage thereof, which is, that when it
cometh directed to him the warrant of the writt cometh there-
20 with most comonly expressing and alwayes intending that the
prisoner goeth as the Warden's prisoner and under keeping, Att
perrill of the Warden to pay the debt if the prisoner doe escape.
This prisoner sometymes lyeing and dyeting in the Fleete, and
sometyme being absent in the country, The question then ariseth
25 whether such a prisoner shall pay his dutyes as if he were really in
the Fleete.

To which may be answeared that if he be in the Fleete and safe
without perrill or extraordinary charge to the Warden he payeth
his extraordinary dutyes without exception, whereby it followeth

that being abroad at more hazard to the Warden, and reapeing more benefitt to himselfe, he ought to pay rather the more then lesse.

The sixt Article of the Constitutions saith:

That if the King or his Councell (that have power) doe send for 5 a prisoner out of London, then he (the prisoner) shall pay all manner of charges of himselfe and him that keepeth him.

If it be alledged that while he is out of London he dyetteth not with the Warden nor possesseth a Chamber, This likewise is answeared that comonly he locketh upp his Chamber till his 10 retorne, if he either esteeme the Chamber or the goods he leaveth behind him, Or if he lock it not upp what prejudice is it to a prisoner absent if any other lye in it, for whensoever he retorneth he is sure the Warden must provide that he have the same or another.   15

But if such a prisoner will conclude and agree with the Warden touching such Chamber and all other his duties (of dyett for which he is to be cast upp as in comons untill he agree for it), And for his outgoings of xxd. per diem, which is then as due as any-thing ells, and theis all (in extremitie) might amount to 30 or 40s. a 20 weeke, If (I say) the Warden and prisoner agree, as comonly they doe before hand in a moderate fashion of 20s. 15s. 10s. 5s. yea nothing at all according as the person is of quallitie, and would yeild benefitt if he tarryed or breede danger to the Warden by his goeing, who in reason can be against it(?) For noblemen and others 25 that have beene licensed to lye abroad in Towne or Country have from tyme to tyme by order and allowance of the Privy Councell paid the Warden reasonable dutyes in regard of dyett, lodging, and other matters, Soe long as he was answeareable for them, As appeareth by infinite presidents.   30

As for the newnesse of theis demaunds from men goeing upon theis writts it is because the writts (in this Comon fashion) are new and not wanted in other Wardens' tymes, when if perhapps they had any it would also appeare that they paied the Warden his

duties dureing those writts even as upon auncyent Comon lawe
writt they did and doe.

Alsoe by the Constitutions at the 13th Article, the Warden
haveing power in himselfe to take or lett some kind of Prisoners
5 to goe downe into the Country in vacation tyme, He should be
prejuditiall to himselfe if such men should not pay or compound
for their duties while they were abroad, For a prisoner is never
discharged of his Fees and dutyes till he be discharged of his
imprisonment, And a *habeas Corpus* doth rather worke a Charge
10 to render him at retorne of the writt then a discharge in the
Interim.

And lett the losses of Escapes and Compositions of prisoners at
under rates in this kind be considered, And it will be found that
it had beene happie for the Warden that noe such writt had beene
15 granted, They haveing procured to him many suits, payments, and
losses of more then ever he can gaine thereby, he haveing already
paied for divers escaped and is sued for others, who takeing
advantage of his now questionning will not render themselves
againe, but leave him to the succour of such bonds and securities
20 as he hath beene ordered to take for his indempnitie, And with an
evill conscyence thinke to avoyd those Bonds by Lawe and all payments of duties accrewed in three or fower yeares for attendance
and victuall in the Fleete, And the Warden cannot deny the
executing of such writt when it is directed to him, Except that
25 Judge which graunted it doth upon information suspend it.

And whereas there was wont to be a great expence to the
Prisoner that goeth abroad by takeing a keeper and provideing
horsmeate and mans-meate for him, The prisoner who can give
sufficient bond (though noe bond be soe sure as to have the
30 Prisoner in the house) is eased of that keeper and his Charge, which
is noe small favour at the Warden's perill.

The Nineteenth Article.

Of men haveing the Kings writts to goe abroad about their
businesses, he exacteth of them for his leave, Of some 40s. 3li. 5li.
10li. or more money or other bribes. A daylie trade never done
by any before, And without yeilding theis fowle exactions they   5
are staied and loose their occasions.

As to the Warden's exactions in this nature, it is onely aggre-
vated against him by such Prisoners who are soe deeply indebted
as they could gett noe competent security for their retorne, and
such in whome was perceaved noe purpose to compound or agree   10
with their Creditors, but endeavoured to stirr suits and trobles in
the Country, whither they intended to goe, For as for leave from
the Warden, it never was denyed to any whome the Lord Chauncellor (being informed) did thinke fitt to grant it unto. Neither
did the Warden take 40s. 3li. 5li. 10li. or more or lesse of any for 15
such purpose. Onely sometymes the Suitors for such writts did
comitt the petition or motion for it to some Secretary or follower
with whom they used to agree what they should have for soliciteing
the same, and soe much they would send them when the business
was effected, Sometymes by the hands of the Warden's servants, 20
sometymes of the Warden himselfe. And at other tymes those not
acquainted would intreat the Warden to carry and put their petition
into the hands of some that had accesse to move it, which he divers
tymes did, and gave them such moneyes as to him was delivered
for that purpose, wherein the Warden will appeal to the Consciences 25
of those that did obteyne the Graunts, for they could not be
ignorant. Soe open and freely did the Warden deale therein
where he thought good would ensue by such libertye, but with
others not likely to do good he would not have intelligence one
way or other, and soe perhapps they rann a costlier course then 30

40s. or 3li. for Sollicitation, but never with the Warden's privity.
And he is ready to make oath that himselfe never appropriated or
tooke such somes to his owne use. Nay, that he never moved or
petitioned the Lord Chauncellor for any writt of *Habeas Corpus* in
5 this kind, save for such poore Beggars as had not meanes to raise
upp others to speake for them. And when as the prisoners were
before the Lord Chauncellor, M^r of the Rolls, Cheife Justices,
Sir Edward Cooke and Cheife Baron, Commissioners from the King
to heare all the prisoners greevances, (amongst others) this was
10 alledged for one, whereupon the Warden acquainted the Lord
Chauncellor and deposed that of 36 Writts which his Lordshipp
had graunted in that terme the Warden had onely 33s. benefitt
for his owne paynes in oversight, that they were formally done and
duely dispatched, wherein he was to peruse his owne bookes of
15 Causes in charge against the Prisoner, and have inspection of the
quallitie and disposition of the Debtor and Creditor and likelyhood
to agree and accordingly to informe To the end that the Writt of
Habeas Corpus might not be abused in idle libertie or defeateing of
creditors.

20   And touching bribes taken by the Warden, Some voluntary
guifts hath beene (*post factum*), but noe condition was made whereby
to pervert right or oppresse the innocent, and therefore it was nee
exaction, but the truth is the Prisoners here meant to have stuck
downe a feather and tooke upp a swann, for he which gave a horse
25 insinuated soe farr as to gett into the Warden's Debt neare 200li.
for meate, drinke, money, and lodging; he which gave a ring 200li.;
he which gave a sword 150li. as appeares by bond of the one,
accompt subscribed of the other, and a judgment for the third.
The Warden would now bribe them with better guifts to have
30 it paied, Soe that indeed the Prisoners have made a new, a daylie,
and a good trade to gett such Creditt of the Warden when they
had broke with all others, and he could call out theis by name
with many whome he hath more or lesse trusted without such
bribes. But here is the pith and marrowe of the busines, that

because the Warden shall not call upon theis Debtors he must be made away by stabbing, pistolling, butchering, or some such stratagem.

Nowe to treate a little of the begining of theis writts, and of the motive whereby the Lord Chauncellor or keeper doth graunt 5 them.

It may first be considered, That untill the first yeare of King Richard the Second, All the Prisoners, though they were in Execution, went abroad with a Baston or with a keeper at the discretion of the Warden.   But then an Act was made for their restraint, 10 After which it being perceaved that this had drawne the prisoners to great extremity, Att their humble suite divers comissions under the great seale were from tyme to tyme obteyned and directed to Commissioners to call before them Creditors from any part of the kingdome and within the prisons of the Fleete and King's Bench, 15 from whence there is noe remove after a man in execution is once come thither to treate and compound betweene Debtor and Creditor transferring and investing on the Creditor the Debtors Estate, and freeing the Debtor out of prison if it were not above such a value.

After this in processe of tyme the King's cheife justice of his 20 Bench, seeing likewise the convenience of a prisoners libertie, did first by a rule in Court admitt the partie in Execution liberty from day to day for many dayes, and at last by *Habeas Corpus* from terme to terme to goe into the countrie.

The Chauncery being the most Imminent Court to releeve men 25 that be in extremetyes. hath not often till of late, and in theis tymes where in Treasure is soe much exhausted and Comerce weakened, much medled with such writts, though there be subordinate to that Courte the Pettibagg and Comon Pleas for privilodged men, where many are properly Comitted in Execution. But 30 of late yeares the same Court, looking upon the desire of prisoners on the one side to satisfie their Creditors and the consent of Creditors to give liberty, and lookeing on some mens inexorablenes to their Debtor, On the fraud and oppression done to prisoners by Feoffees

and freinds in trust, on the weaknes of wives and children to manage imprisoned mens estates (on the one part) and perfidie in
wasting and neglecting on the other part, when husbands and
fathers are surely inclosed and cannot call for an Accompt, looke-
5 ing upon decay of howses, wast of Timber, Imploreing Creditors,
Examining Bayliffs and Stewards, husbands to bury wives, Children
their parents, Inventory their goods, take upp and survey their
Evidence and lands, passe fynes and recoveryes for sale, and many
other matters of convenience.

10   The Chauncery, I say, for theis reasons hath dispensed the King's
grace in such manner As that within theis 3 yeares, wherein there
hath beene graunted writts to 120 persons, One halfe of them have
dispatched themselves out of prison to the good content of the
Creditor, Of which prisoners gon abroad, if any had dyed as some
15 others did dye in prison, Then the Creditor had beene paied by his
Debtor's Carkas and might have made dice of his bones, which
good dispatch of the prisoner hath in noe smale measure prevented
the Warden of many Duties and somes which would have growen.

Many of the residue of the prisoners were well forward in a
20 course to give their Creditors like satisfaccon, and had (noe doubt)
effected it, if some restraints of those writts had not (by the ill
demeanor of a fewe persons and misaprehensions of jealous Creditors)
beene suspended.

For amongst those Creditors which have made voluntary agree-
25 ment with such as went abroad by *habeas Corpus*, who is there
that hath or doth complayne? for *Volenti non fit injuria*, And who
amongst those Creditors to whome their Debtors goeing out by
habeas Corpus hath not yet given satisfaccon is there that did complayne? saveing one, who for a very smale trifle (thorough sur-
30 reptious getting advantage in Lawe) doth oppresse a poore man of
forraigne Nation, Scholler, Soldier, and Protestant who hath
nothing in the world to pay or feed upon but what cometh of
benevolence and Charitie.

One other Creditor complayneth whose Debtor (the prisoner being abroad by *habeas Corpus*) hath obteyned a thrice better Estate then he had before, inhabling him to pay the Debt if the Creditor would either take land, procure a Chapman for it, or tollerate his further libertie, And theis two, besides the watch- 5 fullnes of Majestrates (that lawes already made be not infringed), hath brought the writt of *habeas Corpus* graunted out of the Chauncery into soe much obloquie as now it is, though both theis Prisoners be safely retorned into Custodie in the Fleete and noe prejudice hath followed save to the Warden, who is complayned off 10 on the one side and sued for viij^c^li. on the other side.

Notwithstanding all which his gracious Majesty (the founteyne of compassion to such distressed subjects), wayghing the cases of divers men durceing the vacancy of a Chancellor, hath with the allowance and subscription of the right honourable M^r^ of the Rolls 15 and Judges att the Comon Lawe (Comissioners for the Chauncery), graunted the same writt againe to the exceeding comforte of the Prisoners and hope of the Creditor's suerties and dependants by the good effect which may followe.

The bills of Conformity in the Chauncery were much alike to the 20 Comissions before remembered, for both were compulsory for the Creditor to take what was ordered and appointed him by the Comissioners or Chaunceric.

But the writt of *habeas Corpus* sendeth the Debtor or prisoner home to the Creditor without charge of the Creditor, And there by 25 submission on the Debtor's part, by mediation of well disposed persons, neighbours, or allyes, on the other parte, is procured that peace and voluntary act of Charity which the Coactive bills of Conformity did not doe, Neither was there any prisoner in England Anno 21 Jac. (when the proclamation was made against bills of 30 Conformitie in Chauncery), there delivered out of prison who lay there for non-conformitie, howsoever Creditors were in dread of those bills and weare against those bills for feare they might be imprisoned and checked in their prosecution of Debtors, onely one *Mr. Apis Lapis* or rather *rara avis*, *Mr. Beestone* by name, did gett a libertie non conformable to the proclamation.

The Fleete being the King's prison and an office of that nature
5 as scarcely such another is in this kingdome, Attending all the Courts at Westminster, saving the King's Bench, hath ever beene allowed if not more yet noe lesse priviledges, preeminencyes, and benefitts then other prisons, And therefore may (pleaseing the Superiors) still hould and enjoy (as least equall) with others, For in respect of
10 the Tenure by Graund Serjeancie, which yeildeth warde and marriage and injoyneth personall attendance, the rights and profitts are to be mainteyned, And the Officer of merritt Cherished, Or ells the King's profit is impayred when the Wardshipp falleth.

The Warden is betweene Silla and Caribdis, soe that either he
15 must through that Gulfe of Avarice run upon the rock of Turpe lucrum, or thorough the Syrens allurements of Charity, pitty, and remorse make shipwrack of his owne Estate.

Presidents of his Majesties Prerogative.

The King is not restrayned by any Act or Stattute from the
Actuall Service of his Subjects, For by the Statute of 1 R. 2 by
which meanes persons are restrayned to imprisonment, The words
of the Stattute are,   5

That the Warden of the Fleete shall not suffer any prisoner
being comitted by judgment at the suite of the partie to goe out
of prison by bayle, Mainprise, or Baston, without agreeing with the
party at whose suite he is there, Except it be by the King's writt
or Commandment.   10

By the Stattute of 7 H. 4 the Wardens of the prisons of the
Marshalsey, King's Bench, and other prisons are chargeable accordingly, By which Act there is reserved in the King's power a prerogative to free men from imprisonment, And as occasion hath
beene offered the practise of this prerogative hath been continually 15
Exercised, Of which to omitt the raignes of former princes there
are sundry presidents in the raygne of the late Queene Elizabeth.

First in 4° of her raigne she released one *Thurland* out of the
Fleete, he being at that tyme in Execution there.

In 1588 her Majestie by her Privy Seale discharged *Thomas* 20
Trussell out of the King's, being at that tyme in execution there
for 2,000*li*. Which *Trussell* went presently to Tilbury Campe by
Comandment of the Earle of Leicester.

Her Majesty after discharged *Sir Ri: Skipwith* from the Fleete
by her royall prerogative.   25

Nowe whereas there is often tymes mencon of the Orders or
Constitutions made for the perpetuall Governement of the Fleete
Anno 3° Elizabeth which was formerly obteyned and with such
judgment and circumspection passed the great Seale after consideracon was first taken of the old usages and Customes of the 30

Margin notes:
1 R. 2.
H. 4.
Eliz. 4.
1588.

Fleete: Here therefore (not trobling the reader with the circumstances) are onely sett downe the Articles upon which and the explanation thereof, th'one and th'other being corroborated oftentymes
by the Lords of the most honorable Privy Councell both in his
5 Majesties tyme and in the begining of the Raigne of Queen Elizabeth (of famous memory) the Warden doth found the ordering and
governement of the Fleete, Especially in the two points of Dyett
and allowance for his lodgings, being the mayne revenn'wes by
which he and the place is supported.
10

3ᵈ June, Anno 3ᵈ Elizabeth. 1561.

First that it may be lawfull to the said Warden or his 1.
Deputie to appoint soe many of the howshould Servants as to
either of them shall seeme good to open or shutt the two utter
15 gates of the Fleete at such howers as the gates of Ludgate and
Newgate are accustomed to be opened and shutt and the said
persons to carry in their hands, halbarts, bills, or any other weapon
as shall seeme good unto the said Warden or Deputie within his
Precinct or Libertie.

20   Item the Warden to take such bond of every person that 2.
shall be brought into the Fleete as Prisoner as shall seeme to him
reasonable at his discretion and according as the cause shall require,
As well for the payment of all manner of dutyes there, As alsoe to
be true Prisoners there, and of good behaviour towards the said
25 Warden and all others within the said precinct of the Fleete in
such manner and forme as heretofore hath beene used.

Item that it is and shall be lawfull to the said Warden and his 3.
Deputie to take order from tyme to tyme that noe person comeing
in there doe carry any weapon further then the Porter's lodge
30 there, be he stranger or other, unlesse he shall be licensed soe to
doe by the discretion of such as the said Warden shall appoint to
keepe the gate there.

Item that noe Prisoner shall buy Beere, Ale, wyne, or any other 4.
victuall out of the said howse, Soe long as he may have sufficient Victuall

and good provided within the same howse in such place as shall be
there appointed att such reasonable prices as the same be comonly
sould for within the Citty of London, Except the Warden shall
give licence for any Consideration as to him shall seem good.

5.   Item that it may be lawfull to the Warden to take of every 5
such Prisoner (as the said Warden may lawfully license to goe
abroad with his keeper) for the halfe day, that is to say before
Dinner or after, to the Warden's box fowre pence, and for the whole
day both before Dynner and after eight pence, And for his keeper
that shall be with him for the halfe day six pence, and for the 10
whole day Twelve pence.

6.   Item and if it shall happen the Queenes Majesty and her honorable howshould to be two myles Distant from the Cittyes of
London and Westminster or either of them, and that any Prisoner
shall be sent for by the Councell or any other haveing aucthority to 15
Comand the said Prisoner to be brought before them, That then
the said Prisoner shall beare all manner of such charges as shall
thereunto apperteyne, be it either by water or by land, untill his
retorne, as well for himselfe as any other that shall be appointed his
keeper for the tyme.   20

7.   Item that the said Warden by himselfe or his Deputie shall and
may take and carry downe with him into the Country any such
Prisoner as he may lawfully license to goe abroad with his keeper
at any tymes betwixt the Termes, Except there shall be expresse
Comandment to the Contrarie by such as shall comitt thither.   25

8.   Item that it may be lawfull for the said Warden or his Deputy
and soe many of his howshould as shall be thought needfull to
keepe watch in harness or otherwise within his precinct att all
tymes as he shall see cause for his better safeguard if he shall
suspect any Prisoner within his Custodye to intend to make an 30
Escape.

9.   Item that it may be lawfull to and for the said Warden to take
order at all tymes for such money as shall be gathered at the Box
or otherwise generally given to the poore men there, for the dis-

tribution thereof amongst them if any contention shall arise, And
that the said poore men shall alwayes keepe one key of the Box
and another key to be at the Warden's appointment.

Item that it may and shall be lawfull for the Warden, if there 10.
5 shall at any tyme happen that any person to be comitted, that shall
not be able to maynteyne neither the Parlor Comons nor the hall
Comons, nor alsoe will take part of the box, That then the Warden Lodgings.
may appoint a Bedd and a Chamber for any such convenientlye,
The partie agreeing with the Warden for the same at his reason-
10 able discretion.

Item that if any that will take part of the box will have more 11.
case then for the same is appointed, That then it may be lawfull
for the Warden to appoint any such person or persons a Bedd or
Chamber, the party agreeing with the Warden for the same as
15 shall be thought reasonable.

Item that the said Warden shall take of every man or woeman 12.
that shall sitt at the Parlor Comons Two shillings fower pence
weekely for his Bedd and Chamber, And for every man and
woeman that shall sitt at the hall Comons fowerteene pence
20 weekely for his Bedd and Chamber lyeing like prisoners two in a
Bedd together.

Item whereas by the anneyent Custome, tyme out of memory of 13.
man used in the said Fleete, The Warden or his Deputy for the
tyme being have used and did license such persons as be Prisoners
25 there (not being upon any Condempnation or by expresse Comandment given to the contrary by the Councell or such persons as doe
comitt the said Prisoners thither), to goe abroad about their necessary busines or to their learned Councell or Such like affayres
with a keeper, Therefore it is and shall be lawfull to the said
30 Warden and his Deputy for the tyme being To lycense and permitt
all such persons as be or shall remayne there to goe abroad with a
safe keeper about his or their needfull busines aforesaid, Soe
alwayes as any such prisoner doe not lye there upon any Condempnation or that expresse comandment by the Queenes Majestyes

Councell or such persons as doe comitt the same Prisoners thither
be given or prohibited to the contrary thereof.

About 23 yeares past certeyne prisoners then mislikeing the
Customes and usages put in practise by the Warden there, did
(even as *Mr. Chamberlayne* and *Mr. Rookwood* now doe) Informe 5
against the Warden upon the Statute of 23 H. 6.   Whereupon the
Lords of the Privy Councell tooke the matter to Consideration and
explayned the sence and meaneing of the Constitutions as here
following appeares and put the prisoners to silence.

At the Court at Whitehall the 24th of Aprill, 1598.

PRESENT THE

Lord Keeper	Lord North
Earle Marshall	Mr. Comptroller
Earl of Nottingham	Mr. Chauncellor
Lord Chamberlayne	of the Exchequer

Whereas Information hath beene exhibited by *Robert Brough*
against *George Reynell*, Esquire, Warden of the Fleete, upon
pretence of some exactions and extortions supposed to be comitted
10 by him to certeyne Prisoners in the Fleete, whereof there hath
beene complaint alsoe exhibited both to their Lordshipps and in
the Star Chamber, It pleased their Lordshipps to referre this cause
to the heareing and examination of the Lord Cheife Justice of the
Comon Pleas, her Majesties Sollicitor Generall *Mr. Francis Bacon*
15 and *Mr. Bryan Anslowe, Esquire.*

Forasmuch as it doth appeare by their Certificate to their Lordshipps that the foresaid Comissioners did call before them the
Informer and some others that followed the information against the
said Warden. As alsoe one *Phillipp Smith,* Prisoner in the Fleete,
20 who gave the information ready drawne to the said Informer, and
required of them some proofe and to showe wherein the said
Warden had comitted Extortion or any way broken the exemplified Orders, Their Answeare was that they did not ground their
Information upon the Orders, nor that they did proceed against the
25 Warden for anything done against the said Orders, but their information was for Extortion supposed to be Comitted in takeing of
severall somes of money weekely for sheweing ease and favour to
certeyne Prisoners for their Chambers and lodgings contrary to the
Statute of 23 H. 6.

The said Comissioners being further desireous to be instructed
from those of whome the money is alledged in the Information to
be taken, in what soart the Warden had dealt with them, and
whether he had by any meanes indirectly any payment from them,
The most and cheifest of them did testifie under their hands, 5
which alsoe was notefied by the rest, That they neither consented
nor were acquainted with the said Information nor any of them
forced to any payment, But being desireous of more ease and more
Chambers then the Orders (which bynd them to lye two in a Bedd)
doe allowe the same, For the most of them haveing two Chambers 10
or more made voluntary agreement for them, which was verified by
Mr. Anslowe (one of the said Comissioners) to have beene ever
the Custome, and is alsoe in the opinion of all the aforesaid Comissioners allowed to the Warden by the true sence and meaneing of
the 10th, 11th, and 12th Articles of the said Orders, Soe as by the 15
opinion of the Lord Cheife Justices and the rest, to whome this
cause was comitted, that there is noe just cause of complaint against
the Warden of the Fleete either for Extortion in takeing of theis
somes of money mentioned in the Information or for breach of the
true meaneing of the Orders exemplified in any point.   20

Upon viewe and consideration of the said certificate their Lordshipps comanded the said Informers to be brought before them
to whome the report of the aforesaid Lord Cheife Justice and the
rest of the Comissioners being read, they could not deny but that
they had beene heard by them, nor were able to alledge any 25
further matter against the said Warden then they had delivered
to the Comissioners. In regard whereof their Lordshipps, considering the courses that had been taken by the said *Smith* and others (his
confederates) against the Warden in very malitious soarte, First
alledging that the Orders Sett downe for the Fees of the Warden 30
were not of record in the Chauncery, Then that the hands of
those honorable personages that subscribed the same were counter-
feited, And straineing by theis troblesome courses his unjust
molestation, Their Lordshipps this day have comanded the Infor-

mer to surcease, and noe further to prosecute the said information, Whereupon he yeilded, And this their Lordshipps Order was by their comandment entered (amongst other things) in the Register of Councell, &c.

5   Concordat cum Registro,
                                        C. EDMONDES.

Att the Court at Whithall the 30th of Aprill, 1598.

Lord Archbishop of Canterbury.

Lord Keeper	Lord Buckhurst.
Edward Marshall	Mr. Comptroller.
Lord Admirall	Mr. Chauncellor
Lord Chamberlayn	of the Exchequer.
Lord North.	

Whereas upon Complaint made unto us by *George Regnell,*
Esquire, Warden of the Fleete, That he was unjustly molested and 10
trobled by an informer named *Robert Brough,* who being instructed
by one *Phillipp Smith,* Prisoner there, and some other his adherents,
exhibited an Information into her Majesties Court of the Exchequer
upon pretence of Extortion used to the Prisoners. This matter
being comitted to the hearing and Examination of— 15
   Sir Edmond Anderson, Lord Cheife Justice of the Comon Pleas.
   Thomas Flemynge, Esquire, her Majesties Sollicitor.
   Francis Bacon Esquire, one of her Majesties Learned Councell.
   And *Bryan Anslowe, Esquire,* one of her Majesties Gentlemen
Pentioners, and some tyme Warden of the Fleete. 20
   They did call before them both parties to examyne if the said
George Regnell had unduely extorted from any person, or in anything broken the Orders of that Prison, exemplified under the great
seale, By whose certificate to their Lordshipps because it doth
appeare that they gave full hearing at three severall tymes of all 25
that could be objected against the said *Mr. Regnell,* And that they
could not fynd that he had unlawfully extorted nor any way broken
the exemplified Orders sett downe for that howse, Their Lordshipps enjoyned the said *Robert Brough* not to prosecute the said

Information nor to troble the said *Mr. Reynell* for that cause, whereunto he did submitt himselfe (as by their Lordshipp's Order is to be seene).

And whereas the said Comissioners doe further certifie for the 5 better explayncing of the exemplified Orders, viz.

To the fowerth Article of the Orders which bindeth every Prisoner to victuall himselfe upon the Wardens provision unlesse he agree with the warden to make his owne provision, The said Comissioners doe thinke meete, for better explanation thereof (being 10 according to the true meancing of the same), That the prisoners shall still be reckoned and cast upp as in Comons untill they have agreed with the Warden for it.

And likewise by the 10th, 11th, and 12th Articles every prisoner ought to have his Bedd of the Wardens provision, to lye two in 15 a Bedd together, and to pay as he shall be either of the parlor or hall Comons, or to agree with the Warden if he be of neither Comons. And soe because by the 11th Article it is expressed that if any Prisoner (though he be of the Box) will have more case then is appointed to him, he must agree with the Warden for it, 20 It is to be understood by the Orders, That if any prisoner whatsoever desireth more ease for Bedd or Chamber then the Articles allowe, That then they as well as the poore prisoners of the Box shall agree with the Warden for the same, Their Lordshipps considering their opinion grounded upon the true meancing and sence 25 of the Orders exemplified, and the Testimony of *Mr. Anslowe* (who was many yeares Warden there) that the custome hath ever beene soe, doe thinke meete for better explanation of the same, and takeing away all ambiguityes and cavills, that the aforesaid Articles ought to be soe understood, and shall from henceforth be 30 soe taken and construed, &c.

Concordat cum Registro,

C. EDMONDES.

Whereas *Mr. Edmond Chamberlayne* hath made and excited many Clamours and trobles against the Warden,
The occasion between them hath beene as followeth.

June 16, 1617.   When by Warrant from the Barons of the Exchequer the
Warden seized and took certayne money and jewells betweene the   5
valewe of 3 or 400*li*. from *Mr. George Leicester* and his then wife,
formerly the wife of *Mr. Babington,* Which *Leicester* being in
Execution for debt marryed *Mrs. Babington* there alsoe in Execution, and she found alsoe in arrere to the King's Majesty 46 thowsand pounds, both supposed to keepe an Estate of goods about them   10
in the Fleete.

Mr. Chamberlayne who had removed himselfe from the Kings
Bench to the Fleete for his owne case, And is soe clogged with
almost threescore severall accons and executions to the valewe
of 13 or 14 thowsand pounds, that noe Creditor with reasonable   15
charges can remove him back, fell into consultation with divers
factious Prisoners of the Fleete, how much this seizure made by the
Warden did concerne Chamberlayne himselfe in particuler and all
the Prisoners in generall; wherefore they endeavoured and plotted
to take away the money and jewells from the Warden, whereof he   20
haveing intelligence sent it out of the Fleete and afterwards into
the Court of Exchequer by comand of that Court.

Upon theis occasions and for that *Chamberlayne* had offered to
stabb with a knife a gentleman there Prisoner, the Warden tooke
notice what a Turbulent man *Chamberlayne* was, And finding both   25
that his Estate was made over to other men in trust, and that he
had given noe bond or securitye for his true Imprisonment
according to the Orders of the Prison and yet laye at liberty in the
Wardens Freehould, yea had two of the Wardens owne lodgings, a
Studdy and another roome, where his wife, children, and Servants   30

did (as it were) keepe continuall hospitallitie, gameing and discourseing with others over the Wardens owne Bedd Chamber, Soe as
the Warden when he came weary home at night could neither take
his rest nor be private but be overheard by such an enemye in all
5 the busines of the office, Therefore after many moneths suffering the
Warden himselfe fairely praied *Mr. Chamberlayne* to remove to
some other chamber, whereto (though he seemed to condiscend)
yet haveing said to one *Sir John Meeres, knight,* a Prisoner there,
that he would keepe it in dispight of the Warden, and to another
10 (now dead) he said, that he would not lye there but to that end,
and in divers yeares haveing not paied anything for his lodgings
and Duties there, but began one while to publish that it was the
King's free prison, and the Prisoners ought to pay noe Duties, and
other while they were to pay but ijs. iiijd. a weeke for lodgings how
15 many chambers or roomes soever they enjoyed, And that the
Orders and Constitutions for Governement of the Fleete were false
and gotten by indirect meanes, but such as they were, they were at
most but personall and bound noe more prisoners then such as were
in the Fleete 3° Elizabeth, Att which tyme the same were newly
20 revised and confirmed, And therefore he would shake the fabrick
of the prison and those Constitutions; By which meanes *Chamberlayne* haveing incyted *Sir John Whitbrooke,* and many others, to
say and hold of their lodgings as he had putt in their heads, And
further to vaunt that by withholding their payments they would
25 make the Warden to run away, and voyced it that he was then
already soe farr indebted as he would soon be gon, Upon this and
such like rumours there followed a generall defection of payments
by the Prisoners and a confederacy to oppose the Warden by all
meanes they could. The Warden being thereof very sencible both
30 concerneing himselfe and the governement there, after some
moneths that he perceaved noe accord could be had, he againe
dealt more seriously with *Chamberlane* to leave those lodgings and
to make choyce of any other in the howse, yea wished [him] to doe
it quickly while lodgings were empty.

Each tyme from the 15th of October, untill the 23th of the
same, wryteing downe the messages by those that delivered them,
and never soe much as mencōning any demaund of payment,
that not being soe much the Warden's drift as to have quiett in
his owne roomes, But *Mr. Chamberlayne* answeared uncerteynely 5
and at other tymes negatively, And when the fayrest Chambers in
the howse are taken upp by others he then (too late) made meanes
to the Lord Cheife Justice, whom the Warden attended and fully
satisfied him touching his proceedings, But *Mr. Chamberlayne* still
aspireing to the very best lodgings (which were two and three one 10
within another) where great persons used to lye, and where the
Warden never used to lodge men of suncken Estates, Especially
without bonds given, And perceaveing that he was a man of that
prowde Condicon, thought not fitt to beare his pride and danger
any longer, Wherefore feareing some defeature in putting him out 15
of his lodgings in the day tyme, Aswell because then in the Terme
tyme, the Warden and his servants must all day be abroad about
their attendance, And the Prisoners with their Servants being
many hundreds, were all day within the Fleete, He (the Warden)
about 8 a'clock at night when the severall precincts of the prison 20
were locked and much Company avoyded and *Mr. Chamberlayne's*
wife not there, sent to *Chamberlayne* to pray him to come downe
and speake with him, but he refused to come, Then the Warden
sent him word it was about avoydeing the Chamber.

Then *Mr. Chamberlayne* locking and bolting his dore went to 25
Bedd, and when the Warden sent word that if he would not yeild
the Chamber the dore should be broken open, Then he said, That
he was in God's peace and the King's in his Chamber, which was
his castle, and he could not be put out but by speciall warrant.

But the Warden (well knoweing that if nowe he suffered the 30
repulse it would be taken as a president, and further being informed
how comon a thing this had beene in other Wardens' tymes) Bidd
his servants breake open the dore, who (little thinkeing and lesse
provideing for such resistance) tooke a small fire forke from the

Warden's chimney to wrench open the dore, and thrustinge it
betweene the dore and dore post (soe as if *Mr. Chamberlayne* had
stood in the way it could not touch him), yet untouched and before
the dore was opened, he, to rayse the intended mutiny, cryed out at
5 the windowe, Murther, Murther; Arme, Gentlemen, I shall be killed
in my Chamber by the Warden.

But the Warden satisfied all the howse with present answeare
that there was nothing to be done, but either *Chamberlayne* to goe
or to be carryed to another chamber.

10   After which the Warden's Servants opened the dore by force,
and both they and many of the prisoners did perswade *Mr.
Chamberlayne* to goe to another chamber in the same gallery where
one *Sir Henry Shugsby* had lyen, and where two yeares together
Mr. Chamberlayne himselfe had formerly layen in the other
15 Wardens tymes and had made a Studdy in it and paied 8s. a weeke
for it, and sometymes for it and another xvis.

This Chamber was dressed and a fyer made, onely it tarryed for
Mr. Chamberlayne's bedding, which when he would not suffer it to
come, the Warden's servants and others prayed him to putt on his
20 cloathes, for his Bedd should be carryed away, but he would not.
The Bedd being carryed he wilfully stood in his Shirt and would
not suffer them to put his gowne about him, whereof the Warden
being informed and to prevent his wilfull hurt at such a tyme
caused his gowne to be put on and he therein carryed to his former
25 Chamber, where was alsoe wyne and Attendance to comfort him at
the Warden's cost, and though he faigned to be brused in the
carryage, yet he fedd next day at Dynner upon ordinary dyetts and
would not languish or dye within a yeare and a day to hang the
Warden, but liveth to make a very witty collection of theis 19
30 Articles and thereby to hang the Warden if Comon Bayle or
knights of the Posts oathes may be taken, with whome many
there have very good Intelligence.

When he was removed order was taken that his owne man and a
servant of the Wardens should tarry with his goods untill the next

daye, that *Chamberlayne* might either bestowe them into that one Chamber where he was or elsewhere.

Now the Warden haveing first borne with great patience his pride and haughtines from the 16th of May, 1617, to the 23th of October followeing, and then after his non payment, his menaces 5 soe hatefull and his Conspiracyes untill the xijth of February followeing, he then did appoint him to leave that chamber and to lye in the Comon Prison, for as on the one side *Mr. Chamberlayne* endeavoured to maynteyne the old rights of the Prison, Soe the Warden differed not upon that point but yeilded to it, onely 10 *Chamberlayne*, Seduceing all the prisoners to possesse the Wardens howse, which was built within these 40, 50, and 60 yeares, As if (*ab origine*) it were the Prison, which is of 500 yeares Standing, Therefore it was the Warden's part aswell to maynteyne the free-hould of the Fleete, as *Mr. Chamberlayne* doth lye in Prison to 15 preserve his Freehould in Gloucestershire to discend on his issue, makeing creditors suffer in the meane tyme.

And because that *Mr. Chamberlayne* sett on foote a Cavell, That soe long as a Prisoner lay upon his owne Bedd he neither was to pay ought, neither could the Warden place another with him to 20 lye two in a Bedd according to the Orders of the Prison, Therefore the Warden sent to *Mr. Chamberlayne* a good Featherbedd, Bolster, Covering, Blancketts, &c. to lye upon (as appeares under good Teste), Which Bedding he threwe out of the dore of the Prison into the yard, where some Prisoners layeing hould of it tooke and 25 kept it from the Warden, and therefore the Warden keeping *Chamberlayne's* he presently provided other.

But while *Chamberlayne* was there in the Comon Wards of the Prison (where many better men every way have layen), he practized and laboured in theis fowle Plotts, Evident Testimonyes of the 30 Canker that was groweing, and thereby proved that the Wardens Judgement was not misledd before thorough idle surmise (For *Chamberlayne* did fetch certeyne Records out of the Tower and perswaded the poore Prisoners thereby that the Warden had con-

s ned them of lxixli. p' Ann. which was to be paied to them out of
the King's Customes, whereby he drewe the Warden to such hatred
as the Prisoners did divers tymes Muteny against the Warden.

And not contented with this *Chamberlayne* complayned of it
5 further before the Comissioners as a most fowle deed of the Wardens,
who with one word avoyded it and had made him and others blush
if it had beene possible.

He scandalized the Warden as a Banckrupt, and that he would
run away, and therefore perswaded the Prisoners to hould together
10 against the Warden to the end he should have no command there,
By which meanes the Porter of the Fleete was stabbed, &c.

He consulted with others to take away the keyes from the two
Porters and to turne them and the Wardens company out, And
after consultation it was resolved that it was easy to be don.

15 He and *Sir John Whitbrooke* joyned together, and to make their
faction the greater did possesse themselves of the Box of money
gathered for the poore to dispose it to them, untill the Warden with
some labour gott it from the said *Chamberlayne*, &c.

Theis all, with Axes, hatchetts, Swords, staves, Basketts of stones,
20 &c. brake open all the dores of the wards and Tower Chamber,
Assaulted the Warden and his Servants.

They encouraged *Whitbrooke* to kill the Warden, as before is
declared.

They provoked and hired the Prisoners to rayle at the Warden,
25 praysed them for soe doeing, and wished them to stirr and sett on
foote Complaynts against him, that by multitude they might overcome.

And other matters more fowle then theis are already proved
against *Mr. Chamberlayne* touching killing the Warden, and other
30 fowle Conspiracyes, which is matter on record, and therefore here
omitted.

Whereupon the warden thought good to remove *Chamberlayne*
to another place of the prison, which was upp a payre of stayres by
the Chappell; but he being in the Chappell did [s]trive and resist

and would not goe upp. though the Warden sent some to perswade and move him thereto.

Hereupon hand Irons were put on him about a quarter of an hower to keepe him from striveing, but it avayled not, soe as they were taken off agan.   5

Then two Porters were brought to carry him upp, whome by thretts he deterred from doeing it, Soe he lay in the Chappell till of his owne mynde he went upp to the Chamber where he lodged, with Bedstead, Curteynes, and Traverses, many moneths, And with a fell mynd of revenge drewe his Chamber fellowes to thretten 10 to bynd, whip, and hang their keeper when he came amongst them, Soe that the keeper yeilded upp the keyes of the prison into the Wardens hands, and would noe more attend them.

They therefore fortified the roomes, got chissells and hammers, with which they cutt and tore in sunder the Stones of the dores 15 and the locks and bolt holes, soe as the dores could not be locked and shutt, And *Chamberlayne* was told by them that did it that he was a setter on thereof, Whereupon the warden was inforced to surprize that place, and by strength of his servants to remove the Prisoners untill the locks and dores were mended.   20

At which surprize one of the wardens servants was knockt downe and sore hurt, But the wardens care and direction was that noe Prisoner should be hurt.

Chamberlayne hath beene heard touching theis matters, and comanded to pay his Duties at theis severall tymes, viz.   25

1.   Before the Lord Cheife Baron at large.

2.   Before the Lord Cheife Justice and Master of the Rolls.

3.   Before *Sir Edward Cooke*, Master of the Rolls, and the King's Sollicitor.

4.   Before the honourable Mr. Treasurer and Mr. Comptroller of the 30 King's howshould, *Sir Edward Cooke*, and Master of the Rolls.

5.   Before the Lord Chauncellor aloane.

6.   Before the Lord Chauncellor, the two Cheife Justices, *Sir Edward Cooke*, Cheife Baron, &c.

Mr. Chamberlayne informed on the Stattute and was non suite 7.
upon Evidence in the Court of Exchequer.

There was at receaveing the Communion, some reconcilliacon Feb. 1620.
betweene the Warden and *Chamberlayne*, who againe desired a
5 good chamber aloane to himselfe, giveing faith to deale and pay
like a gentleman; But he lay there Tenne moneths and would pay
nothing, therefore was removed upon the next occasion when the
howse was extreame full, yet in six yeares the Warden or Wardens
could never gett a penny for his lodging, flees and dutyes.

10 The warden was ready to receave any money upon Accompt and
sent an acquittance to that purpose untill further consideration were
had.

The Lord Chauncellors did referre the consideration of *Chamber-*
laynes Duties to be had by a Master of the Chauncery, But *Mr.*
15 *Chamberlayne* refused the referrence though he were brought
thither unto the Master of the Chauncery.

All which alledged against *Mr. Chamberlayne* doth and shall
appeare upon good Evidence, both on record in Starrchamber
and elswhere.

20 Wherefore the warden appealeth to the judgment of all hearers,
whether he could have done more or lesse to such a man of whome
his whole countrymen and neighbourhood can witnes if need be.
And if *Chamberlayne's* first assertions be untrue, as indeed they are
most false, why should he not receave condigne punishment, which
25 did not desist in tumultuous behaviour when he was convinced by
Lawe, neither when he was comanded by those honourable and
worthyes, who have heard the busines from tyme to tyme, but hath
soe farre insisted as (if he report truely) he hath spent 300*li.* in the
pursueing of the Warden, which money were better in his Creditors
30 purses then where it is ?

There is alsoe a Subtle Accusation made against the Warden by one that merrited worse usage at the Wardens
hands, viz.:

One *Edward Rookwood, Esquire*, who removed himselfe from
the King's Bench to the Fleete for ease, and being a prisoner in 5
Execution for great somes, desired to have two of the best lodgings,
which he enjoyed for a fortnight. But when he was to be agreed
withall touching the payment for them, he refused them as too
deare at vjs. viijd. a peece weekely.

Therefore he was removed into the Checker Chamber (A Prison 10
proper for Debtors to the King), and lay there two weekes, but
becoming factious and giveing the Warden noe bond for true imprisonment fees, &c. he was putt into the Tower Chamber the
28th of November.

Upon the 22th of November he came and shewed money to the 15
Warden and tould it out, but would not pay it upon an Accompt, but
that the Warden should conclude himselfe to take xlixs. for his fee
and lodging when there was much more due, Whereupon for want
of money and bond the Warden did not provide Bedd, &c. for him
any longer, but left it to himselfe.   20

The Wardens Servants being informed that out of that Checkquer
Chamber *Rookwood* tooke away Bedd cloathes that were another
Prisoners and carryed them into the Tower Chamber, gave occasion
of takeing away those upper Bedd cloathes from *Rookwood* in the
Tower Chamber, and of his Clamor that his Bedd cloathes were 25
taken from him, A thing unknowne to the Warden, yet justly
done, where he practiseing to seduce (amongst others) one *Downes*
to change religion proffessing power to forgive sinnes, *Downes* his
wife complayned thereof both to the Warden and others.

There alsoe (amongst others) he drewe upp divers things att the 30

windowes with a coarde, Soe as they had gotten a wheelers Axe,
Sword, Staves, &c. and a practize was sett on foote to breake the
prison, whereof the Warden takeing knowledge removed *Rookwood*
into the Boltons wards the xiiijth of May, 1618, where he continued
5 till the 2nd of June, 1618, and then was removed into the place
called the wards or six wardes.

There he conspired with the rest to surprize the Warden and
Officers and to putt them into the strongest wards or prison, and
many other dangerous matters, And for more orderly prosecution
10 thereof he named one *Peck* to be King, and a Duke of Yorke and
Lancaster was designed, and white and redd roses of horne brought
for to make the favourers of each to be knowne, and picklocks
were provided from Newgate by one *John Abell*, who brought
them to *Edward Rookwood*, which he concealed from the Warden
15 untill it was revealed by others, And then *Rookwood* to collour the
matter said that he did informe the Lord Cheife Justice thereof,
which might be perhapps after the Warden had already prevented it.

The 10th of July, *Whitbrooke*, one of the conspirators, yssued
out with a hammer and a stilletto and wounded the Warden (as is
20 often before repeated), wherefore *Rookwood* reproved *Whitbrooke's*
weake execution of the purpose, and said he should have carryed a
Pistoll, and that would have made sure worke.

Then all the dores of the wards being broken open, and the
Tower Chamber Prisoners comeing downe Armed and assaulting
25 the Warden, great tumult was in the howse (*Rookwood* still an
Abettor), And when *Mynors* divers tymes fortefied the prison and
endangered and trobled the howse, *Rookwood* still gave encourage-
ment, And haveing (as the Warden was often informed) divers of
his owne sect repayrcing often to him, the Warden putt him into
30 Boultons Wards and looked the more strictly to him, As by his
Majesties expresse comand 22 November, 1619, Order was given
to keepe straite such prisoners as were Recusants and came not to
Church.

And another reason of strickt lookeing to him was, for that he made many attempts to speake and conferre with one *Thrask*, a dangerous and close Prisoner neare his lodgings.

On the 30th of November, 1618, *Rookwood* complayned to the Lords of the Councell at Whitehall, where the Warden did answeare it, And *Rookwood's* sonne (replyeing for his father) The Lords 5 ordered *Rookwood* to pay 15*li.* to the Warden, and thereupon the Warden to let him have a chamber.

And 2° December, 1618, a Reference at Councell Board was made to the honourable Mr. Treasurer and Mr. Comptroller of his Majesties howsehould, Master of the Rolls, and *Sir Edward Cooke.* 10 and they heard this manus complaint (*inter alia*) att the Fleete afterwards, and understood the reasons of the Warden's doeings.

Rookwood being pressed to come to Church came thither onely once in the morning at sermon, and there without any reverence seemed to lowse himselfe by buttoning and unbuttoning his cloathes 15 and pulling of lice out of his bosome, to the great offence of the people there, and never came thither before or after that day.

At last by often circumspection concerneing *Rookwoods* his malice to Religion and State, was discovered in *Thrask* booke, And the 31th of December, 1618, for his intelligence with *Thrask* and 20 other reports, &c. was committed close prisoner and putt into a Chamber aloane for that night.

The next day to another chamber that was made ready for him, where in the tyme of his being made close prisoner he attempted to seduce the Warden's man (his keeper) to be Papist, offering him 25 500*li.* and his daughter in marriage if he would convert, And when this served not he called out at his windowes and said he was starved, though he abounded with meate at the Warden's charge, as is before declared.

The 20th of Aprill, 1619, being discharged of his close Imprison- 30 ment and refusing to pay for his Chamber and dyett which the Warden had found him about 16 weeks, with a keeper to attend him, he was put into the comon gaole againe.

The 10th of May, 1619, he made meanes to have a chamber

aloane and promised to give satisfaccon for it and for his former
debt, But when he had lyen 3 weekes he offered onely to pay for
that tyme what the Warden durst take, and would not agree to
anything, neither for that tyme nor for his former dyet or Lodging
5 while he was close.

The 31st of May because the prison was full he was put into a
chamber of lesseͬ expense, yet paid nothing, onely talked of money
and would pay none, Except the Warden would take onely xs.
for dyett which he had the last weeke and give Acquittance under
10 his hand, wherewith *Rookewood* meant to have avoyded (in substance
or shewe in any man's understanding) the payment of the former
somes due by takeing an Acquittance for the last before he had
paied the first, and therefore the Warden would not signe the
Acquittance and is yet without the money.

15 The 30th of June, 1619, put againe into the Tower Chamber
where *Nicholas Rookwood* his sonne laye, who conspireing with
others, they with chissells and malletts cutt in sunder the stone-
work's and holdes of the dores where they were locked and bolted,
and grewe soe insolent, thretning their keeper to bynd, kill, hang,
20 &c. and mak'ing way to the outer dores of the prison, as is before
declared.

Whereupon the Warden sent upp his servants to take and sever
them perforce, where *Rookwood's* sonne had a Stilletto and others a
piked staffe and faggott sticks, wounding one of the Warden's
25 servants.

While they had hold of the sonne to bring him away, *Edward
Rookwood* (the Father) being in Bedd did arise and came running
after in his shirt to helpe his sonne, Upon which when the servants
had wished him to put on his cloathes (which he refused to doe),
30 They took him alsoe in his shirt and sent his cloathes after him, and
he was put into the wardes and his Beding sent to him soe soon as
might be, And being in his Chamber there he was very pleasant,
sayeing in a laughing manner he was brought safely and carefully to
his great ease and had good Beding and a Bedstead to lye upon.

In the moneth of July they shutt out 30 of their fellowe Prisoners
and some 10 or 11 of them (the *Rookwoods* being cheife) with
Whitbrooke and *Boughton* kept it soe some dayes.   The Warden
thought restraint of victuall would have made them yeild, but gave
over that course because they had much victuall in store, And not 5
onely other prisoners victualed them, But alsoe upon a Rumor that
Catholiques were oppressed in the Fleete there was much the more
victuall, bread, and money given to them that begged at the box,
Soe that at yeilding one man sent out two dozen of bread away.
Rookwood the Father and some others had meanes to victuall all 10
the rest and did it through a hole of the dore where they lay.

A Serjeant at Armes with his Mace was sent with a warrant
from the Lord Chancellor to comand them to open the prison dores:
they reviled and rejected the Serjeant and the Alderman's Deputy
and Constables altogether, and would by noe meanes yeild.   15

Then this was questioned before the Councell att Somersett
Howse, theire Lordshipps sitting there of purpose divers tymes, and
the Warden cleared himselfe.

Their Lordshipps sent Sir Clement Edmonds with a warrant to
comand the Prisoners to open the dores or ells a proclamacon to be 20
made against them, who after some dispute yeilded and came forth,
And yet againe soe soone as ever the Warden was out of Towne
they forcied the wards againe.

And then upon a complaint *Nicholas Rookwood* was convented
before the Lords of the Privy Councell at Whitehall, and sent to 25
Newgate 11th August 1618, and soe had *Edward* the Father if the
great debts and executions which are upon him had not moved
the Lords to forbeare it, which debts are soe sure a cloake of *Rook-*
wood's Recusancy and other fowle speeches against the comon
wealth as that he dareth more then becometh a good Subject.   30

The 18th of September, 1619, he agreed to pay for a chamber
and to take his dyett and when he had run more in debt about
14*li.* he would pay but 5*li.* and gott himselfe removed to the King's
Bench.   Since which tyme he came againe, and upon his promise

to pay hath a chamber to himselfe, but payeth neither ould or new
debt.

In every Act touching generall breach of prison, killing the
Warden, undermyneing Religion, and Services to be done by the
5 Warden, *Rookwood* hath beene a confederate and an Actor beyond
that which any man would thinke, And therefore if his evill carriage
hath been the cause of straite handleing, the Warden hath therein
done good service in opposeing rather then favoureing him, and he
and *Mr. Chamberlayne* are the onely two who necessarily were in
10 their shirts carryed to other lodgings and might have avoyded it if
they would have put on their cloathes.

And *Rookwood* hath alsoe confessed before witnesses while theis
complaints of the Prisoners were in consideration that they were
things of little truth and moment.

George Lee complained about three yeares past unto
the Lords of the Privy Councell to the effect as
now he doth.

Complaint.	Answeare.
1. That *Lee* hath given bond for true improvement 5 years past.	He gave bond to the othe Warden (not to this) Anno 1613, he broke that bond by many fowle abuses, upon which the other Warden put him close for the most part in the Comon Gaole, where this Warden found him, yet after much counsell and perswasion he let him have a fayre lodging and liberty without money or Condicon.
2. Paid all fees of a Gentleman.	Though he paid his fees at first, it is noc warrant to be irreguler ever after.
3. Demeaned himselfe honestly and continued in all payments.	His demeanor then was bad, and now worse, his payments none at all, his meanes good, but spent in Ryott.
4. The warden with crueltie doth exact.	The warden hath offred that if he can give security for the good behaviour he shall have liberty of the howse, Or if he cannot give security, then if he will retorne to other prisons whence he came and where he hath beene punished for like demeanor, the Warden will not exact any fees or dutyes, but what any indiffrent man shall thinke reasonable.
5. Detayneth his Bedd.	The Warden never detayned his Bedd nor anything ells of his, for he enjoyeth it all.

Complaint.	Answeare.
6. Locked him upp Close prisoner five 5 moneths.	Though he alledgeth to have beene kept upp Close prisoner 5 moneths, he hath had the use of six large roomes and a Court yard, and gon forth to drinke with and accompany his freinds.
7. And of late cast him into a loathsome dungeon, thorough 10 which all sewers doe run.	His last restraint is in a large but strong roome, which is noe otherwise then as any roome in the howse which is next the ground, and hath noe sewer, but onely a necessary vault to itselfe.
8. A place for froggs or Toades not Christian men.	It is as free from Froggs and Toades as any other place.
15 9. Denyeth him Pan or Coales for his health.	He hath not beene denyed but used coales at his will, or faggotts in the chimney there.

Reasons of his latter and more restraint.

1. He was a prisoner in Execution and debt in the Fleete for 20 xiij*li.* The Danger whereof the Warden might not beare or give him liberty in respect he had abused Ladies and other Prisoners in their Lodgings and the Warden's familie.

2. He was often outragious drunck and a busy Agent in all stirres and quarrells, A libeller and traducer of all men night and day, 25 when they have gone about to governe him, dispersed his libells of the Warden.

3. He did stabb the Warden's Servant, and when dyeing men have required the Warden to putt knights and others to silence for wynceing hornes, he hath insisted, fortefied his chamber against the Warden, 30 abetted others, till rescue from abroad armed have come inn for the Warden's safety.

4. Riseing at midnight in his distempers he hath called upon the

neighbours sayeing, Murther. Murther, Rise, Arme, we are starved, yet he abounded with victualls and store in salt as if he kept howse, keepeing therewith strumpetts, &c.

5. He broke downe the windowes and Iron grates of the Prison, and never ceased cloying and stoping the locks of the Prison dores   5
that they could neither be opened nor shutt, which caused the Warden to chaine him to the stocks.

6. He did fortefie the place in Bolton's Wards where he was kept that noe man could come at him, and offered to stabb his fellowe Prisoner if he opened the dore, and he wrott to *Sir John Whit-* 10
brooke and *Mr. Chamberlayne* that they would confirme warre [*sic*] who laye in that roome, that they might keepe the prison shutt against the Warden.

7. He being a Recusant noated prayer and Sermon tyme, and then drumed on the dore soe as divine Service could not proceed.   15

8. He had provided sawes, hatchetts, and other tooles into the Prison and delivered them to other Prisoners that mayneteyned a hold against the Warden in the Fleete, and perswaded them to sawe asunder the tymber of the prison therewith.

9. When the Warden roade into the country he endeavoured to stirr 20
mutynies, reporting the Warden was run away, and durst not come againe but by stealth.

10. He said, That soe often as the Gaoler did lock the prison dores, he would ramm the lock full of stones, for in despite of the Warden he would not be lockt in, And this he hath said and done often 25
tymes.

11. He perswaded the prisoners to trayne the Porter of the Fleete's wife by pollicy within their reach, and keepe possession of her and the prison dores untill their owne wives might come and dwell with them.   30

12. He did with most brutish and uncouth speeches (not to be named) rayle on the Warden, and professed he would sweare anything (how false soever) that would hurt or hang any man to whome he bare mallice.

13. He did incourage all the mutiners in the Wards of the 35

prison to oppose themselves against the Warden and governement
in the wards, to cause Murther, and consulted with other prisoners
to kill the Warden and to gett a Pardon, And that the Prisoners
should hold together and breake downe the back windowes.

5   14. He said that he would frame an Indictment and hang the
Warden for conccalcing a filthy busines touching one *Cranfeild* a
Prisoner whereof the Warden knewe nothing but by *Lees* owne
barbarous relation.

15. The warden was moved to chaine *Lee* to the Stocks to spare
10 the putting of him into the Stocks, because all fetters that were put
on him, he got off and cast them into a privy, and for to keepe him
the said *Lee* in the night tyme from breakeing the Iron grates of
the Prison was he chayned in that manner.

16. Kept away Fees to make the Warden run away.

15   17. Did abett and incourage the breach of prison.

18. Was the first that used incouragement to kill the Warden.

19. Slaundred and rayled at the warden by incouragement of
others.

20. Would wade hell to the knees to have their wills of the
20 Warden.

21. Conferred with others to Cutt the throats of all that gave
intelligence to the Warden.

22. Never paid the Warden anything.

In all which docings of *Lee* he neither would be reformed or
25 Confesse that he did amisse, but by many odious and scurrilous
lies and messages written and sent to the Warden did from tyme to
tyme defye him, and all that he could doe, Soe that for Example
sake the Warden could doe noe lesse, and was soe much justified
in his docings as that *Lee* was thought to be unworthy to live in
30 the Fleete, And therefore sent thence unto Newgate 5 December,
1618.

And whereas it hath of late beene urged as an inhumaine part of
the Warden that a certeyne vault in Boulton's Warde (where he did
lye) was left open, and more (say they) unstopped of purpose by a

CAMD. SOC.   T

servant of the Wardens,   There is noe vault in Boulton's Ward
but the Privy, which whether it had a cover or not was not fitt
office for the Warden to looke unto, But the truth is that this *Lee*
did (in scorne) bid a servant of the Warden's (an honest and able
man) to cover it, and because he did not thereof ariseth this un-   5
savoury complainte, annoyeing all that heare it; And in *Lee's*
complaints heretofore he had not bethought himselfe untill the
witt of men put it into his head.

Sir *Francis Inglefeild, Baronett,* being Prisoner in the Fleete before the Warden himselfe attended the place, did alwayes after adhere to the basest and factious prisoners, And for the first apparant ground he published that the warden by falsefyeing the
5 Lettres Pattents under the Great Scale did cousen the Poore of the viij*d.* per diem, raysed upon Prisoners that goe abroad, and he solely above all others when he went abroad would deliver that viij*d.* to the use of the poore, Whereby he not onely stirred upp the poore but the rest to tumults and to Muteny against the Warden (though
10 he himselfe had paied it, and other Wardens had of him 30 yeares past, and soe had the Warden last before this).

Next that he sett on foote a reproach that the Warden cousond the poore of lxix*li.* per annum which he reccaved out of the custome howse for their behoofe, And this alsoe be sett forward in
15 complainte before the Referrees first, and before the Comissioners next, when they satt upon the busines for the Fleete, both which complaints are braynesick falshoods.

He also published in the Fleete and before the Referrees, and in other places, that the Orders and Constitutions made for the Governe-
20 ment of the Fleete were gotten and obteyned by Corruption and indirectly, and he spake other derogatory speeches touching the explanations of the same made at Councell Board, And that the Warden durst not avouch them, nor take upon him to governe the Fleete thereby. And when by such false suggestions he had (as it
25 were) putt by the power and governement of the Warden, Then he scandalized the Warden that he was but a Deputy and not the Warden, To the end that the prisoners might not relye on him, Nay, that he had not retorne of Proces touching the place.

He often boasted that he had made one Warden run away, and
30 that he would make this Warden do the like, or ells he would spend thowsands of pounds, and boasted of how many thowsands he would

spend for his freind and how many against his enemye.   He sent the
Warden word he would be as busy with him as a Bee in his nose.

Himselfe not comeing to Church, debarred others out of that
place neare his chambers usually appointed for that purpose.

When one *Mr. Holman*, *John Chappell*, and *Rice Powe* were 5
deadly sick (who dyed in the Fleete) they sent to the Warden that
Sir Francis Inglefeild's man might be spoken unto to forbear the
wyncing of a horne there, because it peareed their weake sences
and trobled them. Therefore the Warden first tould *Sir Francis* his
man thereof, wishing him to forbeare, But the next day he doeing 10
it againe the Warden sent two of his servants to bidd him leave,
but his answeare was that he must and would doe it in their dispight.

Then the Warden sent two other servants to *Sir Francis Inglefeild* himselfe, to pray him upon this occasion to take order that
his man might forbeare, but he said that his man should doe it, for 15
the warden had no comand over his servants, but was a Gaoler and
a foole to send to him on such a Message, And this without any
manner of provocation.

He alsoe sent the Warden word that he was a foole and an Asse,
and he would cause him to be canvased in a blanckett.   20

When *George Lee* was (for his drunken demeanor) seized on by
the Warden's servants to be restrayned of liberty, *Sir Francis Inglefeild's* man aforesaid rescued him from them, and *Lee* stabbed the
warden's servant with a knife, and presently *Sir Francis Inglefeild*
himselfe tooke occasion to walke with *Lee* (being one whose 25
society all men shunned) in the very front and opposite to the
Warden's lodgings for a long tyme, as if he tooke the proteccon
of *Lee*.

When *Sir John Whitbrooke* came forth of the wards to murther
the Warden, *Sir Francis Inglefeild's* man colloured his comeing 30
out as to speake to him, and then accompanied him thoroughout all
the Prison to the Warden's stayre foote, where *Whitbrooke* goeing
upp attempted to doe it, as is before sett forth.

When *Mr. Tregian* dyed in the Fleete, oweing the Warden above

200*li.* for meate, drinke, and lodging, *Sir Francis* at the instance and pretence of *Trynion's* sisters receaved out divers evidences and goods in the Wardens absence, and when the Warden did open the dores to put the goods under Inventory in the presence of
5 many witnesses *Sir Francis* thretned the Warden. And lastly, to make a tytle to the goods, asked of the Gentlewoeman one booke of guilt, which when the Warden denyed, *Sir Francis* said that there should be an Accon brought for every particuler booke (whereof there were many hundreds) And soe *Sir Francis* getting a deed of
10 guilt, sent the Warden knowledge thereof, and brought his Accon against him for that one booke, where perhapps were many books and other things might have been discovered for the Comon Wealthes service if *Sir Francis* had not enterposed.

He was comitted 11 June, 1618, he denyed the said Comittment,
15 though the Lord Chauncellor avouched it, and when he had been 5 moneths upon it he tendred the Warden certayne Acquittanes yet extant, confessing to pay soe much as the Warden required for lodging, &c. Soe that the Warden would subscribe that he was noe Prisoner.

20 This proveth his consent for Chamber rent and *Christopher Bryant* testifieth the agreement.

Another Acquittance he tendred as if he were a Prisoner, and then he would pay but xiiij*d.* a weeke or thereabouts for divers chambers for himselfe and familie, And this busines being mediated
25 by freinds (who came from the court to sollicite for *Sir Francis*) yt was upon sight of the orders of the Fleete by them approved with asseveration that if *Sir Francis* would not yeild unto it they would become adverse to him, And it is a impe of *Sir Franciss* owne feather to say that the Warden did scornefully take upon him
30 to be his owne Chauncellor against direccon of the Lord Chauncellor.

Sir Francis kept tabling of knights and Gent. Prisoners in the Fleete, who paied him for it and bereft the Warden of the benefitt, for which cause *Sir Francis* was charged with halfe comons, who

according to the orders of the Lords of the Councell, &c. might
have been charged with the whole Comons.

When he was removed he was put into a good Chamber where
Sir Francis himselfe had formerly lyen and agreed to lye, And for
him, a Gent of worth was put from thence, who at the Warden's 5
request entreated and prayed *Sir Francis* to come thither.

For according as the Prison filleth, and men of honor and
quallity come, Soe men that have neither paied their Fee or other
Dutie (as *Sir Francis Inglefild* had not for that last comittment)
are in equity to be removed above others who pay.   10

And in *Summo Jure Sir Francis* was to have been denyed the
liberty of the howse, because he had paied noe fee, fyne, or Dutie
for lodgings after he had lyen there many moneths, And moreover
by expresse comand from his Majesty, declared and given in charge
by the Lords of the Councell, All Prisoners which came not to 15
Church were to have beene kept straite.

But when he joyned in consent and maynetenance with victual-
ling such Prisoners as blocked upp the dores many dayes, and Con-
tempned the Serjeant at Armes, Excited the stabbing or pistolling
of the Warden at such tyme as desperate persons and murtherers 20
were in that Contention with the Warden, and made their Rende-
vowes in *Sir Francis* his Chamber, And when he was by some
Gentleman reproved for soe sayeing and doeing he still avouched
it, The Warden to prevent such mischeife and abettment confined
Sir Francis for two Dayes within the compasse of his owne and 25
fower other chambers in that severall warde, permitting him notwithstanding to be attended by goers and comers at his pleasure as
is before declared.

When *Sir John Whitbrooke* wounded the Warden and sett the
howse in an uproare, he perswaded the greatest persons and hastiest 30
disposition to joyne in takeing *Whitbrooke* away, who afterward
said, if we had come there had beene noe way but death to the
Warden.

Whereas the *Lady Amy* wife unto *Mr. Edward Blunt, Esq.* The *Lady Blunt.* hath made a great complaint against the Warden of the Fleete, The truth of the busines is as followeth.

5 The said Lady being comitted to the Fleete by the Lords of his Majesties Privy Counsell, desired to be respectively lodged where she and her attendants might have roome convenient, and she would pay as usually was paid for it; she therefore was fitted with an Inner Chamber and an outer roome for her Servants.

10 She tooke her meate att the Warden's table the first weeke, and in that tyme, yea the first moment of her comeing, she acquainted herselfe with the most cuning and factious Gent. in the howse, and continueing in that humour 27 weekes descended to meddle and scann triviall matters, and the meanest usages and Customes of the Fleete
15 touching Prisoners and the Warden.

And as to the fact for which she was comitted she did by her petitions and servants soe troble and misbehave herselfe towards the Lords, that they thought (for her further reformation) to send her from the Fleete unto the Marshalsey prison, and alsoe comitted
20 her servants.

When she was upon her departure and offered the Warden neither fee of Entrance into the Fleete, payment for his meate and drinke, neither for her 27 weekes lodgings, the Warden sent to putt her in mynd thereof.

25 As for the flee she assented to pay as an Earles daughter, but upon Condicon that the Warden would take but ijs. iiijd. a weeke, which was xiiijd. a chamber or roome for lodging of her and her Attendants, A rate inferior to that of one and the meanest that is lodged in the Comon Prison.

Whereupon the Warden prayed her not to stand upon points in behalfe of the factious which laboured in that kind, And as to her ffee if she thought it too much she might rank herself as she pleased.

But she takeing that offer passionately and in derogation (where 5 it was not soe meant) said (as she might well say) that she was honourable and would pay a ffee in that rank, and called the Warden Base Gaoler, whereupon the Warden wished her to remember that Gaolers and Gaole Birds were relatives, and desired her either to doe what was fitt out of her owne motion, Or ells to 10 putt it to consideration, But she persisted in that mynd of payment for her lodging; the Warden would not appoint his Porter to attend the goeing out of her stuffe (of a lesse value then her ffees and dutyes) before he were paid.

Whereupon she tooke an Inventory thereof and left it (her owne 15 howse being in Towne whence she might furnish herselfe when she came at the Marshalsey if she pleased). And the Warden was herein the more cautious aswell for that the said Lady onely of spleene, and at the instance of factious Prisoners was drawne to thinke ill of the Warden, And if her goods went away the act of 20 such a person would have beene taken for a continuall president to the utter overthrowe of the Warden and the office, And further for that she being the prisoner and under covert, her husband, who lived upon a separate estate, neither would or could be drawne to pay her Dutyes.   25

Wherefore ymediately after her departure the Warden (for avoydeing all differences) made suite to the Lord Chauncellor that the variance touching her fees and goods might be referred to consideration, which his Lordshipp did, first unto a Master of the Chauncery, whereof in a civell manner the Warden did advertise 30 the said Lady by a lettre, whereto she answeared and subscribed, that she did not know the Lord Chauncellor could give any man authority to dispose of her money. Yet after that the Warden sent her notice in writeing from the Master of the Chauncery that

a tyme was appointed for hearing the difference whereby her
Ladyshipp might either come or send thither, Unto which she
answeared (as appeares) that she did utterly refuse the reference,
And thereupon she caused an Accon to be brought at Comon Lawe
5 in her husband (*Mr. Blunt's*) name, against the Warden for those
goods.

Upon which the Warden exhibited his Bill in Chancery, and he
(*Mr. Blunt*) or rather (she the Lady) demurring thereupon The
Warden obteyned an Injunction to stay proceedings at Comon
10 Lawe, Then a Peticon was made by her to my Lord Chauncellor
that she might not both be Sued in Court for the Warden's flees
and her stuffe alsoe detayned, to which the Lord Chauncellour
answeared in wryteing, that to satisfye the Lady he did sett aside
the Master of the Chauncery, and referred the busines to one of his
15 Majesties Serjeants at Lawe, and to his Majesties Solicitor Generall
with a proviso that bond should be entred into on both sides to
performe their order, And thereupon directed the goods to be
delivered, But the said Lady refused that order (as she did all the
former), and further she still refuseth to make any reasonable
20 payment.

And whereas she hath made a great complaint at Councell Board
and elswhere about faggotts and coales (things unworthy her great
worth) save that she standeth for a generallitie as is pretended,
Therefore the Warden can doe noe lesse but say in his owne
25 defence that he took notice of six penny faggotts to be brought
into the Fleete by one of her servants late in the night alledged to
be much better then those of the Fleete.

And made
doubt of being
poysened to
the end she
might avoyd
taking and
payeing for
her dyet to the
Warden.

Whereupon the Warden sent for the feweller of the Fleete, and
in the Ladyes servants presence caused fower ordinary (long dryed)
30 three halfepenny faggotts out of a house of the Fleete to be taken
and waighed in a payre of scales against those six sappie and wett
faggotts brought from abroad, And the fower three halfepenny
faggotts of the Fleete did outwaigh them six brought from abroad
by above one in six, Soe as a penny in six pence and her man's

CAMD. SOC.   U

labor was to be saved by takeing those in the Fleete, But as for coales the Warden never heard of such as in his Answeare to the point of fewell appeares.

But when the Warden had done this for his justification he did then doe soe poore a service to the Lady as to lett her faggotts 5 without contradiction to be fetched abroad at her pleasure, and to the great comfort of the Generall Cause which she tooke in hand.

Every of which points touching the said Lady the Warden can approve by good Testimony if it be thought worth the Examinacon.

Mr. Edmond Sharpe, an Attorney, Complayneth alsoe.

And as to him he was comitted to the Fleete, 15 October, 1617, *Edmond Sharpe.* out of the Court of Comon Pleas for misdemeanor, paied the wonted fee of a Parlor Comoner, and afterwards was charged
5 with an Execution for 200*li*. He hath given his owne bond onely to the Warden for true Imprisonment, which is nothing worth (being non solvent) neither to Creditor nor Warden.

He lay on the Greene yard side (amongst other gent) with his brother till 10 November, 1618, which was a yeare and a moneth, And though he agreed for his lodging he never paied one penny for lodging, dyet, and other dutyes, and then was removed to the
10 Tower Chamber.

The Curteynes and vallence which he saith the Warden hath were left with *Sharpes* Brother when he was removed to the Tower Chamber, and he never demaunded them that the Warden heard off, yf he had, and that the same were his owne, his brother
15 might have delivered them to him.

His Brother continued in the Fleete till 5° May, 1619, which was six moneths after this *Edmond Sharpe* was removed to the Tower Chamber, And then was removed from the Fleete to the King's Bench, and left unpaied for his Chamber rent x*li*. at the
20 rates he agreed for, for which the Warden's Servants staied that stuffe (curteynes and vallence) which was in his chamber (being little or nothing worth, yet none of this man's).

Now when *Edmond Sharpe* was in the Tower Chamber (the dores of the Prison being soe broken as the Warden could not
25 lock them) he was forced to send for such Prisoners there as he found refractorie to put them in safetie.

Amongst the rest *Edmond Sharpe* was brought downe and lodged in a roome in the wards 15 July, 1619, where comonly he had the liberty of a court yard 20 yards square, and 5 other large

roomes to walke into, and was offred all his bookes and apparell
whatsoever he had without contradiction, and had them.

Within fewe dayes after his remove to this place he and some
fewe others hadd blocked upp the dores of that prison and shutt
out 28 of their fellowe prisoners that lay in the said six roomes,   5
and then the Warden endeavoured to keepe him and others without
meate and drinke one day, thinkeing thereby to inforce them to
open the dores and lett in the rest of the prisoners, but the
Warden, seeing that though he endeavoured to keep them without
meate and drinke they had it brought them in aboundance (as often 10
before is repeated), proceeded noe further therein.

The Warden never (save now before the Comittees) heard that
Sharpe had left any Gowne or Cloake, neither can his Servants
tell him they ever heard him complayne of anything he had lost.

The said *Sharpe* being an Attorney in the Comon Pleas (for his 15
ill behaviour and misdemeanours towards that court, and for his
shifting tricks) was putt out of the Roll of Attorneys, yet he presumed still to make writts of *habeas corpus* and *Supersedeas* in
other Attorneys names, who would not justifie them, by which the
Warden was often like to fall into great danger, amongst the rest 20
he made a *supersedeas* to the Warden of the Fleete to discharge
a Prisoner out of Execution (there being noe satisfaction acknowledged), and put the name of *Mr. Gulston* an Appronothary
unto it, And caused it to be delivered to the Warden's Clerke to
discharge the Prisoner, to the hazard of the Warden's undoeing.   25

For which offence he, being brought into the Court of Comon
Pleas before the judges, upon Examination the judges blamed him,
and the *Lord Hobart* would have comitted him close prisoner, but
the Warden desired that his Lordshipp (in goeing about to punish
Sharpe the offender) would not punish him the Warden. For if 30
his Lordshipp comitted him close prisoner the Warden must be
much trobled by straite lookeing to him, yet before that tyme
Sharpe was in the wardes, which himselfe calleth close prisoner,
But if noe man be closer, All villany must goe unpunished, There-

fore it it was comanded that he should not make any more writts
in that kind, and that the Warden should keepe him from Pen,
Inck. and paper.

Alsoe the said *Sharpe* being in Execution, and the Warden per-
5 mitting him to goe abroad with an usuall writt of *habeas corpus*
out of the Court of Comon Pleas, which himselfe procured, he
deceaved his keeper of the writt and keeping it brought an accon
of Escape against the Warden, purposeing to bayle himselfe upon
an *Audita Querela*, and thereby he would lay the debt he lyeth
10 for upon the Warden or cousen his Creditor, As appeareth by the
said *Sharpe's* declaracon upon record.

Lastly *Sharpe*, notwithstanding the former comands and thretts
of the judges, did deale with one *Welman*, a poore prisoner liveing
upon the charity, who lay in the Fleete in Execution, and told
15 him he would free the said *Welman* out of Execucon if he would
give him *vili*. to procure an *Audita Querela*. *Welman* agreed to
give him the money soe he might be freed.

Whereupon *Sharpe* went about the busines, and within a short
tyme tould *Welman* (as *Welman* affirmeth) that he had procured
20 him a *Supersedeas* upon the *Audita Querela*, and that he wanted
xxxs. for to finish it, which *Welman* procured and delivered him.

Within 4 dayes after the *Supersedeas* was made by *Sharpe* himselfe (*Welman* standing by), and in a short space he came and
delivered it to him sealed as under the hand of *Mr. Brownlowe* the
25 Appronothary.

When *Sharpe* delivered this Writt to *Welman* he required him
not to tell the Warden's clarke that *Sharpe* had any knowledge of
it or made it, for if he did the clarke would reject it.

The Writt of *Supersedeas* being delivered by *Welman* to the
30 Clarke, the Clarke misdoubted that the *Supersedeas* was unduely
procured (finding it to be *Sharpe's* handwriteing), And the said
writt being shewed to *Mr. Brownlowe* he said that whosoever made
that writt he had counterfeyted his hand, for it was very like but
none of his hand.

Welman is ready to affirme that *Sharpe* had of him about some ix*li.* for this writt, and hath now deceaved him and done him noe good.

Sharpe shewed this *Supersedeas* to *Welman* and *Mr. Brosholme* with *Mr. Justice Hutton's* hand on the back of the writt, which 5 afterwards he razed out againe when it was like to come in question.

For this fact alsoe the said *Sharpe* was by the *Lord Hobart* comitted to the straitest and Close Prison of the Fleete.

Soe that lett a man of honest and Civell Conversation be found that will complayne of the Warden, and then he may be blamed; 10 but, for such as *Sharpe* is, he hopethe he shall never receave rebuke.

One *William Harrey* made a great complaint how he lay 120 *William Harrey.*
nights without a Bedd, whome to Answeare here more then is
formerly said in the general should be needlesse, if that he had
paied his duties to the Warden when he had lyen thrice as long
5 on the Warden's bedding without payment.

On which occasion the warden left him to lye in the Comon
Prison, as reason there was, and besides the distempers in drinke
he was perpetually factious and strooke the warden on the brest,
saying he should never rule him.

10   He haveing a howse in the Towne excellently furnished with all
store, did in an humor mainteyne possession of it and would not
send for his owne Beding, &c. Soe as he lost all his stuffe and
oweing many thowsands had nothing to pay.

When his friends comisscrateing his need and folly did offer
15 privately to pay the Warden for his bedd and dyett, he caused
them to retract it as one that scorned to be beholding to any of
them, though he starved or lay on the boards.

He was alwayes quarrellsome and the Abettor to *Sir John
Whithrooke's* death, stirring *Boughton* to be enraged, by which
20 followed the stabbing of *Whitbrooke.*

He purposely lay without bedd onely to take occasion to complayne, For he was offered a Bedd by one *Coppin* who lay in the
roome with him, And except he had made meanes to the Warden
for one, according to the Orders of the Prison, there was noe
25 reason that it should be thrust upon him when he meant not to
pay for it.

If the peevishnes of the man were as well knowen abroad as it is
in the Fleete, he were fitter to be sent elswhere then to be there,

For now that he hath a Bedd and Chamber he payeth nothing, and besides spends his tyme to perswade others to abstayne from payment.

And better it were to a Warden to be anything then subject to that which of late he suffereth in him, and such like of noe worth of discretion.   5

		An Esquire A gentleman or gentlewoman that shall sit at the Parlour Commons or anie other person or persons under that degree that shall be at the ParlourCommons	A Yeoman or any other that shall lyve at the Hall Commons man or woman	A poore man of the wards that hath his ʒt at the boxe
	William Petre Robert Catlin ght William Cordell ʒt the James Dyer of a Edward Saunder t ... ctor of Tho. Sackford tie or Ge. Gerrard and Robert Rowell of like ... ge hav-			
The Fleete	The ordinarie commons and every estate & gree that shall after be com to the Fleete to the wards & other officers beinge as parti appeareth			
	iiij^d	xxvj^s viij^d	xiij^s iiij^d	Nihil
	viij^s	xxvj^s iiij^d	vj^s x^d	Nihil
	ij^s	viij^s iiij^d	vij^s iiij^d	ij^s iiij^s
	vj^d	x^s	x^s	Nihil
	iij^d	ij^s iiij^d	ij^s iiij^d	Nihil
	ij^d	iiij^d	iiij^d	Nihil
	ij^s	xij^d	xij^d	Nihil
	ij^d	xij^d	xij^d	Nihil
	ij^d	xij^d	xij^d	Nihil
	gallon vyne	One gallon of wyne	One potte of wyne	Nihil

THE FORME OF THE TABLE THAT SHALL HANGE IN THE HALL IN THE FLEETE.

William Pytte
Robert Corbin
William Cordell
James Dyer
Edward Saunders
Tho. Suckford
Geo. Gerrard
Robert Rowell

	An Archbpp. A Duke A Prothere	A Marques A Marquesse An Earle A Countesse A Vicountesse	A Lord spiritual or temporall, A Lady the wife of a Baron or Lord	A Knight, A Lorde for wife of a knight, A Doctor at Domesticke or Lewe and other of like callinge hereos	An Esquire, A gentleman or gentlewoman in that shall be neither Parliament Commons or anie other person winge gret or greter in estate give that shall be at the Parliament Commons	A Yeoman or any other that shall lece at the Hall Doore eftsones some or wee oo	A poore man of the warde that shall hath his grace at the barr
The Warden's fyne for libertie of the House and ironte at the first commyge ...	Tenn pounds	Seaven pounds	Five pounds	iiij s iiij d	xxvj s viij d	xvij s vij d	Nihil
The first week's Commons for himself	Five pounds	iij s vj s viij s	xl s	xxvj s viij d	xvj s vij d	vj s v d	Nihil
The dismission	Three pounds five shillings	Fifty shillings	xxxiij s iiij d	xij s	vij s iiij d	vij s iiij d	ij s iiij d
The ordinarie Commons weekelie with wyne	iij s vj s viij d	xl s	xxxiij s iiij d	xxvj s vij d	v s	v s	Nihil
The Clarkes fee for making the obligacon	Tenn shillings	vij s	v s	ij s iij d	ij s iiij d	ij s iij d	Nihil
The fee for entering the name and cause	Five shillings	iiij s	ij s vj d	xiij d	iiij d	iiij d	Nihil
The Porter's fee	Tenn shillings	vij s	v s	xij d	xij d	xij d	Nihil
The Jaylor's fee	Tenn shillings	vij s	v s	xij d	xij d	xij d	Nihil
The Chamberlaine his fee ...	Tenn shillings	vij s	v s	xij d	xij d	xij d	Nihil
For wyne	Tenn shillings	xiij s	x s	One gallon of wyne	One gallon of wyne	One potte of wyne	Nihil

Sir Francis Inglefeild.
Sir John Whitbrook.
Sir William Aprice.
George Owen.
Francis Tregian.
Edward Bankwood.
Gilbert Beare.
John Hantley.
George Lee.
John Sayne.
John Martin.
John Warren.
Nicholas Bankwood.
&c.

A Petition from the Warden of the Fleete to the Parliament Howse.

To the honourable the Knights, Cittizens, and Burgoses of the Comons howse of Parliament assembled.

5   The humble Peticon of the Warden of the Fleete,

Sheweing,

That the office is a continued Sherriffwick as it were into all shires of the kingdome.

Therefore perhapps obnoxiously taken by many for doeing the
10 services thereof.

Especially when it meeteth with Romish affected persons, with *Sir Francis Inglefeild.* whome the place doth continually abound, and they have beene *Sir John* the onely fomenters of theis quarrells, to the end they may not *Whitbrook.* onely sway the place, but live exempt from all payments there and *Sir William Aprice.*
15 abroad, and have plotted the Warden's death with the adherents of *George Owen. Francis* Mr. *Chamberlayne,* concernciug whome alsoe all Prison keepers *Trygian.* were convented before the Lords of the Councell by especiall *Edward Rookwood.* direction from the king's Majesty, and charged to carry a straite *Gilbert Beare. John Huntley.* hand over such as came not to Church. *George Lee.*
20   The wards and houlds of the King's Prison are such as almost *John Segar. John Martin.* 500 yeares they have beene; And though the accesse of Prisoners *John Warren.* be much of late, yet they have more roome then formerly. *Nicholas Rookwood. &c.*

The usage of Irons, Stocks, &c. contynued from tyme to tyme upon excesses comitted.
25   The Constitutions for Governement often explayned and con-firmed at Councell Table.

A late Comission renewed under the great Scale sheweing that the Governement of that place are consequences of state, And therefore referred to the Councell of State to take care thereof.

Whereupon the Lords themselves have heard all theis Complaints of usage, roomes and fees ;

Sent Comittees, Made References, Satt in Comission themselves.

The Warden stood six tymes to purge himselfe before such, And undergon two verdicts at Lawe in his favour.   5

Wherefore not any way appealeing from this high assembly but submitting myselfe to the very lawes and stattutes in this place made, doe with all most humbly beseech, That the King's Comission, the Councells and Judges paynes may not be in vayne, and that as they have heard, discerned, and shall report, Soe I may 10 stand or fall, for as they Comitt the prisoners, Soe they take Accompt of their usage.

And as to some of the Comittees from this place, If it may stand with the pleasure and course of this howse, I may avowe, That some of them are not discharged of their Imprisonment, and much 15 indebted to the Warden, others have pertictuler Interests and affinitie with the Prisoners, whereof I presume not to inlarge with out speciall leave.

And he shall ever pray for your good happinesse.

Concerning the Fleete.

Imprimis a breife or writt of Certiorari directed to the Warden of
the Fleete or his deputie and returned into the Chaunceerie and there
5 remayninge fyled in the Filisers office, the substance thereof beinge
To cause the Warden and his deputie to Certifie such Records as
they had in their Custodie for the governement and fees lymitted to
be taken of such prisoners as should bee there committed.

There is also in Record in the said Filizers office a certaine
10 Schedule intituled The Constitutions and Orders newly renewed
and to bee established in the Fleete viz: anno dni. 1562, returned
by the then Warden.

There was also a Petition directed to *Sir Nicholas Bacon*, Lord
Keeper of the greate seale of England made by *Richard Tyrrel* esquire
15 then Warden of the Fleete, and in the name of all the then prisoners,
whereby it was desired by both, upon occasion of differences betweene them happeninge, that a Comission might be directed to
some discreete Honble and Worshippfull persons authorisinge them as
well to erect such good and necessaire orders of newe, as they shall
20 thinke convenient. As also to establish all such orders as shall be
approved unto them to have had continuance there tyme out of
the remembrance of man.

Hereupon a Comission was awarded to Sr William Peeter Knight,
Sr Robert Catlyn, kt. Chiefe Justice of our Pleas, Sr William
25 Cordell, Kt. M^r of the Rolles, Sr James Dyer Knight, Chiefe Justice
of our Comon Bench, Sr Edward Saunders, Kt. Lord Chiefe Baron,
Thomas Sackford Esquire, one of the M^rs of our Court of Requests,
Gilbert Gerrard, Esqre our Atturney generall, John Carril Esqre
Atturney of our Dutchie of Lancaster, and Robt. Nowell, Attorney
30 of our Court of Wards and Liveries, or to anie eight seven or six of
them diligentlie to try out what fees, priviledges, liberties, restraints,
orders, Rules, Customes and Constitutions have bine heretofore

allowed or accustomed within the prison of the Fleete or the precinct
of the same, and the same to ratifie, allow and confirme, or the abuses
thereof being perfectlie knowne, to change alter extinguish, and
other newe convenient and meete ordinances, estatuts and usages in
theire place to constitute publishe and establish, and to augment or 5
diminish as well the dyett as the prices of dyet, for all manner of
prisoners there, Willinge and Comaundinge you eight seven or six
Whereof Sr William Peeter Sir Robert Catlyn Sr William Cordell
Sr James Dyer or Sr Edward Saunders or three of you to be three
the same orders or Constitutions to cause to be written fayre in a 10
Table wth your hands thereunto subscribed, and to fixe, place, and
fasten in some part of the Comon Hall of the same Prison, to the end
the Certaintie thereof may bee apparent at all tymes hereafter as
well to the Wardens as to the Prisoners from tyme to tyme.

And that upon the due execucon of this our Comission you eight 15
seven or six of you whereof those before meneoned to be three to
make Certificate unto us into our Chaunceric under your seales
plainlie and at large of your whole doinge therein dated at Westminster the third daie of June in the third yeare of our Reigne.

The Constitutions and Orders newlie renewed and to be established in the Fleete anno dni. 1562.

1. First that it may be lawfull to the saide Warden or his deputie to appoint soe many of the houscholl servants, as to either of them 5 shall seeme good to open or shutt the two utter gates of the Fleete at such howres as the gates of Ludgate and Newgate are accustomed to bee opened or shutt; And the said persons to carrie in theire hands Halberts, Bills or any other Weapon as shall seeme good unto the said Warden or Deputie within his precinct or libertie.

10 2. Item the Warden to take such bond of evrie person that shal bee brought into the Fleete as prisoner as shall seeme to him reasonable at his discrecon and accordinge as the Cause shall require, as well for the payment of all manner of duties there, as also to bee true prisoners there and of good behaviour towards the saide War-15 den and all others within the said precinct of the Fleete in such manner and forme as heeretofore hath bene used.

3. Item that it is and shal bee lawfull to the said Warden and his Deputie to take order from tyme to tyme that noe person com-minge in there doe carry anie weapon further than the Porter's 20 lodge there, bee hee stranger, or other, unlesse they shal bee lycensed soe to doe by the discretion of such as the same Warden shall appoint to keepe the gate there.

4. Item that noe prisoner shall buy beere, ale, or any other victuall, out of the said howse, soe longe as they maie have sufficient and 25 good provided within the same howse in such place as shal bee there appointed at such reasonable prices, as the same be commonlie sould for, within the Citie of London, except the Warden shall give lycense for anie Consideration as to him shall seeme good.

5. Item that it may bee lawfull to the Warden to take of every 30 such prisoner as the said Warden may lawfullie lycense to goe abroad with his Keeper for the half-day, that is to saie before dinner, or

after to the Warden's boxe fower pence, and for the whole day
both before dinner and after eight pence.   And for the Keeper that
shall goe with him for the half-day, six pence, and for the whole
daie twelve pence.

6. Item and yf it shall happen the Queene's Matie and her hon^{ble}   5
howse hould to bee above two myles distant from the Cities of
London and Westminster or either of them, and that anie prisoner
shal bee sent for by the Counsell, or anie other havinge authoritie
to commaunde the said prisoner to bee brought before them, that
then the said prisoner shall beare all manner of such charges as 10
shall thereunto appertaine, bee it either by water or by land
untill his returne, as well for himself, as any other that shal bee
appointed his Keeper for the tyme.

7. Item that the said Warden by himself or his Deputie shall
and may carrie downe with him in the Countrie anie such prisoner 15
as hee may lawfully lycense to goe abroad with his keeper at anie
tymes betweene the Tearmes; except there shal bee expresse Com-
maundem' to the Contrarie by the Councell, or such as shall committ the partie thither.

8. Item that it maie be lawfull for the said Warden or his Deputie. 20
and soe manie of his houshold as shal bee thought needefull to
keepe watch in his Harneyes or otherwaies within his precinct at
all tymes as hee shall see cause for his bettere safeguard, yf he shall
suspect any prisoner within his Custodie to intend to make an
escape.   25

9. Item that it maie be lawfull to and for the said Warden to
take order at all tymes for such money as shal bee gathered at the
boxe, or otherwaies generallie given to poore men there, for the
distribucon thereof amongst them, yf anie Contention shall arise,
and that the said poore men shall alwaies keepe one key of the boxe, 30
and another key to bee at the Warden's appointm'.

10. Item that it shall and may bee lawfull for the Warden yf
there shall at anie tyme happen anie person to bee Committed that
shall not be able to maintaine neither the Parlour Commons, nor

the Hall Commons, nor also will take part of the Boxe; that then the Warden may appoint a bedd and a chamber for any such conveniently, the partie agreeinge with the Warden for the same at his reasonable discretion.

5   11. Item that yf anie that will take part of the Boxe, will have anie more ease, then for the same is appointed, that then it may bee lawfull for the Warden to appoint any such person or persons a bedd or chamber, the partie agreeinge with the Warden for the same as shal bee thought reasonable.

10   12. Item whereas by an ancient Custome tyme out of memorie of man used in the said Fileete, the Warden or his Deputie for the tyme beinge have used and did license such persons as bee prisoners there (not beinge upon any Condemnation or by expresse Commaundem^t given to the Contrarie by the Councell or such persons
15 as doe committ the same prisoner thither) to goe abroad about theire necessarie busines, or to theire learned Councell, or such like affaires with a keeper; Therefore it is and shal bee lawfull to the said Warden and his deputie for the tyme beinge to license and permitt all such persons as bee or shall remaine there to goe abroad
20 with a safe keeper about his or theire needefull businesses aforesaid, soe alwaies that anie such prisoner doe not lye there upon any Condempnacon, or that expresse Commaundem^t by the Queene's Matie, Councell, or such persons as doe Committ the same prisoner thither bee given or inhibited to the Contrarie thereof.

APPENDIX I.

1597.

To the Queenes Matie most honorable Councell.

In most humble and lamentable wyse Shewithe and Complaynith 5
vnto yor honors yor dayly orators the pore prisoners of the Quenes
Maties prison of the flet   That where it hathe bene accustomed
tyme out of mynde that the prysoners there for the tyme beinge
shold haue meate drinke and other nessessary comodyties in the
said flet and be well and decently vsed as it is mete for euery mans 10
degre that is thither comytted, accordinge as it owght and shold
apere by the very orders and constetucions of the said howse whereof
there was wont to be a boke allways Ready to be shewed with all
and euery order and constetution therein conteyned, that all men
that were thyther comytted might se what he owght to haue in the 15
said prison and also what he owght to do touchinge all man^r of
dewties rites constetucions and ordynances to be observed and kept
in the said flet.

But so it is right honorable lordes that now of late contrary to
the good old orders and constetucions of the sayd flet and contrary 20
to all equitie and good conscience the warden now beinge hathe
pryvely let and set to ferme the vittuallinge and lodginge of all
the said howse and prison aforesaid to one John Harvye and
the other profites of the said flet is let to one Thomas Newport
now deputie there vnder the said Warden witch said Newport and 25
Harvye was well knowen at the entrynge in to the said offices to
be very pore men havenge nether lands or any other trade to
lyve by nor yet any certeyne wages of the said Warden, as they
them selfes dothe report, beinge very gredye of gayne dothe lyve
by secrete bribinge and extorcion. By meanes whereof they do 30
not only exacte and extort most shamefully vppon vs the sayd

prisoners and rayse new costomes fynes and payments for theyer
owne advantage and most gredy lucre, but also now of late dothe
most cruelly vse vs yo.r said orators and shut vs up in close prison
for that we dyd myslike and fynde fawte w.th theyer most wicked
5 dealynge, and will neyther suffre vs to have owre lyberty to com
and go w.thin the sayd prison as we ought to have nor yet saffre
our frinds to com into us that shold travell in owre cawses for oure
better Relyffe, but kepithe vs fast locked vp for the witch crueltie
w.th theire bribery extorcion and dyvers other abhomynable and
10 detestable mysdemenors done by the said Newport and the said
Harvye yf there be not spedy remedy provided for the same to be
reformed in tyme by yo.r honors it wilbe to ower vttur vndoinge
and all owers and also to the grete preiudice and myschiffe of all
such as may hereafter be comytted to the sayd prison. In tender
15 consideration whereof and for asmoche as we yo.r said pore orators
are able and can justly prove all the mysdemeanors in this owre
supplicacion allegged, w.th dyvers other abuses agaynst the sayd
Newport and the sayd Harvye, Yt may therefore please yo.r honors
to appoynt Comyssioners in that behalf to com to the said flet and
20 examyne the said Newport and the said Harvey and to sepate the one
of them from the other before theyer comynge that they have no conference togethers, nether that they shall confer w.th any others till
they be examyned severally before the Comyssioners apon Intergatoris
alradye drawen to be ministred to them, and that the prisoners in
25 lik man' maybe examyned towchinge theyer doings and vppon examynacion and deu proffe thereof to take suche good order for the
redres thereof as to yo.r honorrable wysdoms shall seme good and
we accordinge to ower bounden dewties shall dayly pray for the
preservacion of yo.r honorable Estats.

30 [Endorsed.]

Suppl. of the prisoners of y.e fleete, declaring their euill vsage by
Newport & Harvey. And y.t it may please y.e Lords to appointe
Commissioners in that behalfe.

[Lansdown MSS. British Museum 85, Plut. LXXV. D.   fol. 97.]

To the righte honorable the Lorde Burleighe Lorde Treasorer
of Englande and of her Ma^ts most honorable privye Counsell.

In most humble wise beseechen yor L̄p̄e the poore prisone's of
the comon goale of the fleete to showe yor accustomed and honor-   5
able Comisseracōn in furtheringe the bill exhibited into the plia-
mente house touchinge the order and reformacōns of the fleete not
onlie to further so charitable a worke but to be the cheife meanes
it maye be enacted. The substitute warden Joachin Newton by the
greateste indevoric he can (as we are enformed) crosseth the same. 10
Howe requisitt it is and because yor L̄p̄e maye knowe a truthe and
wth more favo^r be induced therevnto we haue presumed (and es-
peciallie I Anthonie Bate in the name of the rest nowe Newton's
close prisonner in the dungeon for the same) Therefore [?] I knowe
not to send the collection of the Articles wch shoulde haue bene ex- 15
hibited by some gentlemen prisoners in the fleete to yor hono^r yf
they had come to the Starchamber the laste teurme as they expected.
The murders horrible and the dailie oppressions extorcions tortures
and other misdemeano's greate more then tyme to be looked vnto
and reformed.   In tender consideracōn whereof and that the most 20
honorable houses of the pliam^t maye iudge howe iuste cause the
prisoners haue to entreate there good likings humblie for enactinge
of the same And for prooffe of the saide articles maye it please yor
good L̄p̄e of yor gratious goodnes to sende her ma^ts learned Counsell
wth Comission to examyn the truthe of the premisses contayned in 25
the Articles gen'allie thoroughe the whole fleete vpon oathe   And
that Jochin Newton & his servant Walter Androwes wth other cul-
pable maye accordinge to Lawe be comaunded to saffe keepinge to
answere the murders mencioned in them And we shall not only

praye dailie wth all devočón for yor Lps preservačón in healthe w^{th}
encrease of worthie honor but will enter into recognisance (yf soe
you please to comaunde) to her ma^{tie} to psecute the suite against
Joachim Newton and the saide Walter Androwes wth pawne of ou^r
5 lives for proffe of the murders and misdemeno^rs aforesaide. Soe
the almightie God graunte our peticon & prayers to be harde w^{th}
further indowem^t to yor and yo^{rs} of all his heavenlie blessings.

ANTHONY BATE.

[Endorsed] 26 Martii 1597 Anthonie Bate prisoner in the fleete.
10 Against Joachim Newton the Deputy Warden.

———————

[Lansdown MSS. British Museum, 85. Plut. LXXV. D. fol. 163.]

To the most honora^{ble} the Lord Treserer of England.

Right honorable we whose names are vnde^r written in teares of
o^r hartes and gryffe of o^r myndes being poore myserable distressed
15 men voyde of anie helpe other then from yor hono^r and othe^{rs} the
lyke and godlie ho^{ble} the charitie at the box wch is not nowe at this
p'sent daily aboue a penny to ech man: Vnderstandinge that in the
names of vs all, the poore of the box, a slanderous peticon is exhibited
to you^r honour, against o^r Warden whos wor^{ps} favo^r to o^r comforts
20 is wekelie bestowed besydes his speciall care for relyvinge any
amonge vs sicke or deseased wth money and all things els nedefull
in right of o^r duties to him, and that yor hono^r may knowe the
skyllfull practises of Mr Smyth & myne^{s}[?] the prinsipall agents in
these doings most hvmblie do pray yor hono^r for Jesus Christes sake
25 that the said peticon may be seen whereby ech mans doings may be
seen in their dobellins & that it may be knowen vnto o^r Warden
that we are none of that factious companye. Whereby by yor hono^{rs}
meanes his wor^p may not w^{th}drawe his [former?] helpes. And [as]

bownden dutie byndes vs wth zelous devocon we shall daylie praye for yor honor.

THO: HAMON
his + mark

THO: SEAGAR cticus.
JOHN ROYMON +

JOHN JONES 5

PETER PARKER
+
his marke

JOHN STURGYS +
JOHN ROBYNSON
HENRY ROFFE

ROBERT COCKE
his + marke

JO: FFELTWELL
+
his marcke

By me JOHN BARBAR
the signe of THO: + BRITTAINE

10

[Endorsed]

The Humble peticon of the porest prisoners in the Wardes and of the box in the comon gayle of the flleete.

Disavowinge the peticon exhibited in ye name of ye prisoners 15 theare against the Warden.

Sept^{br}
1597.

A.D. 1597.

[Lansdown MSS. British Museum, 85. Plut. LXXV. D. fol. 107.] 20

O^r humble duties done to yor Good L: wee haue accordinge to yor L : L^{re} directed vnto vs mett three seu^rall tymes at the flleete and haue therevpon pervsed the orders of the said house which conteyne flees due to the Wardein from the prison^{rs}, and what the prison^{rs} are to expect from the Wardeyn in liew thereof. Wee 25 haue likewise hearde the seu^rall Complaints of some of the meaner sort of the said prison^{rs} against the wardeyn wch they p^rtend to be against the said orders, But wee doe not finde that they haue directly proued against him the breach of any of the said orders notwthstandinge wee thinke that for redresse of some things whereof 30

they compleyn, it were fitt that some addic̃ons were made to the former ordinancs in cases fallinge out not provided for by the former orders, Wherein both the Wardeyns allowancs for Com̃ons and dyett of prisoners might be increased in tymes of dearth accordinge
5 to the occasion and the discrec̃on of the Wardein in matters lefte to his discretion in such measure be moderated and lymited that there might no occasion of complaint be geuen hereafter. Some pticularities whereof wee haue pʳsumed to note in the included, occasioned therevnto by yoʳ L: said lʳᵉ. And soe humbly referringe
10 oʳ laboʳˢ to yoʳ honoʳˢ good acceptance and the supply of the defects to such course as in yoʳ honorable wisdome maye seeme good as well in cases not prouided for as not sufficientlie explaned in the present ordinancs Wee beseech Almightie God to enlenghen yoʳ yeers wᵗʰ continuall encrease of comforte. At the doctors Comons
15 this iiijᵗʰ of August 1597.

Yoʳ honorable good Lordships in oʳ services
humbly at Comaundemᵗ

JUL: CÆSAR

Copie   VINCENT SKYNNER
20   RIC : SKEVINGTON

THOMAS FOWLER.

[Endorsed.]

4 Aug. 1597.
Copie of the Comʳˢ report towchinge the Com-
25 plaint of the prisoners of the flecte.

APPENDIX II.

[From ye Records of ye Privy Council, James I. vol. iv. f. 33.]

(Spelling not re-produced.)

22 November, 1618.

His Majesty having been of late informed that the Gaolers and 5
Keepers of Prisons in and about London do so far misdemean
themselves in their duty to his Majesty and the state as that either
through wilful negligence or corruption they suffer the Prisoners
committed unto their charge and namely Priests and other persons
convicted of Recusancy or upon the statute of Præmunire to go 10
abroad at their pleasure and sometimes without a keeper ranging
whither they list, hath been pleased to recommend the same unto the
Lords of his Privy Council assisted with the Lo. Chief Justice of
England with directions presently to convent before them all the
said Keepers of Prisons and to examine them strictly upon these 15
abuses, according to such particular informations as should be
exhibited unto the Board in that Behalf. Which being this day
performed and only the Keepers of Newgate and the Clink charged
in particular, the one—that is to say the Keeper of Newgate for
permitting one *Hardwicke* who had been committed from the Sessions 20
for refusing the oath of Allegiance, to go abroad without any keeper
at all. The other of the Clink *for suffering Masses ordinarily to be
said within that Prison* . . . .
. . . . . . that forasmuch it was observed *there had been a great
Resort continually in all the Prisons unto Priests and Recusants* 25
which was found to be full of inconvenience. That from henceforth none should be admitted to any private conference with Priest
or Recusant, but in the presence or hearing of the Keeper and the
conference to be in a Language that the keeper should be able to

understand as had been ordered sometime heretofore in the Reign of Queen Elizabeth.

U. s. f. 273. "2 August, 1619.

"An open Warrant directed unto Sir Clement Edmonds, Knight
5 Clerk of the Council and to the Sheriffs of London and to each of them as it shall or may appertain

"Whereas information is made unto us that Sir John Whitbrooke Knight, Nicholas [Rookwood] Ashburnham Peake Esqr. Prisoners in the Fleete, and [sic] have shut themselves up in a strong Prison
10 and by strong hand keep the same against the said Warden and his servants to the disturbance of his Majesty's peace, now in his Majesty's absence and in time of his progress and to the Scandal of the Government. These shall be to will and to command you to repair unto the Fleete to let them know you are sent unto them
15 from us to require them in his Majesty's name to open these doors to come forth and submit themselves, as in duty they ought, to the order and Government of the said Warden, who is required to yield to each of them such civil usuage as to their quality and condition appertaineth. . . . "

20 [On the 3rd of August, 1619, we find the King at Belvoir Castle ; August 10th the King was at Welbeck in Nottinghamshire, on the 12th and 13th he was at Nottingham, on the 17th at Tutbury, on the 18th and 19th at Tamworth, &c.—*Nichols's Progresses of James I.* vol. iii p. 561.]

APPENDIX III.

[The Mutiny in ye Kings Bench.—From y^e *Privy Council Records.*]

At Whitchall the 5th July 1620.

Present:

Lord Chancellor.	Mr. Treasurer.	5
Lord Privy Seale.	Mr. Secretary Calvert.	
Earl of Arundell.	Master Rolles.	
Earl of Southton.	Sir Edward Coke.	
Lord Digbie.		

Letter to the Hiegh Sheriffe and the Deputy Lieutenantes of the 10 County of Surrey.

Whereas wee understand that most of the prisoners in the Kinges Bench having combyned together, do in a most tumultuous manner keepe that prison against the Marshall and his officers, and notwithstanding any means that can be used to draw them to order and 15 obedience, they still persist to keepe the prison by force fforbidding all persons whatsoever save such as are by themselves admitted, to enter into the Prison upon perill of their lives; which being a disorder and presumption of soe hugge a nature as require present and effectual reformaçon for the avoyding of such further in-20 convenience as may insue thereupon. Wee have thought meete hereby to will and require you in his Ma^{tes} name presently upon receipt hereof to rayse Posse Comitatus and so to repare unto the Prison of the Kinges Bench ; where if you shall find the prisoners to continue their foresaid tumultuous and rebellious courses, you shall 25 remonstrate unto them the danger of that their high offence and admonish them to submitt themselves, as in duty they ought, where-

unto if they shal refuse to conform themselves: Wee require you
to cause the Prison to be entered by force and dispose of the prisoners according to the direcōns you shall receive from the Lord
Chiefe Justice of the Court of Kinges Bench, hereof you may
5 not faile and this shall be your warrant and sufficient discharge in
that behalfe, and so, &c.

At Whitehall 9th July, 1620.

Present:

Lord Chancellor.	Lord Digbie.
Lord Privie Seale.	Mr. Treasor.
Lord-Chamberlain.	Mr. Comptroller.
Earl of Arundell.	2 Secretaries.

Sir Ed. Coke.

A Letter to the twoe Lords Chiefe Justices of the Courts of
15 Kinges Bench and Common Plēs requiring them to give present
order for disperseing and removeing of the chiefest of those prisoners in the Kinges Bench that are still mutinous unto other
prisons by writts of Habeas Corpus as far as law will beare: To
require the assistance of the High Sherriffe and Deputie Lieutenants
20 of the Countie of Surrey for execuōn of the said writs, with the
power and strength of the Countie in case of resistance. That as
well the Prisoners that shall be removed as those leaft in the Kings
Bench bee kept closse prisoners, not for the actōns or other causes
for which they stand committed, but for their foresaid mutiny and
25 disorder. And lastly to give special order for removinge of *Robert
Marston* the Prisoners orator unto the Gaole of Newgate there to be
kept closse prisoner and to examine him, &c.

At Whitehall, the 24th of July, 1620.

Present:

Lo. Chancellor.	Mr. Comptroller.
Lo. Privy Seale.	Mr. Secretarie Naunton.
E. of Arundell.	Mr. Secretarie Calvert.
Lo. Digbie.	Mr. of the Roles.

Mr. of the Wardes.

The Prisoners in the Kinges Bench having of late entered into
a mutinous and tumultuous disorder and seized upon the prison
keepeinge *Sir George Reinell* and the underkeepers out from 10
thence, did soe long and with such disobedience continue their
ryotous courses therein, as upon complaint thereof their Lordships
thought fitt to addresse their letters, first to the Hiegh Sheriffe and
Deputie Lieutenants of the Countie of Surrey, requiring them to take
Posse Comitatus and to enter into the Prison and reduce those 15
mutiners to order, and secondly to the twoe Llds. Chiefe Justices
to remove the ringleaders in that disorder, by Writts of Habeas
Corpus unto Newgate and such other Prisons as their Lordshipps
should think meete. Which beinge performed accordingly the said
prisoners so removed did peticon the Board to be heard in such 20
greevaunces as they pretended they underwent in the Kinges Bench ;
whereunto their Lordships condiscendinge and givinge order for
bringing them to the Table by Habeas Corpus, complaint was made
by them, upon the hearinge, of a windowe shut up by *Sir George
Reinell* whereby they were debarred from takinge in their victuall 25
out of the streete and consequently compelled to take their victuall
from *Sir George Reinell's* servaunts, to their great charge and inconvenience, as beinge farr deerer than that which they could buy
abroade. For aunsweare whereunto *Sir George Reinell* there
present replyed that the windowe was shutt upp for the safe keepinge 30
of the prisoners and for their meate though it were true that at his
comeing to the Prison there was taken 2*d.* upon every joynt as in

other places; yet that was now le.(t of and had not been used for
theis 7 years last, and therefore humbly prayed their Lps. to give
order that theis particulars might be duly examined. Whereupon
it was ordered that *Sir Thomas Fowler*, *Sir Henrie Spiller* Kte.
5 *Edmond Dubbleday* Esq⁰. Justices of Peace of the Countie of Mid-
dlesex ; *Sir Edmund Boyer*, *Sir Nicholas Carie*, and *Sir Thomas
Grymes* Kte. Justices of Peace of the Countie of Surrey or anie
fower of them shall with their first convenience meete together
either at Kinges Bench or anie other fitt place and examine such
10 greevances and complaints as the prisoners have to offer. And upon
due informaçon of the true state thereof and upon what just causes
the same are grounded shall sertifie their opinions thereof to the
Board that such further order may bee taken as shalbe meete.
For the better performance whereof the Lord High Chancellor of
15 Englande, if in his wisdome his Lp. shall conceive it expedient,
may grant HaLeas Corpus for such of the prisoners as are fitt to be
at the heareinge and shall petiçon to his Lp. for the same.

APPENDIX IV.

1621.

20   [Lansdown MSS. British Museum 85, Plut. LXXV. D.   fol. 109.]

An awnswere to the questions gyuen by the Comissioners wᵗʰ
their certificat to the right honorable the lord keep.

Question. Whether a prisoner lyenge in the wardes should paic
for his lodginge accordinge to the orders he beinge of abilitie.

25   Awnswere. This question is cleered by manie reasons first *Mr.
Anslow* and other wardens will witnes the like payment. The in-
uentarie of the old *Tirrell* doth also testifie that there weere beds
in euerie rome in the wardes wᵗʰ weere not gratis to the prisonᵗˢ.

An old woaman havinge bin Thirtie yeares seruante to the prison[rs] produced by them before the Comissioners affirmed that the prison[rs] did euer paie some what in that place, there be also dyuers prison[rs] yet in the fleete that haue paied lyenge there to dyuers wardens, and the xi[th] article in the orders playnely warranteth 5 that if anie prisoner at the boxe will haue more ease than is appointed for him that then the warden maie appointe him a bed and a chamber the partie agreeinge for hit wth the warden at his reasonable discretion and it was neuer harde that anie such poore prisoner laie out of the wardes, lastlie since the wardes is indeede the prison 10 and where those of greatest charge and daunger are lodged, howe cann yt be thought reasonable that the warden should take charge of them and haue no benefitt by them they beinge of great abilitie.

Seconde question. Whither the warden maie receaue the dismission fee before the prisoner be discharged by colour of custome 15 or tradition from former wardens?

Awnswere. This ffee hath euer bin paid wth the other fees if the prisoner be of abilitie and that for the most parte at his departure, if he staie not past three moneths, the poore neuer paie it vntill their departure, when if one paie there are ffower that for 20 wante must be forgyuen, and if anie of them die the warden must both loose that fee and also paie for his buriall.

Third question. Whether the rate of chambers be arbitarie at the wardens pleasure as at x[s] xv[s] xx[s] xxx[s] or more, or to be moderated by the Comissioners.   25

Answere. The house of the Fleete is no parcell of the gaole, but proper to the warden who maie lett it altogither or in parte as those howses in ffleetyard now called ffleete lane w[ch] is parte of the fleete and prisoners are sometymes lodged there yea if they be in execucon the warden beinge secured from breakinge awaie. The 30 Tenants paie rente to the warden yearely and the warden keepeth the keys of the viter gates and shutteth and openeth them wth a guard euerie eueninge and morninge and this is mencioned in the exemplified orders. In cases of dower the house hath bin devided

and former wardens have sometymes lett chambers to such as were
no prisoners by the weeke moneth or yeare, all wch in my vnderstandinge maie proue that the house beinge not proper to the
prisoners but as other land of Inheritance cannot be rated by Comis-
5 sioners. Neuerthelesse I wilbe contented to be moderated by whome-
soever if yt can be proued that I haue euer taken for one chamber
as is mencioned in this question or inforced anie man to paie
more then his owne voluntarie agreement when he desired a
pryvate chamber or haue taken more then the former wardens haue
10 continuallie accustomed for manie yeares since or aboue the rates
of other meaner prisons if the psons be equall; or els if those
Comissioners could moderate the penaltie of an escape (whereof
euerie warden before hath tesed [?]) or assure me from the harme of
fire or sickenes or desperate detts, [*sic*] or could lessen my necessarie
15 charge for his Ma^{ts} seruice in all casuall tymes. All wch I doubte
not but yor L^p (wth those graue men by whome the orders were
first established and latelie confirmed) will holde more worthie of
regarde towards me hauing a place of such charge and trust then
th' other towards malefactors.

APPENDIX V.

20

[From ye MSS. in ye Library of ye House of Lords.]

To the R^t Honble the K^{ts} Cittizens and Burgesses of the
House of Commons, in Parliament assembled.

The humble petiticion of the distressed prison^rs in the
Kinge's Bench and Fleett, and all others His Ma^{ts}
distressed sub^{ts} nowe prison^s, w^{thin} His M^{ts} Realme
of England and Walls.

25 In most Lamentable manner sheweth vnto yor Hono^rs that
whereas heretofore many good and Laudable Acts and Statuts
have byn made for the releif and pvision of maymed soldiers, and also

for the releife of the poore in eu^y pishe. But as yet no pvision
or releife for poor distressed prison͂s in this Realme, wch are many
thousands in England, whereof at this present remaynes in the 15
prisons in and about this Cittie of London the number of 3,500 able
subjects for His Ma^{ts} service if occasion of any employments. [*sic*]   5

And forasmuch as this Honble House is nowe making and
establishing of many good lawes for the peace and good of this
Comon Welth wch may well concurr and agree wth the grave saying
of that worthy and hono^{ble} member of this House (*Sir Edward Cooke*,
Knight) in his 4th booke of reports geveth this Christian advice to 10
all Judges and Justices, that *boni judicis interest lites dirimere*.

> Most humbly beseeching yor Honors to comisserat o^r
> distressed Estate and to take into your honorable and
> charitable consideracion this o^r bill here in Parlia-
> ment offered and in yor grave wisdomes to make 15
> and establishe some good and charitable Lawe for
> the speedy releife and releasment of all such p^rson͂s
> now in distresse or hereafter shalbe so imprisoned
> (as all other Christian Nations hath done) in this
> case most humbly beseeching this Hono^{ble} House to 20
> further this o^r charritable suite.
>
> And yor poore peticion͂s will nowe and ever here-
> after be bound on their bended knees to praye
> for these Hono^{ble} Houses of Parliament.

An Acte for the better and more spedier payment of Debts 25
from men Imprisoned nowe and eu͂ hereafter, in any of his mats:
Prisons wheresoeu͂ w^thin the Realme of England and Dominon
of Walls. And for releasement and discharging of prison͂s and all
others in danger thereof for the better imployments and service to
his matie and Realme.   30

Whereas by the Auncient Common Lawe of this Realme no
Subiects bodily could haue byn Imprisoned for debte betweene ptie

and ptye. And that these Latter Statute Lawes & ordinanes for
Imprisoning of mens boddyes for debt haue increased, mayntayned,
and cherished soundry oppressions. And the horrible trade of usury
(expresly forbidden by God's word) and in former times utterly
5 detested and abhored w'hin this Kingdome, as appereth by many
Cannons of the Church, Acts and Statuts made against the same.
And whereas in fforren Countryes and Doñïnons (where trade and
commerce doeth most abound) And even amongest the Turks and
infedells their is no continance of mens boddyes in prison for debte
10 Longer than one yere and a daye. But that some charitable and
consionable course is theire taken to enlardge such prisoñs, the
better to enable them to satisfye their debts by such Labour and
industry in their señ all facultyes and pñ shions as by their liberty
they may atchive and peure vnto them. Whereby the King
15 and Realme may haue vse of their boddys for the defence of
their Country and for other services according to their señ.all
fitnes and pñession. And for that daily experience pveth that
Banckroupts and prisoñ's did never so much as now abound.
Notw'hstanding the strickt and severe Laues made and pvided
20 in that behalf as aforesaid. And being a matter well nowen that
the Imprisoning of mens boddyes cannot make him or them
anything the better able to paye his or their de'ts. But contrary wise by Longe Imprisonm', by trust in vnfaiethfull and
vnconsionable frinds neglecte of thier callings expressions of
25 vnconsionable creditors defence of multiplicity of suits. And the
horrible extortions and barbarous vsaige of Goalers and keepñ s
of Prisons, and their officers and many violent extremetyes
in pcesse of tyme (of civill men) they growe and become
deboyst by Idleness and Riott and so become in short tyme vnfitt
30 ether for their formñ callings or for any other service to the King
or Comon Welth. Missery by custome growen into habitt, that
many being (once disgraced) rather desyers to leeve still in prison
then otherwise to be Imployed for getting of his releise And
meanes to paye his debtes, whereby the creditoŗs are hopeles ever

to recover any pte of his or their debte arising for the most pte at
the first from the obstinacy of some fewe refectory creditors to the
piudice of all. And somtymes to the vndoing of many a creditor
as well as of the debtor. Ffor remedy and redresse whereof and
to the end that some good p'sent Christian and Charritable course 5
may be taken for the good both of the creditor and enlardgment of
the p'son's.

Be it enacted by the Kings most excellent Ma^te the Lords Spirit-
uall and Temporall and the Comons in this present Parliam^t
assembled: That to the end from hensforth an Indifferent care be 10
hadd both of the creditor and debtor. All his Mat^s Justices of
Peace w'hin the Citty of London Countyes of Middx and Surrey
or w'hin fyve myles of the said Citty of London or any 6, 4, or 3
of them shall by this Acte be required and enioyned w'hin Thirty
dayes next and Imediately after this Sessions of Parliament to 15
Repayer and go in and to his Ma^t^s prisons of the Ffleett and Kings
Bench.   And also in & to all other prisons and Goales w'hin and
about the said Citty of London, and the libertyes and subberbs
theirof the Citty of Westminster the Burroue of Southwarke and
all other prisons in and w'hin the said Countyes of Midelsex and 20
Surry. Their to call before them or any 6, 4, or 3 of them all
and eu'y p'son and prison's as now is, are, or at that at any tyme
hereafter shall be Imprisoned in any of the said prisons or Goales
aforesaid for or vppon any Judgment execution accion or accions for
debte whatsoeu [ether by Statut, Recognizance, Judgment, ellegitt 25
Bond, bill, Booke pmise, assumsett or contracte or by any other wayes
or means whatsoeu.] Wherein any prison is indebted by himself or
wth any surety or suertyes whatsoeu. And that for the speedier
releasing of the said prison's as also for the sooner satisfacion of the
said Creditor and Creditors. They the said Justices or Comis- 30
sions shall in eu'y Sheire, County, Cittyes and Corporacions Devyde
them selves by the said nombers of 6, 4, or 3 of them as need and
occasion shall requier. Which said 6, 4, or 3, of them shall haue
full power and aucthority by this present Acte to Mynister an

oath as well to the debtor or debtors as to the Creditor or Creditors
or to his their or any of their wyttnes or wytnesses on ther syde or
vppon Interrogatoryes to be mynistred by the said Justices on
either pte. And to examyne them the said prisoñs, Creditors or
5 wytness's or any or eñy of them vppon oath for the better sifting,
serching and fynding out of the truth what estate or habillity the
said prisoñ or prisoñs or any of them, or any other pson or psons
to their vse or vppon trust for them or for their benefitt hath or
haue eicther in Lands, goods, Chattels, Leases, Rents, ffees,
10 Annuityes or debts whatsoeu̅ for the enabling of them for the
payment of his and their debte or debts. And what their seu̅ all
Just and true debts be or shalbe owing to their said creditors or
any of them. After wch examynacion so made and the prisoñs
vttermost estate thereby found out it shall be Lawfull for the said
15 Comissioñs having some reasonable respecte and consionable
consideracion for the mayntaynance and Lyvelyhoodd of the prisoner his wyf children and famely in such consionable sort that they
maye not be any wayes burthensome to the pishe ever afterwards. To
distribut and satisfye to the Creditor and Creditors pte and pte like
20 according to the quality and true some of their principall debte
that to eache Creditor is due in the said whole estate. And all
those prisoners whose estate by the said Justices haue byn examyned
and so ordred and decreed for the satisfying of their creditors as
aforesaid to be forthwth by them absolutly ffreed and sett at liberty
25 and never afterwards to be Imprisoned againe for the said debts.
And that from hensforth no Goaler or Keep of any prison shall
deteyne or keepe any the said prisoner or prisoners for any ffee or
ffees or dutyes whatsoeu^r. And whereas the prison^r or prisone^{rs}
whose estate and meanes vppon due examynacion shall appere to be
30 nothing worth, they to be Absolutly ffreed and dischardged by the
said Justices and Comiss^{rs} p^rsently out of prison. Whereas otherwise his ma^{tie} Loaseth his subiects and his service the Comon Welth
their members and many Thousands of wyves children and famelyes
shall and wilbe still in penury, missery and ppetuall beggery. And

the poore prison[r] him self lead a misserable vnprofitable and discontented life by their dollerous durance and Crewell Imprisom[t].

Be it also further enacted by this p[r]sent Parliament That frome hensforth The Custos rotturolu of eu[y] Sheire and County w[th]in this Realme of England and Dominon of Walls, Or in his Absence flower of the Auncients Justices of the peace there in person at the Sessions once eu[y] yere shall haue full power and Aucthority by this p[r]sent Acte of Parliament to nominate and appointe 6. 4. or 3 of sufficient wyse discreet men of Understanding and Judgment either Knights Esquiers Justices of peace or gent[e] of good quallity next or nere adioyning to any place or places where any Goales or prison[n]s are in, w[ch] place or prison any prison[n] or prison[n]s are Imprisoned for any debte or debts aforesaid as well w[t]hin any liberty or libertyes Burrowes or Corporacions wheresoeu[r] w[t]hin his ma[ts] said Realme of England or Dominion of Walls. And then and their the said Comissio[n]s to call before them or any 6. 4. or 3. of them all such prison[n] and p[r]sons w[ch] doe or shall at any tyme hereafter lye or remayne in prison for debte or debts vppon any execution, Judgm[t] Statut, or by any of the aforesaid securityes aboue pticulerly declared and specifyed And they the said Comiss[rs] or any 6. 4 or 3 of them to haue all such full power and aucthority to examyne the debter and debters, Creditor, and Creditors, wytnes and wytnesses and p[r]es on either syde by oath in eu[y] respecte for the satisfying of the creditors. And releasement of the prisoner and freeing of his suertyes in eu[y] respecte as fully lawfully and as Lardgly in eu[y] respecte as is by this p[r]sent Acte of Parliament geven and before declared to all and eu[y] the said Justices of peace aboue said or any 6. 4 or 3 of them and to all intents and purposses as aforesaid. And so to free any such prison[n] or p[r]sons as before is specifyed and declared. And also it is hereby further enacted that yf any Creditor or Creditors being summoned and warned by warrent from the said Justices of peace or Comissio[n]s or any 6. 4. or 3 of them shall refuse to come and to appere in pson before the said Justices or Comissio[n]s or any 6 4 or 3 of them. That then

the said Justices or Comiss^{rs} or any 6 4 or 3 of them shall by this
p^{r}sent Acte haue full power & Aucthority hereby to free the said
p^{r}soñ out of prison for the said debte. And such Creditor &
Creditors to stand to such order and decre as the said Justices or
5 Comiss^{rs} or any 6 4 or 3 of them shall in their discretion sett downe
and agree vppon, And that the said Justices for their pte and also
the said Comissioñs aforesaid be by this Acte enioyned to execut
& performe the Aucthority of this said Acte for the spedier deliū y
and enlardgment of prisoñs aforesaid at 4 seū all tymes in cū y
10 yere, or fouer or oftner (yf need shall requier) Viz the ffeast of St.
John Baptist, St. Mickhell Tharkeaungell the Birth of o^r Lord
God And the Anuciacion of o^r Blessed Lady St Mary the virgin
(or wthin Tenn dayes before cū y of the said seū all ffeasts). And
also the said Comissioñs in cū sheire and County shall nominate and
15 appoint one sufficient Clerke to be Regester in cū y seū all shiere and
County to Regester and record all such orders matters and agree-
ments as shalbe made decreed and sett downe by the said Justices
and Comissie^{rs} at all tymes, or by any 6 4 or 3 of them where vnto
any of his mat^s sub^{ts} and Creditors maye repayer there to take
20 knowledge and see the pceedings orders and decres by the said
Justices or Commission^{r}s sett downe and made for their satisfacion.
And that the said Regester may be by them sworne truly to sett
downe and Regester the same, and so to keepe a true and pfecte
record theirof. And that they shall haue power to allowe the said
25 Regester such reasonable ffee for his paynes and attendance to doe
the same as they in their discretions shall thinke meete, And the
same to be equally payed by the Creditors and debtors Indifferently.
Provided allwayes that yf any Creditor or Creditors shall refuse to
stand to such order and decre as the said Justices or Comissioñs or
30 any 6 4 or 3 of them shall make and sett downe and by them appointed to be entred and Regestred by the said Clarke That then
the said Justices or Comissioñs or any 6 4 or 3 of them shall have
full power and Aucthority by this Acte absolutly to ffree and dis-
chardg the said prisoñ or prisoñs so by them the said Creditor or
Creditors Imprisoned. And whereas diū se attornyes in his mat^e

Courts doe appere for diū.se his mat' sub'' w'ʰout warrant from the
ptye so to doe, to the great p'iudice and somtymes vndoing of
diū.se his mat' said sub'' Be it theirfore enacted from hensforth
that no attorny in any of his ma' Courts shall hereafter appere for
any his mat' sub'' in any accion or siute whatsoeū. hereafter to be 5
brought or commenced against them or any of them w'ʰout he hath
a Lawfull warrant vnder the Hand of the said ptye for whome he
is to appere or comence any suit vppon payne to Loase his practiz
eū. after And to fforfitt to the Kings mat'' C'' And the siut so
brought w'ʰout warrant as aforesaid to be voyde against these his 10
ma'' sub'' w'ʰ shalbe their uppon sued. Provided allwayes that the
form' acte for releasment of prisoñs nor any thing theirin Conteyned
shall not in any wyse bynd the Kings mat'' his hyers or successors
for any debte originally due to him or them, but that such order or
course shalbe taken for the recoū.ing and Levying of his ma'' said
debts his heyers and successors as were vsed and hadd before the
making of this Acte, any thing theirin Conteyned to the Contrary
theirof not w'ʰ standinge.

APPENDIX VI.

15

The Condition of the Fleet in 1691.

The following extract is taken from a rare little volume kindly
lent me by Mr. Thoms, entitled,

20

THE CRY OF THE OPPRESSED.

Being A True and Tragical Account of the Unparall'd Sufferings
of Multitudes of poor Imprisoned Debtors, in most of the Gaols
in *England*, under the Tyranny of the Gaolers, and other 25
Oppressors, &c.

*   *   *   *   *

London, Printed for *Moses Pitt*, and sold by the Booksellers of
London and Westminster, 12mo. 1691.

A relation of some of the Barbarities of Richard Manlove Esq. the present Warden of the Fleet, which has lately been found guilty of Oppression and Extortion by a Jury of twelve men.

The said Warden lock'd up (till opend by the Worthy Mr.
5 Justice *Lutwyche*) threescore gentlemen and others, in a loathsome Place called the Wards, for non-payment of excessive chamber-rent, where was a noisome House of Office near their lodgings, not allowing the King's beds, but forcing them to procure beds, or lie on the ground: and keeping men dead among'' them, for his pre-
10 tended Dues till they infected others, Witness. *James Mott* then a Stranger, and of the Jury.

Richard Brockas Esq. was carried down thither, for not paying Excessive Chamber-rent, and his wife and servants denied to bring him victuals or physic: and when he died the jury summoned, could
15 not but find his death occasioned by cruelty and they were dismissed by contrivance with the Coroner: and when he was buried, a new jury summoned, he taken up again and an Inquisition returned contrary to law. Witness *Mrs. Elizabeth Brockas* his widow.

Sir John Pettus of Suffolk, Baronet, for not paying extorting
20 dues, was forced from his Chamber; his books, Cloths, and Monies seized, and he turned into a little Room (now the Warden's Coach-man's Lodging,) who being a learned studious person for want of those necessaries, he melancholly died, and was kept many days above ground: his friends being denied his body till they paid
25 the Warden's pretended dues. Witness *Mr. John Warren*, *Mr. Briggs*, Clerk of the Fleet, now Marshall of the King's Bench.

Sir William Ducy, Baronet, was kept by the Warden in his Coachhouse till he was drawn out with Ropes, being so offensive, that none could come near him. Witness *Mrs. Anne Facey* Cham-
30 berlain.

Symon Edolph Esq. Seventy-Eight years of age, the son of *Sir Thomas Edolph* of Kent, for not paying 42 pounds demanded of him, when he proffered thirty pounds, which was for a little room about twelve foot square, after the rate of Six shillings per Week

besides payment of the Chamberlain was dragged down to the Wards,
in the hard weather & there not allowed a bed, but must have lain
on the ground had he not (at his own charge) procured one, and is
now in the Wards. Witness, *Richard Hare*, *William Higginson*,
Waiters, *Mr. John Machen*, *Mr. John Pemberton*, *Mr. Manning*,   5
Mr. Warren.

Walter Cowdrey Gaoler of Winchester, for about 2 or 3 months
Chamber Rent, kept above ground till it caused a sickness in the
next room, and his friends denied to take his body without paying
extorting Fees.   10

By which, may be perceived the Inhumanity of this Gaoler, not
only to gentlemen, but one of his own trade & calling.

Sir George Putsay Serj: at Law, dying of a dropsie: and being
a very great fat Man, was kept (for extorting Fees,) till a judges
Warrant was procured for his delivery.   15

Moses Pitt of London. Bookseller, being committed Prisoner to
the Fleet, April the 20th 1689, lodged on the Gentleman's side in
a chamber which the Warden values at eight shillings per week,
tho of right its but two shillings and fourpence, the rest being exaction (and the said *Moses Pitt*, at the time of writing of this 20
has two Chambers within the rules of the Kings-Bench for one
shilling three pence per week, twice as good as the said Chamber)
he the said *Pitt* continued in the said Chamber from the said 20t
of April 1689 to the 26th of August 1690 which was seventy weeks,
and three days, in which time the said *Pitt* had paid the Warden 25
his commitment Fee, Two Pounds four shillings and sixpence,
where as there is but four pence due; *Pitt* also paid him fourteen
shillings for two day-writs, and was to pay him eight shillings,
fourpence at the going out of the Gate, (Every Prisoner there in
Execution pays eleven shillings and two pence a Day when he goes 30
abroad about his business) but the said Warden kept his said
fourteen shillings, and would not let him go out of the gates of
the prison by which the said *Pitt* lost his tryals, which was many
thousand pounds damage to him. The said *Pitt* also paid the said

Warden for Chamber rent fifteen pounds, and the said Warden had of *Mr. Stephen Upman*, Fellow of Eaton College, and brother to *Pitt's* wife (who was committed Prisoner upon a false oath sworn in the open Court of the Common Pleas, by two of *Pitt's* adversaries, 5 on Nov. 15, 1689 an account of which is at large related in PITTS CASE herewith printed) and of *John Pitt* Son of the said *Moses Pitt*, and of *Mr. Lock*, and *Mr. Bland*, the said *Pitt's* friends, £17. 6. 8. for one nights lodging. Notwithstanding the said Warden of the Fleet had received of the said *Pitt* and his friends (which was all 10 upon *Pitt's* account) £35. 5. 2. when there was due to him, and the Parson of the Fleet, besides the one nights lodging for the said *Pitts* four friends but £9. 8. 4. from the said 20th of April 1689 to the 26th of August 1690, upon which day he threw down the said *Pitt* into the Wards or Dungeon of the said Prison and there 15 lock'd him up within the Door of the said Wards for five days without allowing him any bed or any thing else to lodg on: and altho' the said *Pitt's* wife came to see her husband in this miserable place, he the said Warden would not permit the said *Pitt* to come up into the yard of the Prison to speek with his wife, upon which 20 the said *Pitts* wife was forc'd to send him a bed to lodg on & there the said *Pitt* continued and lodg'd in a room with twenty seven more Prisoners most of which livd on the basket and beg'd at the grate: one of which said Mendicant Prisoners after he had, in order to take the benefit of the Act sworn himself not worth more than £10 25 died at the said *Pitts* bed head, (he was a Man full of Vermin, of a corrupt body, and bursten), at 12 of the Clock at night. And one day the said *Pitt* being at prayers in the Chappel of the said prison, was taken with a Delirium or Apoplectic fit, and getting into this noisome cell threw himself on his Bed, and so lay some hours, 30 upon which one of his friends goes to the Warden and acquaints him in what condition the said *Pitt* lay & desired him that the said *Pitt* might have a chamber till he was well, paying him for it. But the said warden denied the said friend of *Pitt* that request. In this same dismal place did the said *Pitt* continue from the 26th of

August 1690 to the 16th of May 1691 in all which time he was not
able to keep himself clean from vermin, being forced to Louse himself
most commonly twice a day either in the open ward or in the house
of office: For at any time if the said *Pitt* had the use of any of the
Gentlemen's Chambers for his Devotions, study, and louseing him- 5
self, if the said Warden came to hear of it, both he and his wife
would be very angry with the said gentlemen, and would hunt him
thence as a partridge upon the mountains.   And that the Reader
may be satisfied that it was impossible for the said *Pitt* to keep
himself clean from Vermin, whilst he continued in the said wards 10
of the Fleet Prison he doth assure his readers that many of his
chamber fellows were so lowsie, that as they either walked or sat
down, you might have pick'd lice off from their outward garments.
But enough of this least my Reader scrubs and scratches at the
reading of it.   The said *Pitt* was removed from the Fleet Prison
to the Kings Bench on the 16th May, 1691.   15

     *   *   *   *   *

NOTES.

P. 9, l. 25. *John Calton* appears as Warden of the Fleet in 1584, and was certainly Warden as late as 27 June, 1586. (*Cal. Dom. Eliz.* 1581-1590, pp. 170, 336.) About his death I have been able to discover nothing. *Edward Tirrell* was Warden in 1581 (21 June), *u.s.* p. 21. For *Joachim Newton* see App. p. 163. For *Brian Anslowe* and *George Reynell* see p. 115.

P. 9, l. 31. But in this time . . . See Appendix p. 168.

P. 12, l. 3. *See the Lord Chancellor moved his Majesty, &c.* This was on the 26 July, 1618, as appears by the Privy Council Records.

P. 18, l. 30. . . . *they have not only paid (taking nothing for it) but yet further exhibited to the Warden, i.e.* paid the fees, found themselves, and given the Warden *a douceur* into the bargain (see p. 105, l. 20). The Warden probably alludes to *Dudley, Lord North*, who had recently been committed to his custody : viz. on the 21 May, 1620 (*MS. Records of Privy Council*). The cause of his committal seems to have been a quarrel with *Lord Digby* mentioned in *Birch, Court and Times of James I.* vol. ii. p. 202.

P. 19, l. 26. . . . . *a certayne reverend bishopp* . . . . Apparently *Cuthbert Scott*, Bishop of Chester, committed to the Fleet in 1561 (*Cal. Dom. Add.* 1547-1565, p. 524). He appears to have given a bond to remain within 20 miles of Finchingfield in Essex (*Cal. Dom.* 1547-1580, p. 247). The bond must have been forfeited, for he escaped and died at Louvain some time before 1564, for in a document of that date he is called "the late Dr. Scott." (See *Brady's Episcopal Succession*, vol. i. p. 106.)

P. 23, l. 29. *Mr. Leicester.* George Leicester, see p. 120.

P. 23, l. 29. *Thrask.* This eccentric personage managed to attract much attention to himself, as the following extracts will show:

"Master *John Thrask*, born in the county of Somerset and a schoolmaster there, being about four and thirty years of age, came to London about the year of our Lord 1617, where being zealously affected in the path of nonconformity he fell into divers points differing from the way of the Church. One was that he ranked men into three distinct estates: 1 of Nature. 2 of Repentance. 3 of Grace. According to which three degrees was his order of preaching. To recover men out of a state of nature he preacht repentance so earnestly that he caused many of his Auditors to weep yea to roar in that manner that inhabitants in several places of the city were disquieted many times in the night season by his converts. . . . . . .

"Now there being a young man named *Hamlet Jackson* a tailor, who according to the former direction, supposing that he should walk by law in everything, came at last to believe that the Word of God did prescribe him what to eat and what to refuse . . . . . . He presented his opinion to *Mr. Trask* and had the ill-luck to be too hard for his master, and to pervert his judgment so far that *Mr. Trask*, instantly upon it, labours to persuade his auditors to the same opinion . . . . . .

"Upon which came in a number of laws ceremonial, touching building, planting, wearing of Apparel, and sundry other things as well as eating . . .

"So Mr. Traske elects from among those of his third estate four men . . . . . . On these four he in a Pontifical manner layeth hands, sends them to preach, and they take upon them to cure diseases by anointing with oil and Mr. Traske to give the Holy Ghost by imposition of Hands . . . . *John Traske* for his Judaicall opinions was censured in the Star-chamber to be set upon the Pillory at Westminster and from thence to be whipt to the Fleet, there to remain prisoner: three years after he writ a recantation of all his schismatical errors." (*Ephraim Pagitt's Heresiography*, 4to. *London*, 1645. p. 125, &c.)

"On Friday last the 19th of the month [1618], one *Thrasko* a minister, who hath been long a prisoner for divers fanatical opinions by him maintained, was censured in the court of Star-chamber, *where I was present*, besides the Lord Chancellor [*Bacon*], the Lord Archbishop [*Abbot*] and the Bishops of London [*King*] and Ely [*Andrews*] spoke much against the prisoner there present. The Bishop of Ely was altogether in confutation of his opinions, that especially of the Jewish Sabbath, and of different meats, and rather theological than political. The Bishop of London was wholly narrative in making a relation of his life, his secret and schismatical conventicles, his making proselytes, his imprisonment and just proceedings against him. The particulars would stuff a letter too much. His censure was, in a word, to stand on the pillory, with his ears nailed, and branded in the forehead, so that he that was *Schismaticus* might also be *stigmaticus*, it was the Lord Chancellor's phrase, to pay a thousand pounds fine, and to remain a close prisoner during life." (*Sir Henry Bourgchier to Abp. Usher, Usher's Works (Elrington), vol. xvi. p. 359*. Compare *Birch, Court and Time of James I*. vol. ii. p. 63, and *Spedding's Bacon. Letters*, vol. vi. p. 315.) The poor wretch seems to have been first thrown into prison in Feb. 1618, for in a letter dated the 28th of that month (*Dom. J. I. S. P. O.* vol. xcvi. No. 38) *Nath. Brent* writing to *Carleton* says: " . . . . His Majesty makes merry with the opinions of a new sect called *Thraseists;* their leader *Thrasco* is in prison, and the Ecclesiastical Commission has them in chase."

Three years after this *in the Parliament* of 1621 . . . "*Thursday, May 24.* . . . . At the Conference with the Lords.

"Their Lordships did desire to alter the Title of the Bill for the Obser-

vation of *Sunday;* and where it was expressed for the better observation of
the Sabbath Day, commonly called *Sunday,* their Lordships would have the
word Sabbath day left out, and that it should be for the observation of the
Lord's Day, commonly called Sunday: their Reason was, because people now-
adays so much inclined to take hold of Words of Judaism; *as did lately
Traske and his Adherents . . . . . ."* (*Proceedings and Debates of the
House of Commons in 1620 and 1621.* Oxford, 8vo. 1766, vol. ii. p. 97.)

P. 23, l. 31. *Rookwood.* This is *Edward,* son and heir of *Nicholas Rookwood,* of
Euston, co. Suffolk, Esq. He was born in the first year of Q. Mary, and appears to have lost his father when he was a child. He married *Elizabeth,*
daughter of *William Browne,* of Elsing, Esq. and when Q. Elizabeth paid
her visit to Norfolk in 1578 she was entertained at Euston, on the 10th
August. What return Mr. Rookwood received for his hospitality at the
hands of the Queen may be read in my work, *One Generation of a Norfolk
House,* where (in the note to chap. iii.) I have given some account of this
unfortunate man. He spent the greater part of his life in prison, and was
subjected to continual fines and other annoyances for his nonconformity. I
find his name occurring again and again as summoned to appear at the
Bishop's court in Norwich, or before the Privy Council, wherever they chanced
to be sitting, and, even when permitted to return to his house, confined to a
circuit of five miles from his own door. He became more and more em-
barrassed by the expense to which he was put; but I have some reason for
believing that the occasion of his being committed to the Fleet was a suit for
recovery of a debt for which he was surety, though it had been incurred by
another. By his first wife he had a family of three sons and four daughters. The eldest son, who succeeded to the estates at Euston, was the *Nicholas*
of these pages; the second was *William,* who appears to have been killed
while in the service of Charles I.; the third, *Robert,* became a Catholic priest
and died at Rouen in 1668, æt. 82. Of the daughters, *Elizabeth* became a
nun and died at Brussels in 1621. *Alice* married *Julius Zanchi,* private
secretary to *Gondomar. Susan* and *Dorothy* were living at Euston unmarried
in 1605. When *Robert Rookwood* left England in 1620 his father was still
in prison, and he says (in the autobiographical account of himself, printed by
Mr. Foley) that his eldest brother [*Nicholas*] was then the only member of
his family who was not a Catholic. This seems to explain the curious passage
at p. 130, l. 18-21, and other expressions which *Harris* applies to him.
Edward Rookwood spent his last days at Euston, and was buried there 19
Jan. 1633-4, being then 79 years of age. (*One Generation of a Norfolk
House.* See the Index. MS. *Records of the Privy Council. Presentments
of Recusants in the Archives of Norwich Cathedral.* Dacy's *MSS. Brit.
Mus. Foley's Records,* S. J. vol. i. p. 198, *et seq.* vol. iii. p. 785.)

P. 23, l. 32. *Peck.* *Ashburnham Peck,* son and heir of *John Peck,* of Winchelsey,
co. Sussex, by *Mary,* daughter of *James Blechenden,* of Aldington, co. Kent.
He had been in prison for 19 years; p. 72, l. 26.

P. 26, l. 26. *Chamberlayne*. *Edmond Chamberlayne*, second son of *Sir Thomas Chamberlayne*, of Prestbury, co. Gloucester. He was of Mangersbury House, in that shire, where his descendants are seated to this day. He was High Sheriff of the county in 39 Elizabeth. He had been for at least six years in the Fleet in Feb. 1620-1 (p. 127, l. 8). Harris says he was in debt to the extent of thirteen or fourteen thousand pounds, and yet lived at some expense in the Fleet and kept up a great deal of riotous hospitality (pp. 120, 121). He himself says he was in prison by being surety for his brother Sir John Chamberlayne (*Cal. Dom. James I.* 1611-1618, p. 561, n. 51).

P. 29, l. 15. *Sir John Whitbrooke*. He was the son of *John Whitbrooke*, of Bridgewater, co. Salop, and of Water Newton, co. Huntingdon, Esq. by *Margaret*, daughter and sole heir of *Thomas Lunn*, of Pocklington, co. Ebor. He married *Joan*, daughter of *Simon Horspoole*, of   co. Kent, and by her had a large family. By his Inq. p.m. taken at Huntingdon, 23 March, 1619, it appears that he was a man of very extensive landed property, which, however, was heavily encumbered when his father died in 1587. He was knighted at Greenwich 12 May, 1604, but when the new oath of allegiance was enforced upon the Catholics he refused it, and for the rest of his life became numbered among the Popish Recusants, who were the prey of the hungry courtiers. Accordingly I find, 19 March, 1610, " Grant to *Clement Corbet* of the benefit of the Recusancy of .... *Sir John Whitbrooke*, of Bridgenorth, co. Salop." He must have been thrown into the Fleet about this time, for he had evidently been many years in prison at the time of the brawl which terminated so disastrously. He received the fatal wound on 7 Oct. 1619, and died the same day. Chamberlain writing to Carleton on the 16th alludes to the fray and adds, " .... the matter has not yet come to trial, and that I do not thoroughly understand the evidence." The jury found Boughton guilty of manslaughter. (*Cal. Dom. J. I. P R. O.* 1604-1618. *Birch's Court and Times of James I.* vol. ii. p. 193. *Visit. of Hants. Camden Soc. Privy Council Records Jas. I.* vol. iii. p. 190. The Father's *Inq. p. m. Chancery,* 29 *Eliz. Salop,* 185. The Son's, 18 J. I. part i. No. 158. See *App.* p. 167.)

P. 32, l. 7. *The Lady Whitbrooke in her petition*. The petition " To the Lords of his Maties most honorable Privy Council . . . of Joane La: Whitbrook . . . " is to be found in *Dom. Add. Jas. I.* vol. xli. n. 86.

P. 33, l. 2. In March 1621 there was . . . A grant to *Lionel Batty* of the goods and chatels of *Henry Boughton* forfeited for felony and for Manslaughter of *Sir John Whitbrooke*. (*Cal. Dom. Jas. I.* p. 234, for this year.) He appears by p. 36, l. 10, to have been committed as a Popish Recusant.

P. 35, l. 15. Please correct " fortications " to "*fortifications.*" The order of the Privy Council will be found in App. p. 169.

P. 37, l. 7. *Sir John Meres*. He was of Auborne, co. Lincoln, son and heir of *Anthony Meres*, of Auborne, by *Katharine*, daughter of *Sir Everard Digby*. He married (1) *Barbara*, daughter of *Sir William Dallison*, Judge of the

King's Bench, and (2) *Barbara*, daughter of *John Nevill*, of Grove, co. Notts.
He was High Sheriff of Lincoln in 1596, and was buried at Washingborough,
co. Lincoln, 16 May, 1630. (Kindly communicated by Mr. A. Larken, Portcullis.) He was knighted by James I. 23 July, 1603. (*Nichols's Progresses of
J. I.* vol. i. p. 211.)

P. 38. l. 21. *Sir Francis Inglefield.* He was son and heir of *John Englefield*, of
Wotton Basset, co. Wilts, Esq. who was a younger brother of *Sir Francis
Englefield*, of Englefield, co. Berks. On the accession of Q. Elizabeth his
uncle, Sir Francis, who had been one of the Privy Council and was a devoted
friend to Q. Mary, retired to Spain, and threw in his lot with Philip II. By
a special Act of Parliament passed in the 38 Eliz. his estates were declared
forfeited to the crown, and by a legal artifice his nephew, the Sir Francis of
these pages, was deprived of them. James I. seems to have restored them to
our Sir Francis, who was created a Baronet 25 Nov. 1612. It appears that he
was committed to the Fleet in July 1618 as a defaulter in a matter of some
property for which he was a trustee, and was fined 500*l.* for "contempt of
Court." *Buckingham* wrote a letter in October to *Bacon* interceding for him,
and in Dec. of the same year again wrote, begging that he might have liberty
for a fortnight. Two years later (July 1620) *Bacon* writing to *Buckingham*
says—"I have stayed the *thousand pounds* set upon Englefield for his
Majesty, and given order for levying it," so that apparently another fine had
been laid upon him in the meanwhile. This second fine seems to have been im-
posed in consequence of his refusal to contribute to the "musters;" for *Lord
Hertford* writing to the Council on the 26 June of this year says that he had
so refused and "advises that he be dealt with." In *Bacon's* "Confession and
Submission" (1621) he says "there have been many orders since caused by *Sir
Francis Englefield's* contempts." In February 1623-4 he was still in the
Fleet and was again fined, this time 3,000*l.* "for touching the Lord Keeper
(*Williams*) with bribery." How long he continued in prison I cannot discover,
but he died in 1631, and was buried at Englefield, where there is still a splendid
monument to his memory. *Hacket* tells us that *Abp. Williams* forgave him
the fine of 3,000*l.* and became eventually a friend to him. How nobly the
great lawyer *Plowden* behaved to *Sir Francis*, how ungrateful the latter was
to his benefactor, and how that shameful conduct of the young man killed
the old one, may be read—and it is a sad and pathetic story—in *Blakeway's
Sheriffs of Shropshire*, pp. 222 *et seq.* (See *Cal. Dom. James I.* 1618, p.
558. *Spedding's Bacon's Life and Letters*, vol. vi. pp. 342, 448, vol. vii. pp.
110, 258. *Burke's Extinct Baronetage*. *Birch's Court and Times of James
I.* vol. ii. p. 449. *Hacket's Life of Williams*, part i. §. 96. *Lords' Debates*,
Camden Soc. pp. 23, 33, 34. *Statutes at Large* (folio), vol. iv. pt. ii. p. 851.
The Inq. p. m. upon his father sets forth that *John Englefield* died 1 April,
9 Eliz. and that *Francis* his son and heir was aged 4 years 9 months and 2
weeks on the 7th May.)

P. 45, l. 25. *Sir Edward Cleare.* He was son and heir of *Sir Edward Clere*, of Blickling, co. Norfolk, by *Frances*, daughter of *Sir Richard Fulmeston*, of Thetford. He was baptized at Blickling 1 Jan. 1563-4. He succeeded his father in August, 1606, and is said to have married *Margaret*, daughter of *William Yaxley*, of Yaxley, Esq. by whom he had a son Henry, who applied for and obtained a baronetcy sometime in 1623, which he did not live long to enjoy. See *No.* 31 of *The Genealogist*, where I have attempted to unravel some of the confusion in the popular accounts of this family.

P. 58, l. 16. *Beare.* *Edward Beare* (p. 7, l. 25). Query of Ash in the parish of Brawnton, co. Devon. (*Foley's Rec.* iv. 645.)

P. 58, l. 16. *Jennyson.* *Michael Jenison*, of Walworth, in the Bishopric of Durham. He was 3rd son of *John Jenison*, of Walworth, by *Mary*, eldest daughter of *Sir Thomas Gerard*, of Bryn. The Jenisons were very stubborn Recusants, and their names are frequently occurring in the Records of Eliz. and James as suffering fines, imprisonment, and other inconveniences. There were no fewer than eight members of this family who became Jesuits. Of course Mr. Foley has a great deal to say about them. In the House of Lords' Library there is a Petition from this *Michael Jenison* addressed to *Henry, Earl of Huntingdon,* dated 18 May, 1621, complaining of his treatment in the Fleet. This petition seems to have produced no effect, for in the following February he addressed another to the Lords of the Council, in which he describes himself as "*Michael Jennison, of Grays Inn,* Prisoner in the Fleet," and prays "for release and permission to prosecute by law his complaint against *Sir Edw. Coke,* who caused him to be severely treated in prison." He seems to have died some time in 1628. (*Surtees' History of Durham,* vol. iii. p. 320. *Foley's Records,* vols. iii. and iv. see Index. *Cal. Dom. J. I.* (1611-1618), pp. 185, 513. *Dom. Add.* 1580-1625, p. 497 (1619-1623), p. 345. *Hist. MSS. Com. Report,* vol. iv. p. 20, vol. iii. p. 23.)

P. 58, l. 24. *Lee.* *George Lee.* See p. 134, *et seq,*

P. 61, l. 9. *With* blame .... Query, "*without* blame."

P. 67, l. 22. *Dr. Fryer.* This is *Dr. Thomas Fryer,* son of *Dr. John Fryer,* who with his wife and several children died of the plague in 1562. Both father and son were strict and conscientious Catholics. The father was thrown into the Tower for attending mass in 1561. The son compounded for his recusancy more than once and paid heavy fines. There is an account of both men in *Dr. Munk's Roll of the College of Physicians.* See, too, *One Generation of a Norfolk House,* ch. ix.

P. 68, l. 32. *The Lord Chancellor.* Bacon. The Lord Chief Justice. *Sir Henry Montague,* afterwards Earl of Manchester.

P. 77, l. 9. Thirty years past *Sir Francis Inglefield, &c.* This must have been at the time when measures were being taken to despoil *Sir Francis* of the property inherited from his father. See note on p. 38, l. 21. The expression in the next line baffles me. I can only conjecture that "prisoners of 3 or 4 pills" must be some *slang* expression, and that "pill" must mean *robbery* or *rascality*.

P. 86, l. 19. *Bishopp of Gloucester.* Apparently *Richard Cheyney*, Bishop of Gloucester from 1562 to 1579. For an account of him see *Cooper's Ath. Cantab.* vol. i. p. 100.

P. 99, l. 30. *When the Thames was twice frozen over.*

"The Thames is now quite frozen over, so that people have passed over to and fro these four or five days; but not so freely as in the great frost, for the winds and high tides have so driven the ice in heaps in some places that it lies like rocks and mountains, and hath a strange and hideous aspect. It hath been seldom seen that this river should be twice frozen over in one winter; and the watermen are quite undone to lose the benefit of term and parliament both.

Letter from John Chamberlain, Esq. to Sir Dudley Carleton, dated London, February 3, 1620-1. (*Birch's Court and Times of James I.* vol. ii. p. 217.)

P. 108, l. 14. *Dureing the vacancy of a Chancellor.* Sir *Francis Bacon's* confession was read in the House of Lords on 24 April, 1621; the great seal was put in commission on the 1st of May. *Bp. Williams* received the great seal by the title of *Lord Keeper* on the 10th July.

P. 108, l. 30. *Anno 21 Jac. &c.* The date given is wrong, it should be 18° Jac. The Proclamation for the Abolition of Bills of Conformity was issued 31 March, 1621. It may be found in the eighth vol. of *Rymer's Fœdera*, xvii. 290. "Bills of Conformity . . . . . . were exhibited into his Majesty's Court of Chancery and other his Courts of Equity by sundry persons against their Creditors, *of purpose to enforce them to accept less than their just debts and damages or to give longer days or times of payment than the said Creditors were willing to do.*" The Proclamation was issued to remedy the evils that had arisen in consequence of the increase of these Bills of Conformity. [I am indebted to *Mr. Gardiner* for the reference to this passage.]

P. 110, l. 21. *Sir Ri. Skipwith.* He was of Ormesby, co. Lincoln. In 1582 he received a grant of the office of Clerk of the Treasury of the Court of Common Pleas. He was ancestor of the Skipworths of Newbold Hall, who became extinct in 1790, after keeping the Baronetcy upwards of a century. The Queen rewarded him for his twenty years' service by granting him the lease of Gransden Manor, co. Cambridge, *late parcel of the Bishoprie of Ely* (?), on March 31, 1602. (*Cal. Dom. Eliz.*)

P. 118, l. 9. *George Reynell.* He appears to have succeeded *Joachim Newton* as Warden about 1597, and to have become Marshal of the King's Bench Prison in the following reign. James I. knighted him, but when I have not been able to discover. About a year after the prisoners in the Fleet mutinied and complained of Harris, the prisoners in the King's Bench did precisely the same, and in the P. R. O. there is a narrative of their outbreak which affords a curious parallel to that of Harris (*Dom.* vol. cxvi. N. 46. See App. III.) *Sir George Phillips* reporting in the House of Commons on *Bacon's* malpractices says: "That there was also much corruption said to be in the suit betwixt *Peacock* and *Sir George Rheuill*, which is not examined;" and *Bacon* in his confession says to the nineteenth article of the charge, "videlicet, In the cause between Reynell and Peacock, he received from Reynell two hundred pounds and a diamond ring worth five or six hundred pounds."

"I confess and declare, That at my first coming to the Seal, when I was at Whitehall, my servant Hunt delivered me two hundred pounds from Sir George Reynell, my near ally, to be bestowed upon furniture of my home, adding further, that he received divers former favours from me; and this was as I verily think before any suit begun.   The ring was received certainly *pendente lite*, and though it were at new year's tide yet it was too great a value for a new year's gift; though, as I take it, nothing near the value mentioned in the article."

In *Bacon's* will he mentions this diamond " .... To my wife a box of rings, save the great diamond I would have restored to Sir George Reynell." (*Cal. Dom.* J. I. 1618-1620, pp. 168, 172. *Add.* 1580-1625, p. 552. *Oxford Debates*, vol. i. p. 207. *Spedding's Bacon*, vol. vii. pp. 228, 258).

P. 120, l. 6. *Mr. George Leicester*, &c.

Uriah Babington was a London merchant, who appears to have been concerned in extensive Government contracts at the close of Queen Elizabeth's reign and at the beginning of that of James I. In 1609 his wife having been left a widow was in some way involved in losses which her husband had sustained. She is described as "a very wilful woman," and is hard pressed by her creditors. The proceedings against her extend over some years, and on her marriage with George Leicester, apparently early in 1617, he became involved in the suit. (See *Cal. Dom.* J. I. 1604-1618.) Among the Lords' MSS. is her petition to the House of Commons, praying for discharge from prison, and setting forth her grievances, in 1620. (*Hist. MSS. Com. Rep.* vol. iv. p. 120.)

P. 123, l. 13. *Sir Henry Slugsby* (*sic*.) Probably *Sir Henry Slingsby*, of Scriven, co. York, who was M.P. for Snaresborough in several Parliaments during the reigns of James I. and Charles I. Sir Walter Scott published his Commentaries in 1806.

P. 128, l. 27. *Downes*. Another victim of the penal laws against the "Popish Recusants." He was son and heir of *Robert Downes*, of Melton Hall, co. Norfolk, Esq. concerning whom see *One Generation of a Norfolk House*, ch. iii. n. (10) and (11). In 1601 an Act was brought into the House of Lords "for the sale of certain lands of *Edward Downes*, Esq. for payment of his debts," which was rejected on the 3rd reading (3 July). The draught of it is in the P. R. O. (*Certiorari Bundle, No.* 66). After this I lose sight of him, and conjecture that he died in the Fleet.

P. 140, l. 34. *Mr. Tregian.* *Francis Tregian*, eldest son of Francis *Tregian*, of Volvedon alias Golden, co. Cornwall, Esq. See the painfully-interesting narrative in Mr. Morris's *Troubles of our Catholic forefathers*, series i. pp. 61-143. Francis the father was in prison from 1577 to 1605. Soon after the accession of James I. he was liberated and banished. He retired to Lisbon, where he died 25 Sept. 1608. *Francis*, the son, appears to have been sent across the channel when his father's troubles began. On the 31 Sept. 1586 he entered at the English College, at Rheims, when he was described as having been "in Angensi schola eruditus." He appears to have remained at Rheims for the next six years, and left it 11 July, 1592. The next two years he seems to have spent in travelling on the Continent; but 23 May, 1594, *Beard*, the spy, writes that "*Tregian's* eldest son is coming over shortly." When he was thrown into the Fleet I have not been able to discover, but he evidently had been there many years when he died there in 1619. (Morris, u. s. *Cal. Dom.* 1591-1594, p. 506. *Add.* 1619, p. 613, 1598-1601, p. 520. *Douai Diary*, under the dates given.)

P. 143. *The Lady Amy Blunt.* She was third daughter of *George Tuchet, Earl of Castlehaven and Lord Audley*, and wife of *Edward Blunt*, of Arleston, co. Derby, Esq. Sometime in the summer of 1619 she had, or thought she had, reason to complain of injustice at the hands of Sir Francis Bacon, then at the zenith of his power, and she addressed a Petition to James I. complaining of the treatment she had received. Summoned before the Council 9 June, 1619, she was asked to deliver up the writer of the petition, and on her refusal she was committed to the Fleet on the 6th July. She was detained there for 27 weeks, and then transferred to the Marshalsea, where I find her as late as Nov. 1620. (From information kindly furnished by *Mr. Larken*, Portcullis. *Hist. MSS. Com. Rep.* iii. p. 285. *Cal. Dom. J. I.* 1619, 1620, pp. 53, 68, 144, 190. *Privy Council Records*.)

INDEX NOMINUM.

Westminster: Printed by J. B. NICHOLS AND SONS, 25, Parliament Street.

www.ingramcontent.com/pod-product-compliance
Lightning Source LLC
Chambersburg PA
CBHW030734280326
41926CB00086B/1432